A-Z WINC

CONTEN

REFERENCE

Motorway	M27
A Road	A33
B Road	B3335
Dual Carriageway	
One-way Street Traffic flow on A Roads is also indicated by a heavy line on the driver's left.	
Road Under Construction Opening dates are correct at the time of publication	
Proposed Road	
Restricted Access	
Pedestrianized Road	
Track & Footpath	
Residential Walkway	
Railway	Station, Level Crossing, Heritage Sta., Tunnel
Built-up Area	UNION STREET
Local Authority Boundary	
National Park Boundary	
Posttown Boundary	
Postcode Boundary (within Posttown)	
Map Continuation	16 / Large Scale City Centre 50
Airport	
Car Park (selected)	P
Church or Chapel	†
Cycleway (selected)	
Fire Station	■
Hospital	H
House Numbers (A & B Roads Only)	13 8
Information Centre	i
National Grid Reference	130
Park & Ride	East Winchester (Barfield) P+R
Police Station	▲
Post Office	★
Safety Camera with Speed Limit Fixed cameras and long term road work cameras. Symbols do not indicate camera direction.	30
Toilet: without facilities for the Disabled	
Toilet: with facilities for the Disabled	
Viewpoint	
Educational Establishment	
Hospital or Healthcare Building	
Industrial Building	
Leisure or Recreational Facility	
Place of Interest	
Public Building	
Shopping Centre or Market	
Other Selected Buildings	

SCALE

Map Pages 4-49

1:15,840 4 inches (10.16cm) to 1 mile 6.31cm to 1km

0 — ¼ — ½ Mile

0 — 250 — 500 — 750 Metres

Map Page 50

1:7,920 8 inches (20.32cm) to 1 mile 12.63cm to 1km

0 — ⅛ — ¼ Mile

0 — 100 — 200 — 300 — 400 Metres

Fairfield Road, Borough Green, Sevenoaks, Kent TN15 8PP
Telephone: 01732 781000 (Enquiries & Trade Sales)
01732 783422 (Retail Sales)
www.az.co.uk

Edition 4 2012

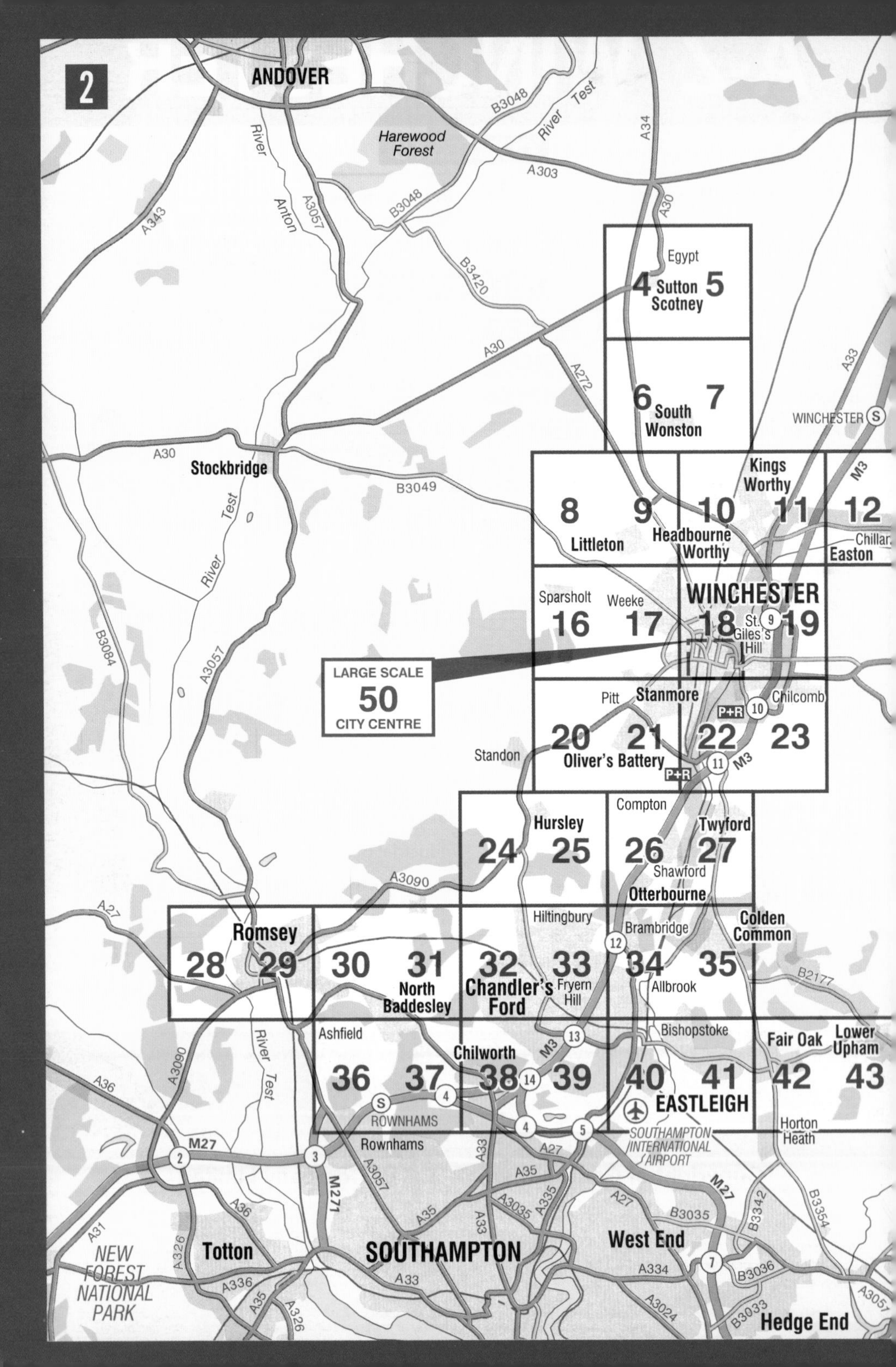
ANDOVER
Harewood Forest
River Anton
River Test
B3048
A34
A303
A30
A343
A3057
B3420
Egypt
4 Sutton Scotney 5
6 South Wonston 7
A272
A33
WINCHESTER
A30
Stockbridge
B3049
8 Littleton
9 Headbourne Worthy
10 Kings Worthy
11
12 Chilland Easton
M3
Sparsholt
Weeke
16
17
WINCHESTER
18 St. Giles's Hill
19
LARGE SCALE
50
CITY CENTRE
Pitt
Stanmore
Chilcomb
P+R
20 Oliver's Battery
21
22
23
Standon
B3084
Compton
Hursley
24
25
26
27 Twyford
Shawford
Otterbourne
A3090
A27
Hiltingbury
Brambridge
Colden Common
Romsey
28
29
30
31 North Baddesley
32 Chandler's Ford
33 Fryern Hill
34 Allbrook
35
B2177
Ashfield
Chilworth
36
37
38
39
40 EASTLEIGH
41 Bishopstoke
42 Fair Oak
43 Lower Upham
ROWNHAMS
Horton Heath
SOUTHAMPTON INTERNATIONAL AIRPORT
A36
M27
Rownhams
M271
A35
A3035
A335
B3035
B3342
B3354
West End
Totton
SOUTHAMPTON
A31
A326
NEW FOREST NATIONAL PARK
A336
A334
B3036
A3024
B3033
Hedge End

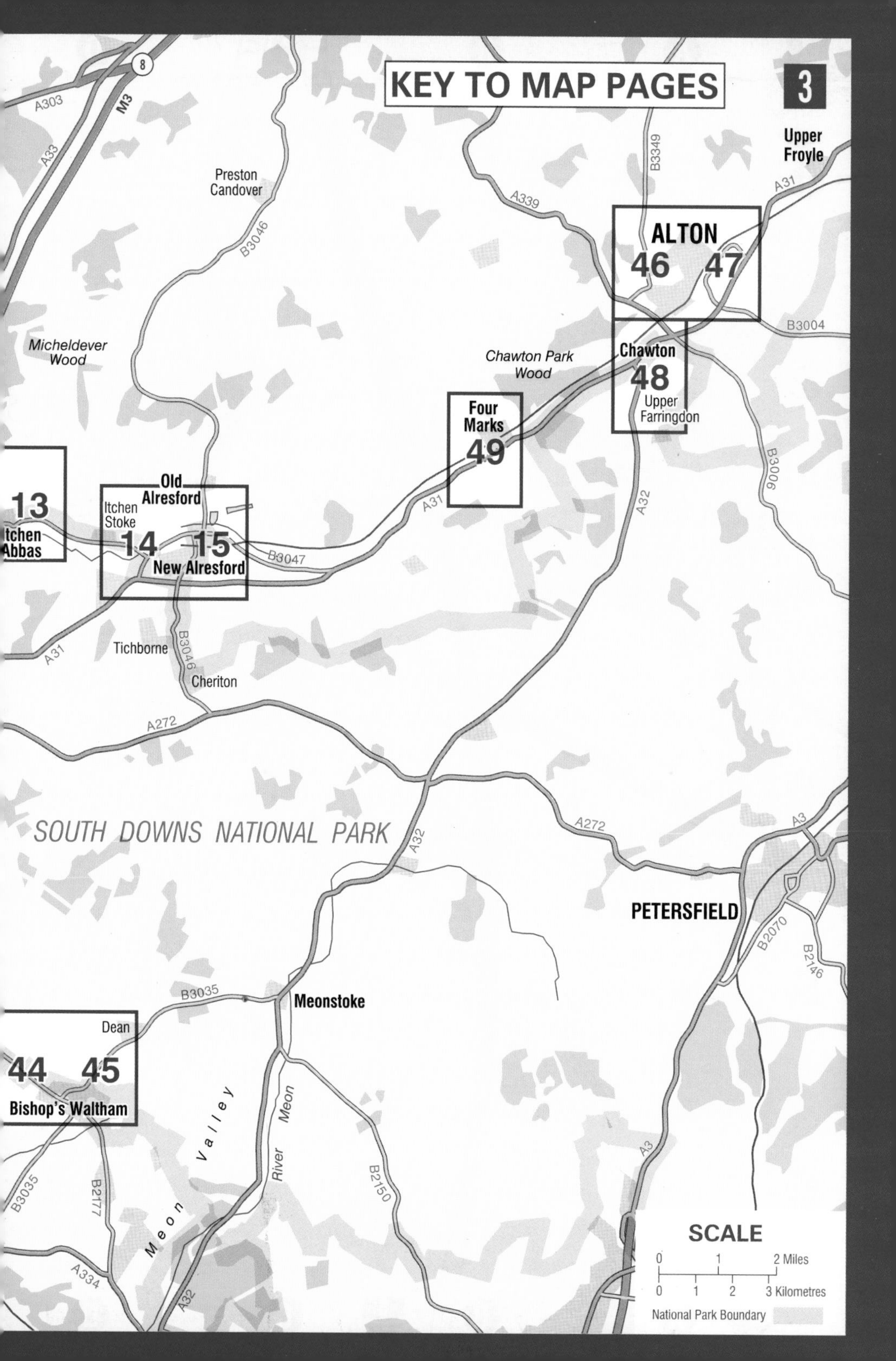
KEY TO MAP PAGES
Upper Froyle
A31
B3349
A339
ALTON
46
47
B3004
Chawton
48
Upper Farringdon
Chawton Park Wood
Four Marks
49
A31
B3006
A32
Preston Candover
B3046
A303
M3
8
A33
Micheldever Wood
13
Itchen Abbas
Old Alresford
Itchen Stoke
14
15
New Alresford
B3047
A31
Tichborne
B3046
Cheriton
A272
A272
SOUTH DOWNS NATIONAL PARK
A32
A3
PETERSFIELD
B2070
B2146
B3035
Meonstoke
Dean
44
45
Bishop's Waltham
Meon Valley
River Meon
B2150
B3035
B2177
A334
A32
A3
SCALE
0
1
2 Miles
0
1
2
3 Kilometres
National Park Boundary

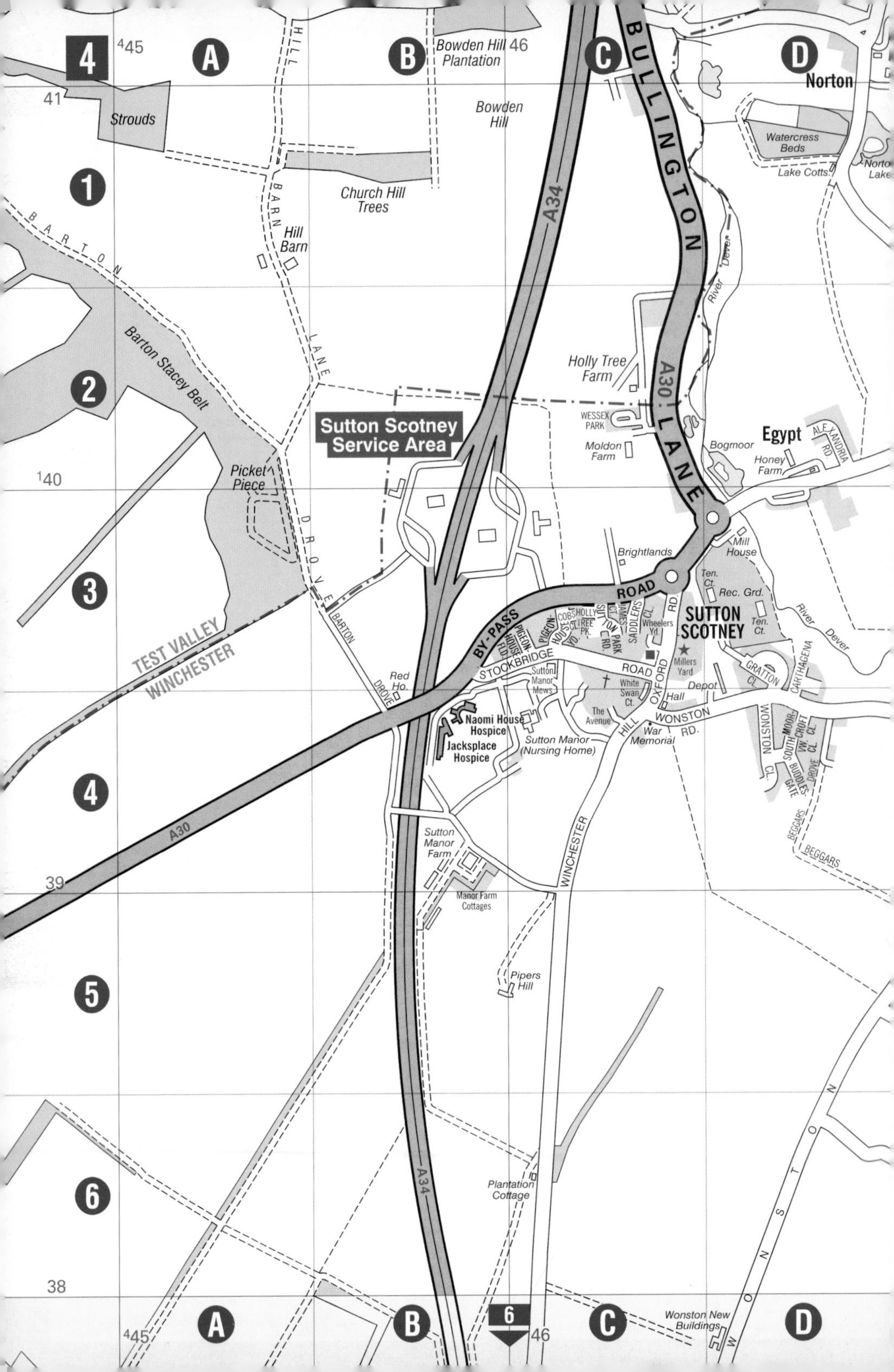
4
A
B
C
D
Bowden Hill Plantation
Norton
Strouds
Bowden Hill
BULLINGTON LANE
Watercress Beds
Lake Cotts.
Church Hill Trees
A34
BARN LANE
Hill Barn
BARTON
Barton Stacey Belt
River Dever
Holly Tree Farm
A30 LANE
Sutton Scotney Service Area
WESSEX PARK
Moldon Farm
Egypt
ALEXANDRIA RD.
Bogmoor
Honey Farm
Picket Piece
DROVE
Brightlands
Mill House
ROAD
BY-PASS
Ten. Ct.
Rec. Grd.
SUTTON SCOTNEY
Wheelers Yd.
SADDLERS CL.
Millers Yard
River Dever
STOCKBRIDGE ROAD
OXFORD RD.
TEST VALLEY
WINCHESTER
BARTON DROVE
Red Ho.
Sutton Manor Mews
White Swan Ct.
Hall
Depot
GRATTON CL.
CARTHAGENA
Naomi House Hospice
Jacksplace Hospice
The Avenue
HILL
WONSTON RD.
War Memorial
Sutton Manor (Nursing Home)
WONSTON CL.
SOUTH MOOR
CROFT VW. CL.
DROVE CL.
BUDDLES GATE
A30
WINCHESTER
Sutton Manor Farm
BEGGARS
39
Manor Farm Cottages
5
Pipers Hill
6
A34
Plantation Cottage
WONSTON
38
6
Wonston New Buildings
445
46
41
140

E
F
G
H
5
48
49
47
Manor Farm
Norton Manor
Counsellor's Walk
41
Hunton Grange Farm
1
New Cranbourne Cottages
Moat
Cranbourne Grange
Grove Hill
Chestnut Villas
DOWN LANE
2
Norsebury Ring
40
Norsebury Ring Fort
Hunton Manor Farm
Hunton Lodge
Cranbourne Lodge
Wonston Grange
Hunton Manor
Hunton
3
Norsebury Farm
Norsebury House
HUNTON LANE
Giddy Bri.
River Dever
Watercress Beds
The Old Ho.
Wonston
Wonston House
Upton House
Stoke Charity
4
Measures Gate
Southwinds
Winchester
39
SO21
5
6
Wonston Manor Farm
OLD STOKE ROAD
LANE
38
E
F
7
48
G
H
49
47

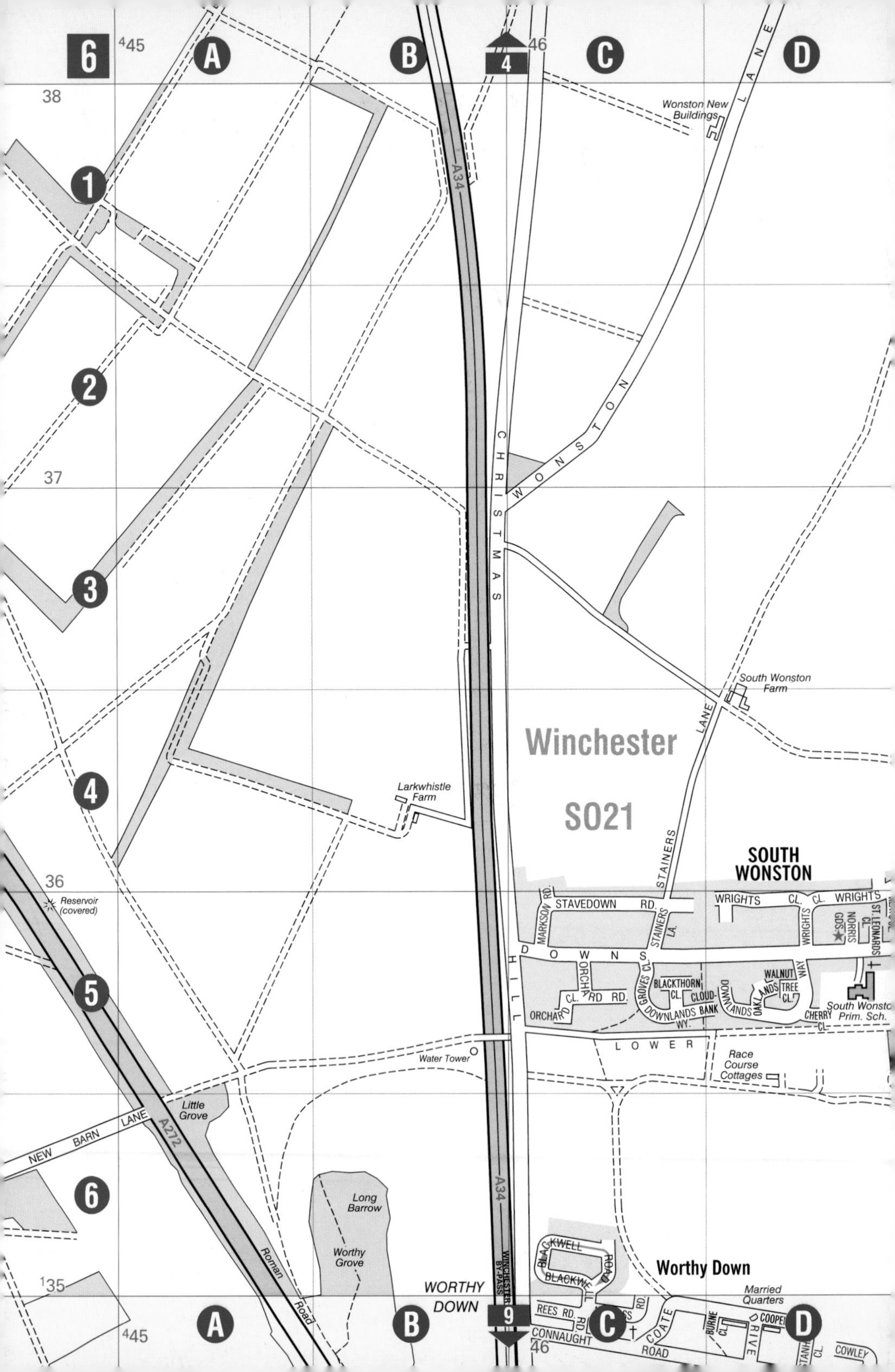
A
B
4
C
D
445
46
38
37
36
135
Wonston New Buildings
LANE
WONSTON
CHRISTMAS
A34
Winchester
SO21
South Wonston Farm
STAINERS
Larkwhistle Farm
SOUTH WONSTON
STAVEDOWN RD.
MARKSON RD.
STAINERS LA.
WRIGHTS CL.
NORRIS CL.
ST. LEONARDS
DOWNS
HILL
ORCHARD RD.
ORCHARD CL.
GROVES CL.
BLACKTHORN CL.
CLOUDBANK
DOWNLANDS WY.
DOWNLANDS
OAKLANDS
WALNUT TREE CL.
WAY
CHERRY CL.
South Wonston Prim. Sch.
LOWER
Water Tower
Race Course Cottages
Reservoir (covered)
NEW BARN LANE
A272
Little Grove
Long Barrow
Worthy Grove
Roman Road
WINCHESTER BY-PASS
BLACKWELL ROAD
Worthy Down
WORTHY DOWN
Married Quarters
REES RD.
CONNAUGHT ROAD
COATE
BURNE CL.
DRIVE
COOPER
COWLEY
9
1
2
3
4
5
6

7
5
10
E
F
G
H
47
48
49
38
37
36
35
1
2
3
4
5
6
Wonston Manor Farm
West Stoke Farm
STOKE ROAD
Windy Nook
Belle Vue
Sanctuary Farm
Ruby Cottage
Wallers Ash
ALRESFORD DROVE
ALRESFORD DROVE
OLD STOKE
Greenacres
Bayley's Clump
Southridge Copse
WEST HILL ROAD
LA FRENAYE PL.
GOLDFINCH WY.
FINCH CL.
CHAUCER CL.
CHAUCER WAY
SPRUCE CL.
BARROW CL.
LONG
BURNS CL.
NORTH WAVERLEY
HORNBM CL.
ROWAN CL.
WAVERLEY DR.
PADOK CL.
PINE CL.
ROAD
BORMAN WY.
HUNT CL.
W. HILL RD. STH.
LOVELL CL.
ANDERS RD.
STRONG CL.
ARM
GREEN CL.
OX DROVE
ROAD
Pav.
Playing Field
Tennis Ct.
Playground
CHARITY ROAD
Kingsway Farm
Little Stoke
North Winchester Farm
Depot
RILEY
ROAD
CONNAUGHT ROAD
Worthy Down Camp
Railway Cottages

43
A
B
C
D
135
New Barn Cottages
NEW BARN LANE
44
New Barn
CRAWLEY
Whitethorn House
Crawley Pond
Morns Field Cottages
Morns Field
SO21
Beeches Farm
The Beeches
34
Littleton House
Long Park
The Paddocks
Long Park Cottage
Long Park Farm
Winchester
STOCKBRIDGE
33
Church Garage
BALLDOWN CARAVAN & CAMPING PARK
Cradle Copse
Long Wood
Northwood Cottage
Lyne's Plantation
Winsley Cottage
NORTHWOOD PARK
Northwood Park Farm
Sparsholt College
Garston Farm
TRACK
GARSTONS
Garstons Buildings
Ball Down Farm
Chilcott's Plantation
B3049
LANE
Telephone Exchange
Bushmoor Copse
Smith's Plantation
32
Garston Cottages
Westley
HILLSIDE RD.
WESTLEY
Lodge
ROAD
Water Tower
WATLEY LANE
1
2
3
4
5
6

16

9
Worthy Down
WORTHY DOWN
Worthy Grove
Roman Road
Married Quarters
BLACKWELL
REES RD.
MALPASS RD.
CONNAUGHT
COATE DRIVE
BURNE CL.
COOPERS CL.
STANHAM CL.
COWLEY DR.
ROAD
Gallop
WINCHESTER BYPASS
A272
A34
Gas Valve Compound
Lower Farm
Lower Farm Cottages
Lower Farm House
Drovers Way
Earthwork
DOWN FARM LANE
Down Farm
Underpass
B3420
Roman Road
Littleton Stud
Stud Lodge
Littleton Stud Cottages
LANE
CHURCH
Littleton Manor
MAIN ROAD
OLD STABLE MEWS
SO22
Bowling Green
Tennis Cts.
Playground
Rec. Grd.
Hall
NEW RD.
PADDOCK VW.
ROZELLE CL.
HOLM OAK CL.
FAIR-CLOSE DR.
HOLLANDS CL.
THE HALL WAY
PITTER CL.
UPHILL RD.
WESTFIELD RD.
HILLTOP
LAWN RD.
HILLSIDE
FLOWERDOWN MOBILE HOME PARK
Playing Field
Ten. Cts.
Pav.
HILDEN WAY
FYFIELD WAY DRIVE
THE COURTYARD
LITTLETON
DALE CL.
RUTLEDGE DR.
VALLEY RD.
NORTH DRIVE
BERCOTE CL.
CHESTNUT AVENUE
SIR JOHN MOORE BARRACKS
ANDOVER ROAD
Sewage Works
WELLHOUSE LANE
HARESTOCK ROAD
BURITON
PRIORS DEAN RD.
MINSTEAD CL.
HICKORY
GRAYSHOTT CL.
CLOSE
NORTH
SOUTH DRIVE
MEADOW RI.
KENNEL
DROVE
Flowerdown House
Flowerdown Barrows
LITTLETON
6
10
17
E F G H
1 2 3 4 5 6
45 46 47
135 34 33 32

10
A
B
C
D
1
2
3
4
5
6
7
18
9
47
48
135
34
33
32
Worthy Down
Worthy Down Camp
North Winchester
Railway Cottages
Sewage Works
SO21
SO22
Down Farm
Underpass
WINCHESTER
DOWN
FARM
A34
Woodhams Farm
Springvale
Winchester
Headbourne Worthy
Upper Farm
Vokes Cotts.
Watercress Beds
The White Cottage
Manor House
Headbourne Worthy House
Taylors Corner
Lower Farm
Well House Farm
Headbourne Worthy Grange
Green Cl.
CONNAUGHT
RILEY ROAD
ROAD
STOKE
CHARITY
STANHAM CL.
COWLEY DR.
SHRONER WY.
CLOVERBANK
THE PASTURES
VALE WY.
KINGS CL.
ROBERTS CL.
Elan Ct.
CUNDELL
LARCH CL.
CEDAR CL.
WAY
MAPLE DR.
HOOKPIT FM. LA.
SYCAMORE DR.
FIRS GR.
ILEX CL.
LABURNUM DR.
CHURCHILL CL.
ELIZABETH CL.
NORTH RD.
BROOKE CL.
FORBES
TUDOR WY.
BOYNE
SPRINGVALE AV.
BENTLEY CL.
GLENDEEP CL.
ST. NICHOLAS RI.
NATIONAL
SPRINGVALE ROAD
BY PASS
BEDFIELD LANE
LONDON
PUDDING LA.
SCHOOL LANE
LANE
WELLHOUSE LANE
ANDOVER ROAD
ROAD
B3420
HARESTOCK
CLOSE
NORTH
GRAYSHOTT CL.

11
E
F
G
H
1
2
3
4
5
6
12
19
450
51
135
34
33
32
Depot
Southstoke Farm
Down Farm
Yearly Cotts.
Burntwood Cotts.
Burntwood Farm
Burntwood Cotts.
BRIDGETTS LANE
A33
ROAD
Burntwood Cottages
Bull Farm
Bank Fm.
Copse Farm
Depot
Meadow Farm
M3
M3-MOTORWAY
SO21
BASINGSTOKE ROAD
ROMAN ROAD
Rec. Grd.
Club
Recreation Ground
Playground
Hinton Cott.
Play. Fld.
Kings Worthy Prim.Sch.
Hinton House
KINGS WORTHY
SO23
Grace's Farm Cottages
Grace's Farm
The New House
Princes Mead Sch.
Homewood
WORTHY PARK
B3047
EASTON LANE
Abbotsworthy House
ABBOTS WORTHY
Worthy Park Home Farm
The Worthys
Mill
Ford
Subway
New Bridge Cott.
Easton Bridge
SOUTH DOWNS NATIONAL PARK
Nursery
Kingsworthy Ct.
Hall
Wks.
WATER LA.
M3 MOTORWAY
Pumping Station
Weir
The Old Rectory
CHURCH LANE
The Terrace
EASTON DOWN
LONG WK.
Hall
Sports Grd.
CHAPLE LA.
MALTHOUSE CL.
EASTON

12
A33
51
A
B
52
C
D
135
Rutherley Copse
Subway
Chillandham Farm
BRIDGETTS
1
urntwood Cotts.
Rutherley Copse
M3
Pavis Copse
CHILLANDHAM
M3-MOTORWAY
Roman Villa (site of)
2
Reservoir (covered)
Bridget House
Bridget's Experimental Husbandry Farm
34
3
11
Winchester
SO21
LANE
4
SHEPHERDS FLD.
Chillandham Cottages
Garage Cottages
Couch Green
Grace's Farm
Grace's Farm Cottages
33
Freefolk House
Martyr Worthy Place
COUCH GRN.
Rec. Grd.
Sports Grd.
B3047
Cygnet House
B3047
Manor House
MARTYR WORTHY
Chilland Barn
Upper Chilland House
Hall
CHURCH LANE
5
EASTON LANE
Chilland
Chilland Ho.
CHILLAND LANE
Lower Chilland House
New Bridge Cott.
RIVER ITCHEN
Easton Bridge
Weir
SOUTH DOWNS
Weir
6
AVINGTON LAKE
Power House
Easton Lodge
Old tory
CHURCH LANE
The Terrace
EASTON
MALTHOUSE CL.
32
Hall
CHAPEL LA.
Earthwork
Sports Grd.
High Down
EASTON
51
52
Low Grounds

Courtney's Copse
E
F
54
G
H
455
135
Itchen Stoke Down
1
2
3
4
5
6
ROAD
Itchen Down House
Itchen Down Farm
Lone Farm
34
Spreadoak Cottages
NORTHINGTON
RECTORY
Veterinary Centre
Oxdrove Way
Rectory Lane Dairy
New Farm Cottages
ITCHEN ABBAS
Winton Cottages
BARING CL.
Abbey House
LANE
Railway Cottages
The Elms
33
Clock Cottage
SCHOOL LA.
Little Hayes
LITTLE HAYES LANE
Hazeldene Gds.
STATION CL.
Station Approach
OLD STATION RD.
ROAD
The Paddock
Itchen Abbas Prim. Sch.
ABBAS BUS. CEN.
Itchen Abbas Ho.
Hall
STATION
HILL
SHELLEY CL.
Fish Farm
Fish Farm
Park Farm
B3047
AVINGTON
Itchen Abbas Manor
Chalk Pit
Waterfall
NATIONAL PARK
AVINGTON PARK GOLF COURSE
Avington Lodge
LANE
The Pavilion
Avington House
The Rectory
AVINGTON PARK
Yavington Farm Cottage
Club Ho.
Pinder Centre
Lonsica
Earthwork
TEMPLE
The New Houses
Yavington Farm
LOVINGTON
Yavington Mead
AVINGTON
The Row
32
DRIVE
LANE
West Hill Dairy
53

14
A
B
C
D
56
57
34
33
132
31
1
2
3
4
5
6
Dog Kennel Row
Watercress Beds
Andover Water Plantation
Oxdrove Way
ABBOTSTONE ROAD
Fobdown Farm
Fobdown
Lodge
Folly Hill Farm
Alresford
SO24
New England Cott.
Keepers Cott.
Fob Down
Fish Farm
RIVER
DROVE
LANE
Fish Pond
Arlebury Park
ITCHEN STOKE
Longcrate Cottages
Rectory
ITCHEN VW.
151
Manor Farm
Itchen Stoke Manor
Watercress Beds
Woodlands
West Lodge
Round House
ROAD
BRIDGE RD.
B3047
Itchen Stoke House
Garden Cottages
WATER LA.
Cricket Grd.
Pav.
Borough Farm
WINCHESTER
NEW
DE-LUCY
AV.
Willowfield
Steward's Bri.
SOUTH CL.
Nicholson Pl.
SOUTH FARM
DORIAN GRO.
JESTY RD.
COVEY
PERINS
NEW IND.
RIVER ITCHEN
Ford
Fish Farm
Lady Croft Cottages
LADYCROFT
ALRESFORD ROAD
Itchenstoke Mill
Yew Tree Cottages
Lady Croft Farm
Watercress Beds
WATERCRESS MDW
Kingsley Bogs
LOVINGTON LANE
Thatch Cottage
OVINGTON
Hall
Park Farm
EAST LANE
North Lodge
East Lodge
East Lane Cott.
East Lane Down
Pumping Sta.
Vernal Cotts.
A31
Ovington House
SOUTH DOWNS NATIONAL PARK
South Lodge
RIVER ITCHEN
Vernal Farm Cottage
Park Lodge
Vernal Farm
Winchester Lodge
Trodd's Copse
The Crawls

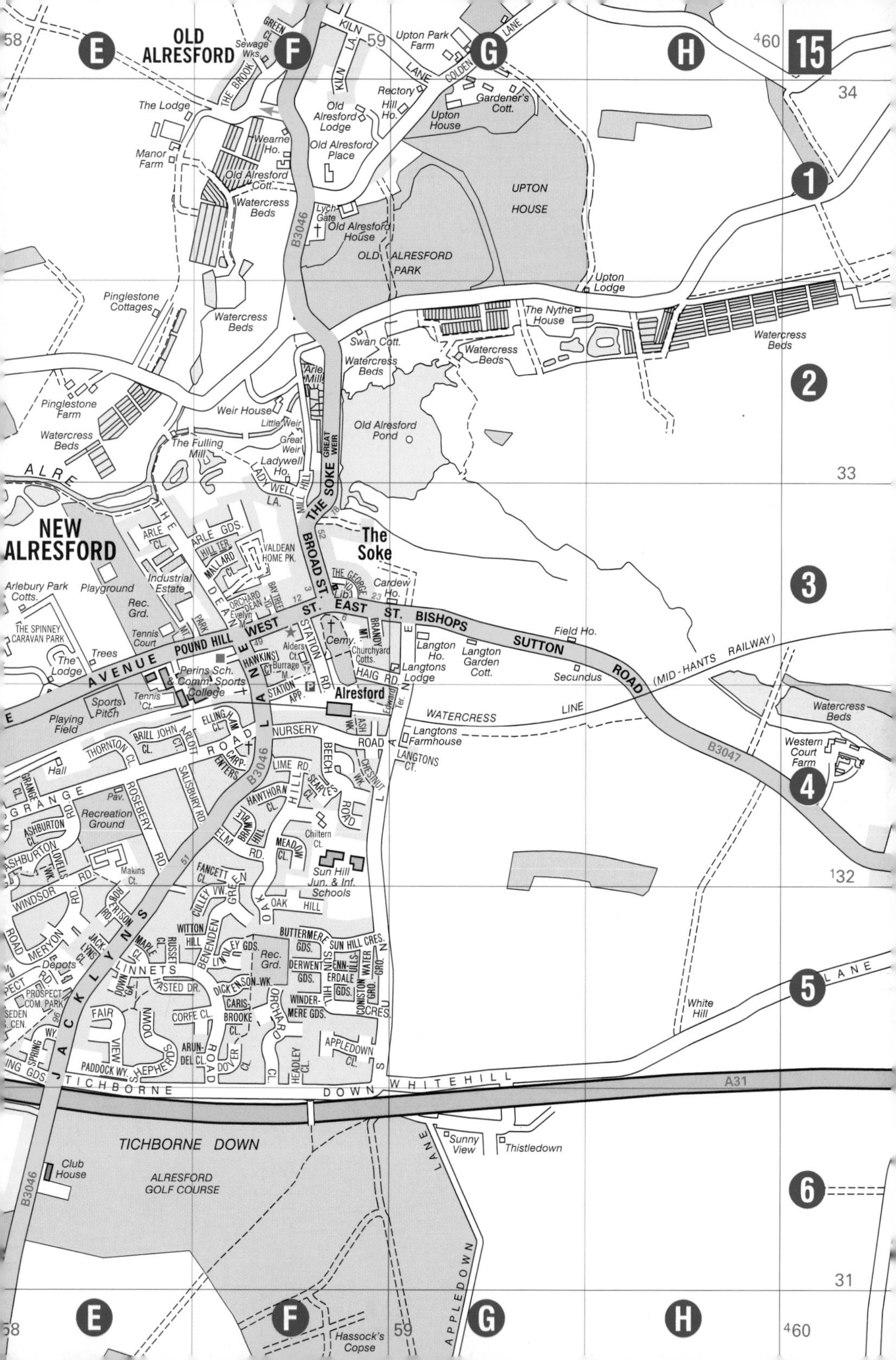

OLD ALRESFORD
NEW ALRESFORD
The Soke
Alresford
UPTON HOUSE
OLD ALRESFORD PARK
Old Alresford Pond
TICHBORNE DOWN
ALRESFORD GOLF COURSE
Watercress Beds
Upton House
Upton Lodge
The Nythe House
Old Alresford Place
Old Alresford Lodge
Old Alresford House
Old Alresford Cott.
Manor Farm
The Lodge
Pinglestone Cottages
Pinglestone Farm
Weir House
The Fulling Mill
Ladywell Ho.
Swan Cott.
Field Ho.
Secundus
Langton Ho.
Langton Garden Cott.
Langtons Lodge
Langtons Farmhouse
Western Court Farm
White Hill
Sunny View
Thistledown
Club House
Hassock's Copse
Upton Park Farm
Rectory Hill Ho.
Gardener's Cott.
Perins Sch. & Comm. Sports College
Sun Hill Jun. & Inf. Schools
Recreation Ground
Playing Field
Sports Pitch
Industrial Estate
Arlebury Park Cotts.
THE SPINNEY CARAVAN PARK
VALDEAN HOME PK.
PROSPECT COM. PARK
BROAD ST.
THE SOKE
WEST ST.
EAST ST.
BISHOPS SUTTON ROAD
POUND HILL
AVENUE
JACKLYNS LANE
TICHBORNE DOWN
WHITEHILL LANE
APPLEDOWN LANE
GRANGE ROAD
NURSERY ROAD
SALISBURY RD.
ROSEBERY RD.
MID-HANTS RAILWAY
WATERCRESS LINE
B3046
B3047
A31
E
F
G
H
1
2
3
4
5
6
58
59
460
34
33
132
31

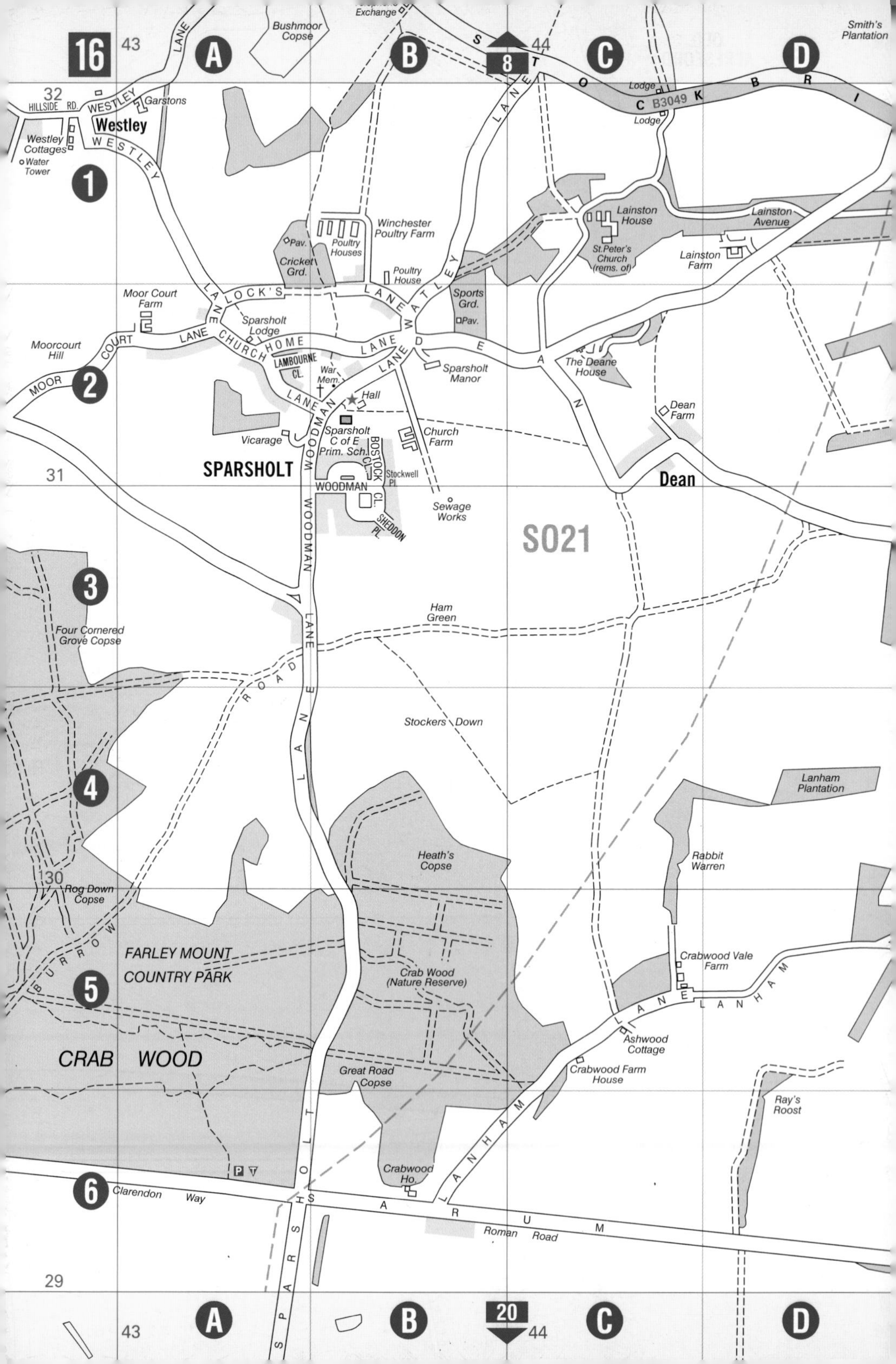
Exchange
Bushmoor Copse
Smith's Plantation
43
44
A
B
C
D
8
STOCKBRIDGE
B3049
Lodge
Lodge
32
HILLSIDE RD.
WESTLEY
Garstons
Westley
Westley Cottages
Water Tower
WESTLEY LANE
1
Lainston House
Lainston Avenue
St.Peter's Church (rems. of)
Lainston Farm
Winchester Poultry Farm
Poultry Houses
Pav.
Cricket Grd.
Poultry House
WATLEY LANE
LOCK'S LANE
Sports Grd.
Pav.
Moor Court Farm
Sparsholt Lodge
Moorcourt Hill
MOOR COURT LANE
CHURCH LANE
HOME LANE
DEANE
The Deane House
LAMBOURNE CL.
War Mem.
Sparsholt Manor
2
Hall
Dean Farm
Vicarage
Sparsholt C of E Prim. Sch.
BOSTOCK CL.
Church Farm
SPARSHOLT
WOODMAN
Stockwell Pl.
Dean
31
WOODMAN CL.
SHEDDON PL.
Sewage Works
SO21
3
Four Cornered Grove Copse
Ham Green
ROAD
WOODMAN LANE
Stockers Down
4
Lanham Plantation
Heath's Copse
Rabbit Warren
130
Rog Down Copse
BURROW
FARLEY MOUNT COUNTRY PARK
Crabwood Vale Farm
Crab Wood (Nature Reserve)
5
LANHAM LANE
Ashwood Cottage
CRAB WOOD
Great Road Copse
Crabwood Farm House
Ray's Roost
Crabwood Ho.
P
6
Clarendon Way
SPARSHOLT LANE
SARUM
Roman Road
29
20

LITTLETON
Harestock
WEEKE
Winchester
SO22
TEG DOWN
ROYAL WINCHESTER GOLF COURSE
Sleepers Hill
SIR JOHN MOORE BARRACKS
Flowerdown Barrows
Flowerdown House
Little Harestock Farm
Crabwood Cottage
The Down House
Apley House
Harestock Corner
Terwick
Wyke Mark
Salters
CROUCHER'S CROFT
Harestock Prim. Sch.
Weeke Prim. Sch.
Peter Symonds Coll. (ACE)
Henry Beaufort Sch.
Adult Education Cen.
The Westgate Sch.
Western C of E Prim. Sch.
WEST DOWNS STUDENT VILLAGE
Univ. of Winchester (West Downs Campus)
ROYAL HAMPSHIRE COUNTY HOSPITAL
University of Winchester (King Alfred Campus)
HMP WINCHESTER
SARUM RD. BMI HOSPITAL
Reservoir (covered)
Lanham Down
Weeke Down
PINSET CAMP SITE
Old Butt
Old Butts
Sewage Works
Earthworks
Royal Winchester Mews
Club House
Teg Down Farm
Sarum Farm
Flagstaff Stables
Tower Arts Cen.
Kings School
Knights Lodge
Sleeper's Hill House
Melbury Lodge
Alwyn Hall
Milnthorpe
Roman Road
B3049
B3041
B3040
B3420
ANDOVER ROAD NORTH
CHILBOLTON AVENUE
STONEY LANE
HARESTOCK ROAD
LITTLETON ROAD
DEANE DOWN DROVE
KENNEL LANE
SALTERS LANE
LANHAM LANE
TEG DOWN MEADS
DEAN LANE
BEREWEEKE ROAD
ROMSEY ROAD
SARUM ROAD
CLARENDON WAY
KILHAM LANE
9
18
21

WINCHESTER
Abbotts Barton
Hyde
Fulflood
WEEKE
West Hill
The Close
The Soke
Wharf Hill
SO22
SO23
ROYAL HAMPSHIRE COUNTY HOSPITAL
University of Winchester (King Alfred Campus)
Univ. of Winchester West Downs Campus
HMP WINCHESTER
Peter Symonds' College
Henry Beaufort Sch.
Cathedral
Wolvesey Castle
Wolvesey Palace
Winchester College
Winchester City FC
Rugby Football Ground
North Walls Recreation Ground
River Park Leis. Cen.
Riverside Indoor Bowl. Club
Winnall Moors Nature Reserve
Winchester Gallery
Univ. of Southampton
City Mill
Cemetery
Osborne Sch.
The Westgate Sch.
Western C of E Prim. Sch.
Weeke Prim. Sch.
Peter Symonds Coll. (ACE)
Adult Education Cen.
ANDOVER ROAD B3420 NORTH
STONEY LANE
BEREWEEKE ROAD B3041
STOCKBRIDGE ROAD B3049
ROMSEY ROAD B3040
WORTHY ROAD B3047
LONDON ROAD B3047
NORTH WALLS
FRIARSGATE
WELLHOUSE LANE
PARK ROAD
ST. CROSS RD. B3335

Winchester
SOUTH DOWNS NATIONAL PARK
SO21
Junction 9
M3
M3-MOTORWAY
EASTON DOWN
WINCHESTER BY-PASS
A34
SPITFIRE LINK
A272
LONG WALK
EASTON LANE
CHAPEL LANE
CHURCH LANE
Pumping Station
Rectory
The Terrace
Hall
Sports Grd.
Chapel Field
Cocket's Mead
Dairy Farm
Dairy Cottages
Lone Barn
Easton Manor Farm
Winnall Cottage Farm
White Hill Cott.
Shoulder of Mutton Farm
Harfield Farm
RIVER ITCHEN
THE WYKEHAM INDUSTRIAL ESTATE
Works
Depot
Gasholder Sta.
Warehouse
Erasmus Park
WINCHESTER TRADE PARK
Superstore
SUN VALLEY IND. PK.
WINNALL TRADING ESTATE
Mus.
Dennett Ho.
Craddock Ho.
Braxton Ho.
Earle Ho.
WINNALL VALLEY RD.
Winnall
Comm. Cen.
Winnall Prim. Sch.
Fairdown
St. Giles's Hill
Cemy.
Highcliffe
Winnall Down Copse
Winnall Down Farm
Roseacre
No Man's Land
Magdalen Hill Farm
Glencross
St. Swithun's School
Tennis Cts.
LEIGH HOUSE
B3404
ALRESFORD ROAD
MAGDALEN HILL DOWN
Lodge
Magdalen Hill Cemetery
PETERSFIELD ROAD
A31
KINGS LANE
Rec. Grd.
Pav.
Sports Ground
11
23

43
A
B
16
44
C
D
Roman Road
SARUM
SPARSHOLT LANE
29
1
2
28
3
4
27
5
6
26
LANE
ENMILL LANE
Enmill House
Enmill Bungalow
Enmill Barn
Enmill Cottage
Enmill Farm
Pit View
Vale Farm
The Strawberry Fields
Sunbeams
Grovelands Copse
Winchester
White House
Yew Tree
ROMSEY
MILLERS
The Green
Pitt Copse
Stopham's Copse
Larkfarm Plantation
A3090
SPARSHOLT
Standon Fm.
Standon
Juniper Bank
Nan Trodd's Hill
SO21
Butcher's Plantation
Down Farm
Chalk Pit
PORT
25

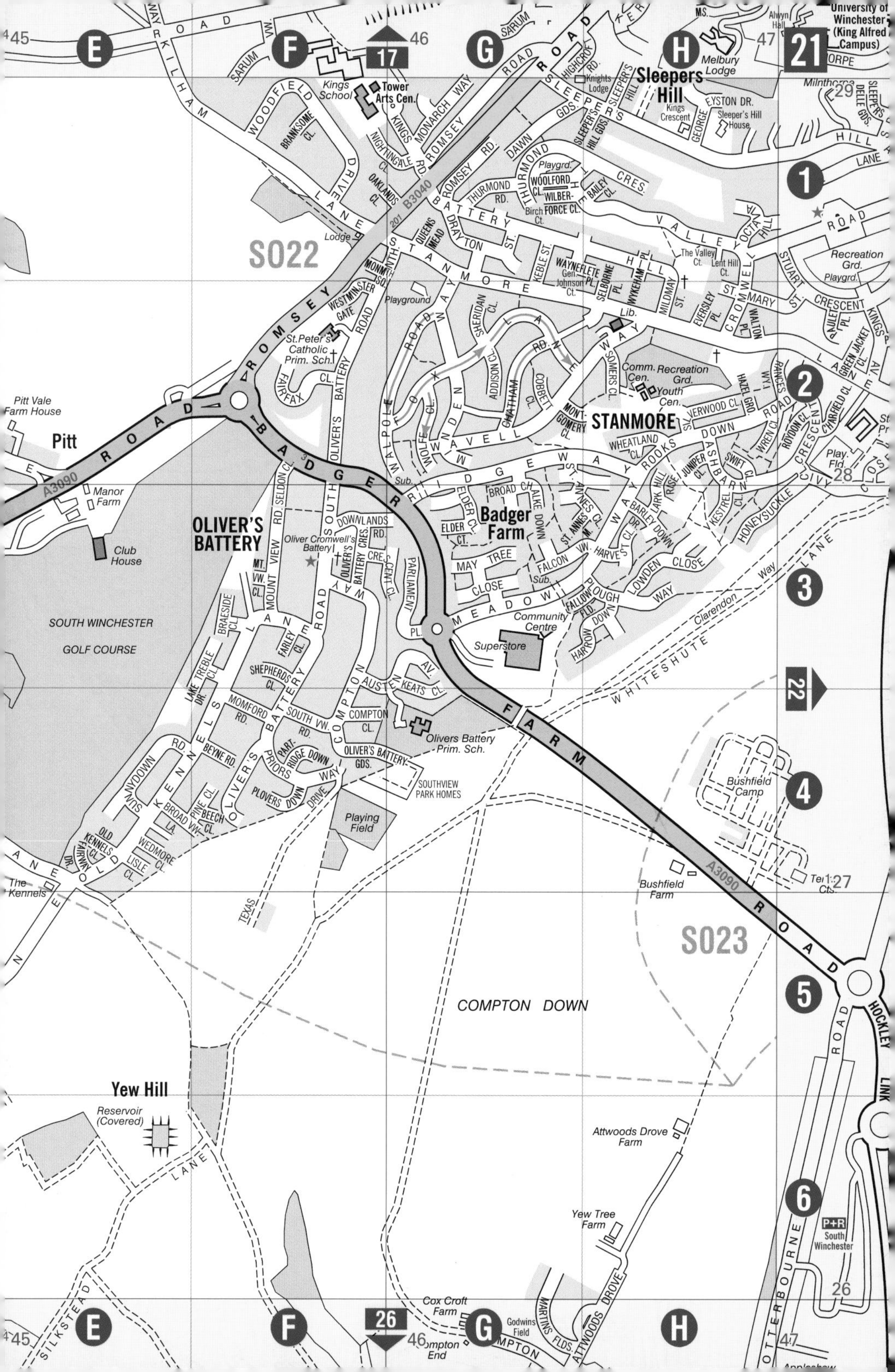

21
17
22
26
Sleepers Hill
S022
S023
STANMORE
Badger Farm
OLIVER'S BATTERY
Pitt
Yew Hill
COMPTON DOWN
SOUTH WINCHESTER GOLF COURSE
University of Winchester (King Alfred Campus)
Kings School
Tower Arts Cen.
Melbury Lodge
Knights Lodge
Kings Crescent
Sleeper's Hill House
Recreation Grd.
Playground
St.Peter's Catholic Prim. Sch.
Pitt Vale Farm House
Manor Farm
Club House
Oliver Cromwell's Battery
Comm. Cen.
Youth Cen.
Community Centre
Superstore
Olivers Battery Prim. Sch.
SOUTHVIEW PARK HOMES
Playing Field
Bushfield Camp
Bushfield Farm
The Kennels
Reservoir (Covered)
Attwoods Drove Farm
Yew Tree Farm
Cox Croft Farm
Godwins Field
P+R South Winchester
ROMSEY ROAD
BADGER FARM ROAD
A3090
B3040
STANMORE LANE
WHITESHUTE LANE
Clarendon Way
HOCKLEY LINK
OTTERBOURNE ROAD
KILHAM LANE
WOODFIELD DRIVE
SLEEPERS HILL
VALLEY
CROMWELL RD.
ST. JAMES
OLIVER'S BATTERY ROAD
SOUTH VIEW
COMPTON WAY
KENNELS LANE
SILKSTEAD
ATTWOODS DROVE
MARTINS FLDS.

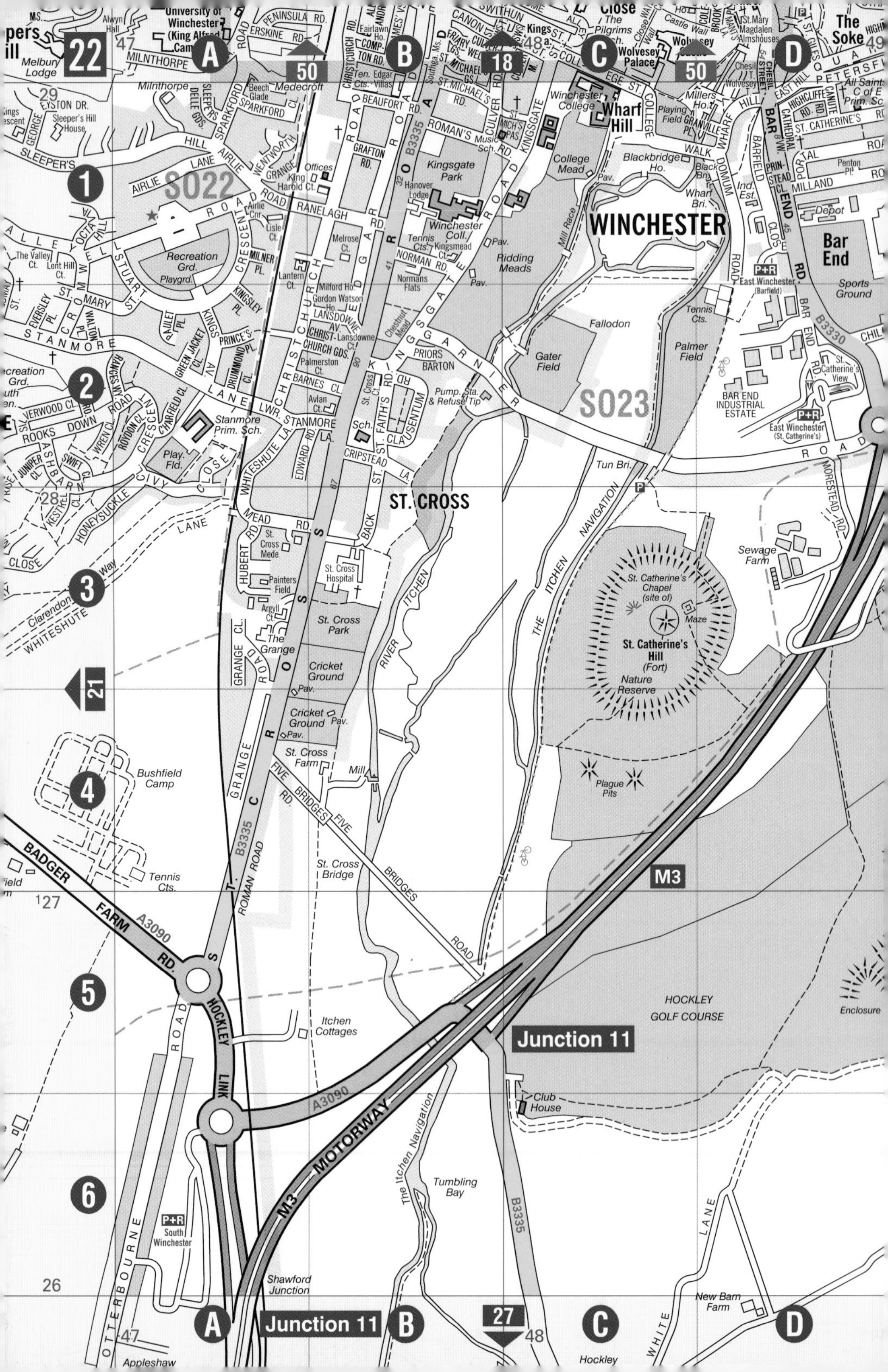

22
WINCHESTER
ST. CROSS
SO22
SO23
Recreation Grd.
Kingsgate Park
Winchester Coll.
Ridding Meads
College Mead
Wharf Hill
Winchester College
Wolvesey Palace
Gater Field
Palmer Field
Fallodon
Bar End
Sports Ground
BAR END INDUSTRIAL ESTATE
East Winchester (Barfield)
East Winchester (St. Catherine's)
St. Catherine's Hill (Fort)
Nature Reserve
St. Catherine's Chapel (site of)
Maze
Plague Pits
Sewage Farm
St. Cross Hospital
St. Cross Park
Cricket Ground
St. Cross Farm
St. Cross Bridge
Bushfield Camp
Itchen Cottages
Tumbling Bay
HOCKLEY GOLF COURSE
Club House
Enclosure
Junction 11
M3 MOTORWAY
A3090
B3335
B3330
South Winchester
Shawford Junction
New Barn Farm
Hockley
Appleshaw
Stanmore Prim. Sch.
RIVER ITCHEN
THE ITCHEN NAVIGATION
The Itchen Navigation
STANMORE LANE
BADGER FARM RD.
HOCKLEY LINK
OTTERBOURNE ROAD
WHITE LANE
FIVE BRIDGES ROAD
KINGSGATE ROAD
CHRISTCHURCH ROAD
EDGAR ROAD
ST. CROSS ROAD
GRANGE ROAD
ROMAN ROAD
GARNIER ROAD
MILNTHORPE LANE
SLEEPER'S HILL
AIRLIE LANE
RANELAGH RD.
CROMWELL RD.
BAR END RD.
WHARF HILL
COLLEGE WALK
ST. CATHERINE'S ROAD
MORESTEAD RD.
50
18
21
27

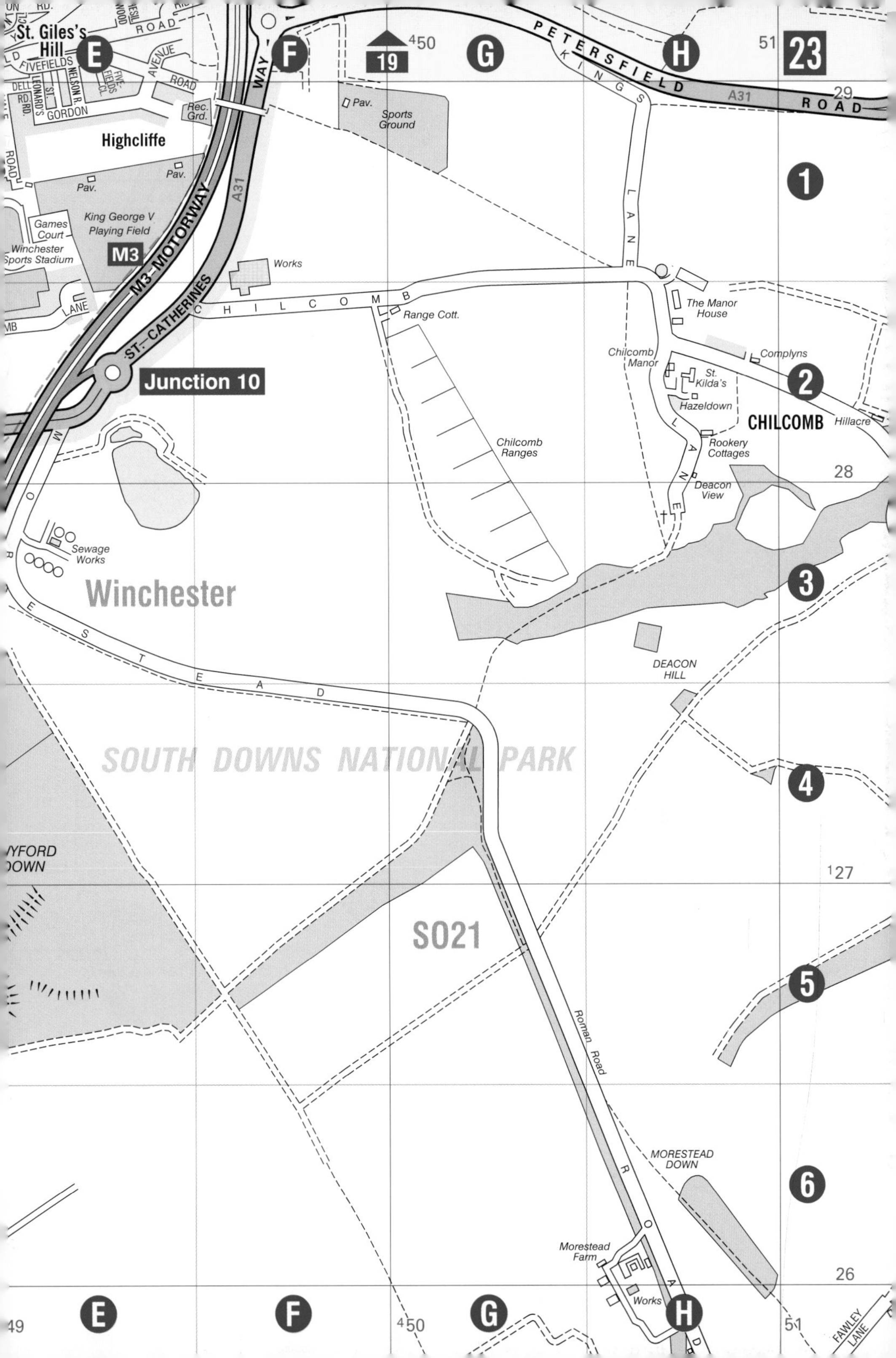
St. Giles's Hill
E
F
19
450
G
H
51
PETERSFIELD ROAD
A31
KINGS LANE
ROAD
FIVEFIELDS
AVENUE
ROAD
NELSON R.
FIVEFIELDS CL.
DELL RD.
LEONARD'S RD.
ST.
GORDON
Rec. Grd.
Pav.
Sports Ground
29
Highcliffe
WAY
Pav.
Pav.
King George V Playing Field
Games Court
Winchester Sports Stadium
M3
M3 MOTORWAY
A31
Works
ST. CATHERINES
CHILCOMB
Range Cott.
The Manor House
Chilcomb Manor
Complyns
St. Kilda's
Hazeldown
CHILCOMB
Hillacre
Junction 10
Chilcomb Ranges
Rookery Cottages
Deacon View
LANE
28
Sewage Works
Winchester
MORESTEAD
DEACON HILL
SOUTH DOWNS NATIONAL PARK
TWYFORD DOWN
27
SO21
Roman Road
MORESTEAD DOWN
Morestead Farm
Works
26
ROAD
FAWLEY LANE
1
2
3
4
5
6
E
F
G
H
49
450
51

Pillinch Copse
Anmery Cottages
Chalk Pit
Waterloo Plantation
Sunlight Cottages
Home Farm
Cromwell House
KEBLE CL.
PORT
Catways
HEATHCOTE PL.
HURSLEY PARK ROAD
Recreation Ground
Rifle Range
HURSLEY PARK
Vicarage
HURSLEY
MEREDUN CL.
Pelican Ct.
Home Farm Row
Pavilion
Sports Ground
Tennis Court
Hall
SOUTH END CL.
Hursley Park
Cricket Ground
John Keble C of E Prim. Sch.
Keeper's Lodge
Little Fir Hill
A3090
Ampfield Copse
Hawker's Fir Hill
Portland Bank
Portland Copse
Deer Park Farm
Ladwell
Square Copse
HUNTERS RIDE
Bushy Copse
Petty Priest Copse
Snow's Copse
Fitts Copse
RATLAKE LANE
Red House
AMPFIELD WOOD
Kent's Copse
B3043
Ampfield Plantation
Nevil's Copse
Lower Ratlake Farm
WINCHESTER
TEST VALLEY
Ratlake Hall
Ratlake
Romsey
Lake Court
Purdue's Copse
Ryder's Row
Upper Ratlake Farmhouse
POTTERS HERON LA.
HOOK ROAD
White's Copse
Hawstead Farm
HURSLEY ROAD
Buddy's Barn
SO51
POTTERS HERON CL.
Sandpit Copse
Hook Row
Hocombe
Hocombe Upper Plantation
ROTHVILLE PL.
A B C D
1 2 3 4 5 6
41 42
26 25 24 23

32

43
E
F
20
44
G
H
445
25
26
PORT LANE
LANE
LINS LANE
Shawlands Farm
Cemetery
Parsonage Farm
Winchester
SO21
Bunstead
BUNSTEAD LANE
Bunstead Farm
SILKSTEAD LANE
SHEPHERDS LANE
Upper Silkstead Farm
Silkstead
Silkstead Farm
125
1
2
3
4
5
6
Brooks Copse
Blacklands Copse
Weedacre Copse
Hursley Forest
Cullys Copse
Windmill Copse
Strowdens Copse
POLES LANE
Lower Silkstead Farmhouse
Club Ho.
Driving Range
OTTERBOURNE GOLF COURSE
24
Freemantles Copse
Wells Bow
Barn Copse
Field House
Matthew's Copse
Greenclose Copse
Longmoor House
Great Pond
Cranbury House
Hessians Copse
The Gardens
Home Farm
Great Moorlands Copse
23
Hocombe Bridge
Hocombe Lodge
The Lodge
33
CRANBURY PARK
Upper Pond
Hocombe
ASHDOWN DR.
Little

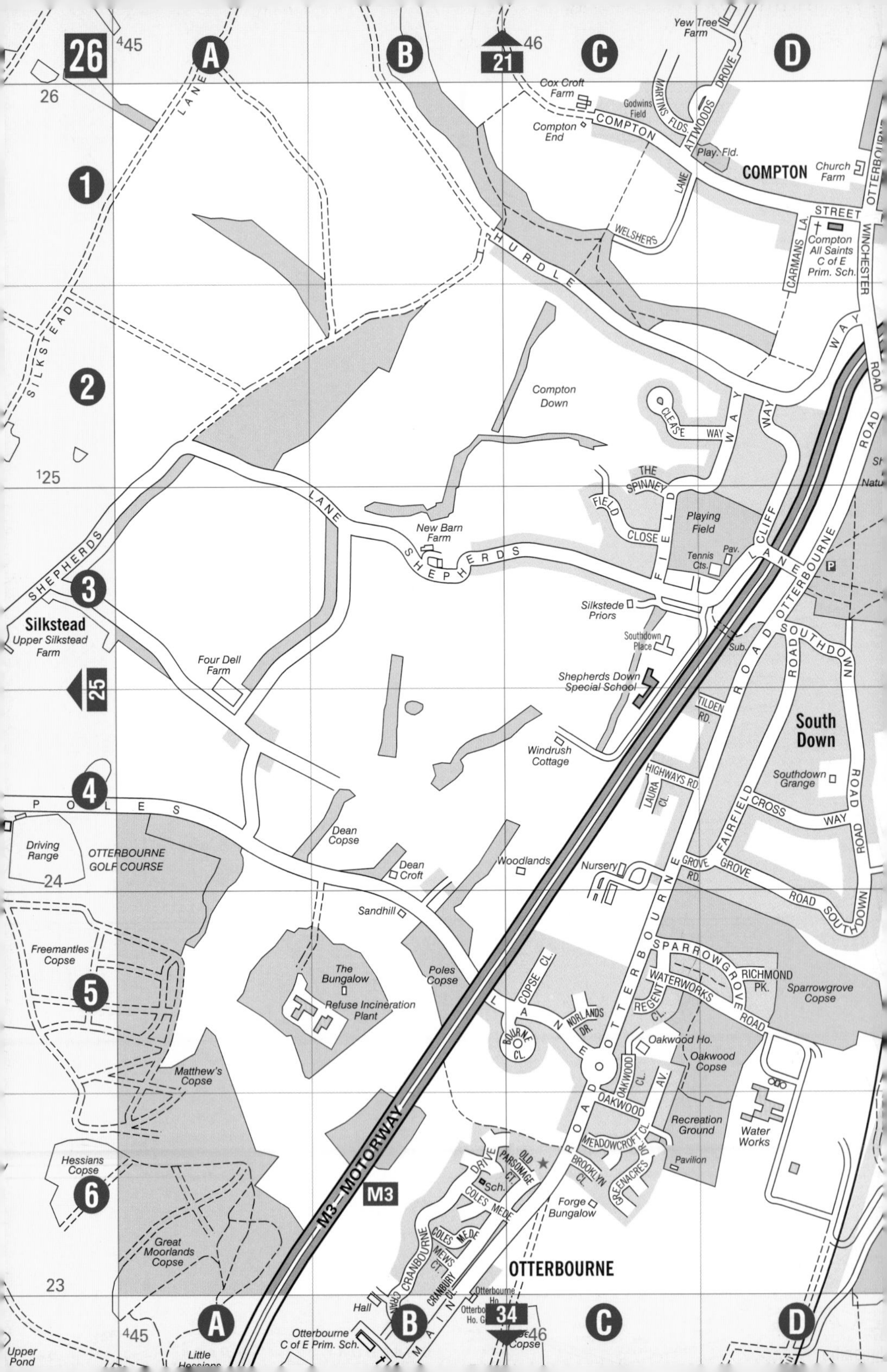
A
B
C
D
21
445
46
26
1
2
3
4
5
6
125
24
23
25
34
Yew Tree Farm
Cox Croft Farm
Godwins Field
COMPTON
Compton End
MARTINS FLDS.
ATTWOODS
DROVE
Play. Fld.
COMPTON
Church Farm
OTTERBOURNE
LANE
STREET
WELSHERS
HURDLE
CARMANS LA.
Compton All Saints C of E Prim. Sch.
WINCHESTER
WAY
ROAD
SILKSTEAD
Compton Down
CLEASE WAY
WAY
THE SPINNEY
FIELD CLOSE
FIELD
Playing Field
Tennis Cts.
Pav.
CLIFF
LANE
New Barn Farm
SHEPHERDS
LANE
SHEPHERDS
Silkstead
Upper Silkstead Farm
Silkstede Priors
Southdown Place
Sub.
OTTERBOURNE
ROAD
SOUTHDOWN
ROAD
Four Dell Farm
Shepherds Down Special School
TILDEN RD.
South Down
Windrush Cottage
HIGHWAYS RD.
LAURA CL.
Southdown Grange
FAIRFIELD
CROSS
WAY
ROAD
POLES
Driving Range
OTTERBOURNE GOLF COURSE
Dean Copse
Dean Croft
Woodlands
Nursery
GROVE RD.
GROVE
ROAD
SOUTHDOWN
Sandhill
Freemantles Copse
The Bungalow
Refuse Incineration Plant
Poles Copse
COPSE CL.
LANE
SPARROWGROVE
RICHMOND PK.
Sparrowgrove Copse
WATERWORKS
ROAD
REGENT CL.
NORLANDS DR.
BOURNE CL.
Oakwood Ho.
Oakwood Copse
OAKWOOD CL.
AV.
OAKWOOD
Matthew's Copse
Recreation Ground
Water Works
M3 — MOTORWAY
M3
DRIVE
Sch.
OLD PARSONAGE CT.
MEADOWCROFT CL.
BROOKLYN CL.
GREENACRES DR.
Pavilion
Hessians Copse
COLES MEDE
Forge Bungalow
Great Moorlands Copse
CRANBOURNE
COLES MEDE
MEWS CT.
CRANBURY CL.
OTTERBOURNE
Hall
Otterbourne Ho.
Otterbourne Ho. G.
MAIN
Otterbourne C of E Prim. Sch.
Copse
Upper Pond
Little Hessians

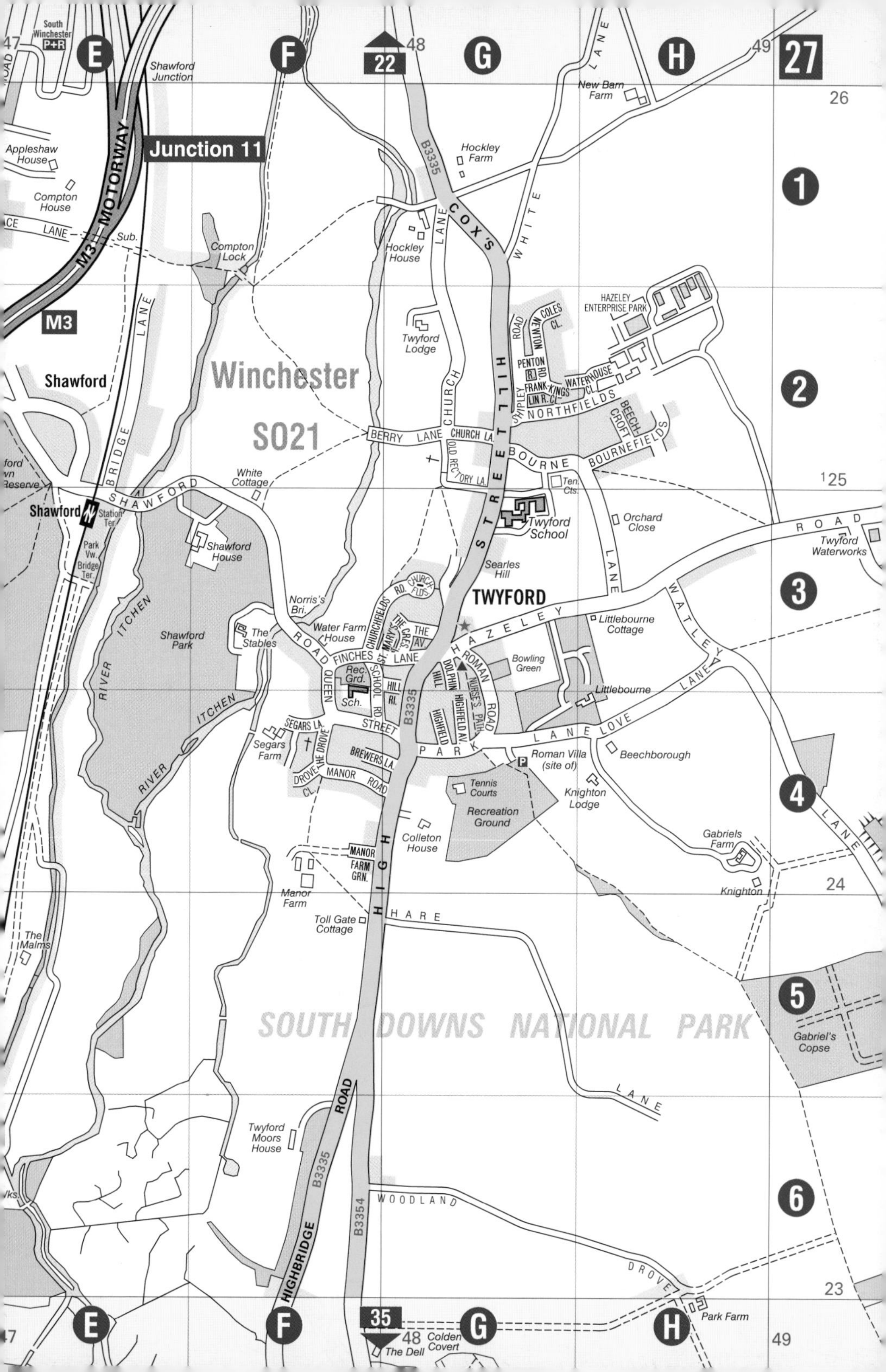

Winchester
SO21
TWYFORD
Shawford
SOUTH DOWNS NATIONAL PARK
Junction 11
M3 MOTORWAY
M3
South Winchester P+R
Shawford Junction
Appleshaw House
Compton House
Compton Lock
Hockley Farm
Hockley House
New Barn Farm
Twyford Lodge
HAZELEY ENTERPRISE PARK
White Cottage
Shawford House
Shawford Park
The Stables
Norris's Bri.
Water Farm House
Twyford School
Searles Hill
Orchard Close
Twyford Waterworks
Littlebourne Cottage
Littlebourne
Bowling Green
Beechborough
Roman Villa (site of)
Knighton Lodge
Tennis Courts
Recreation Ground
Colleton House
Gabriels Farm
Knighton
Segars Farm
Manor Farm
Toll Gate Cottage
The Malms
Gabriel's Copse
Twyford Moors House
Park Farm
Colden Covert
The Dell
RIVER ITCHEN
B3335
B3354
COX'S HILL
STREET
HIGH
HIGHBRIDGE ROAD
SHAWFORD ROAD
BRIDGE LANE
BERRY LANE
CHURCH LANE
CHURCH LA.
OLD RECTORY LA.
BOURNE
BOURNEFIELDS
BEECHCROFT
NORTHFIELDS
WHITE LANE
HAZELEY ROAD
WATLEY LANE
LOVE LANE
PARK LANE
ROMAN ROAD
HARE LANE
WOODLAND DROVE
FINCHES LANE
QUEEN STREET
SCHOOL RD.
HILL RI.
SEGARS LA.
THE DROVE
DROVE CL.
MANOR ROAD
BREWERS LA.
MANOR FARM GRN.
DOLPHIN HILL
HIGHFIELD AV.
HIGHFIELD
NURSE'S PATH
CHURCHFIELDS RD.
CHURCH FLDS.
ST. MARY'S
THE CRES.
THE AV.
Rec. Grd.
Sch.
PENTON R.
FRANK RD.
LIN R. CL.
KINGS CL.
WATERHOUSE CL.
NEWTON
COLES CL.
SHIPLEY
Ten. Cts.
Station Ter.
Park Vw.
Bridge Ter.
22
35

A
B
C
D
1
2
3
4
5
6
33
34
23
22
21
20
Playing Field
SOUTH DRIVE
Conegar Row
Lone Barn Fm
OLD SALISBURY LA.
B3084
LANE
South Lodge Farm
OLD SALISBURY
Roke Manor Farm
Greatbridge
Roke Manor Fm. Cotts.
Palmer's Copse
Tennis Court
Roke Manor
Bull's Copse
SQUABB WOOD
Monks' Cottages
Foxbury Cottages
RIVER TEST
The Romsey Comm. Sch
Mead Mill Farm
Trout Farm
Test Mill
HOLLMAN DRIVE
MILL
MILLSTREAM RISE
Playing Field
Mill Stream
LITTLE MEADS
RIVERMEAD CL.
Rivermead Ho.
THE MEADS
Spursholt Farm
Spursholt House
Spursholt Cottages
SALISBURY ROAD
A27
Playing Field
Tollgate Cottage
GARDENERS LANE
Burnt Grove Cottages
Sewage Works
Greenhill View
Greenhill Ter.
War Memorial Park
Pav.
Saddler's Mill
Mill Race
CAUSEWAY
Middle Bridge
Green Hill
MAINSTONE
Mainstone Farm
FOREST EDGE
PK
Hallswood
HALL COPSE
Luibeg
BURNT GROVE
HILL
A3090
PAUNCEFOOT
Test Way
Pauncefoot House
The Round House
Forest Lodge
The Grotto
Furze Cottage
RYEDOWN LANE
Sounding Arch
Pauncefoot Cottages

29
E
F
G
H
435
36
37
120
1
2
3
4
5
6
30
23
22
21
40
Romsey
SO51
ROMSEY
Cupernham
Harefield
Whitenap
May's Island
Baroona
Abbotswood
Great Bridge
Island Cott.
Island Ho.
Mill Race
Fishlake Cottage
Garden & Aquatic Cen.
Trout Farm
Fishlake Meadows
Fish Lake
Barge Canal
Oxlease
Oxlease Farm
Minchin Hill
BUDDS LANE INDUSTRIAL ESTATE
FROBISHER INDUSTRIAL CENTRE
Serendipity Sam's Play & Party Cen.
ROMSEY IND.EST.
Romsey Prim. Sch.
Romsey Junction
The Red House
The Plaza Thtre.
Plaza Pde.
Mottisfont Lodge
Superstore
Coachmakers M.
King John's Ho.
Bus Sta.
Stirling Wk.
Eastwood Ct.
Wakeford Ct.
Hanover Cl.
Coun. Offs
Lib.
Cherville Mews
Cherville Ct.
Playing Field
Cupernham Jun.Sch.
Cupernham Inf. Sch.
Works
Chirk Lodge
ROMSEY HOSP.
Nightingale Ho
Tadburn Meadows Local Nature Reserve
Romsey Cemetery
Rec. Grd.
Football Grd.
The Rapids Swimming Pool
Romsey Spts. Cen.
Ten. Cts.
Pav.
Reynolds Ct.
David Ct.
James Ct.
Whitenap Farm
Montfort Ct.
The Mountbatten School & Language College
Beggarspath Wood
BROADLANDS PARK
Broadlands
River Test
Southampton Lodge
Keepers Cottage
Homemead Ho.
Stephens Ct.
Berthon Ho.
Ashley Ho.
Paimpol Pl.
Mt. Pleasant
Tadburn Grn.
Hall
GREATBRIDGE ROAD
A3057
B3398
DUTTONS RD.
MALMESBURY RD.
ALMA ROAD
WINCHESTER ROAD
WINCHESTER HILL
A3090
CUPERNHAM LANE
MEADOWS
FISHLAKE
BUDDS LA.
HUNDRED
PALMERSTON ST.
BY-PASS
SOUTHAMPTON ROAD
A27
LUZBOROUGH LANE
BROADWATER RD.
NEW ROAD
MERCER WY.
NELSON CL.
LATHAM RD.
GREAT WELL DRIVE
BRAISHFIELD RD.
WOODLEY LANE
GANGER FARM LA.
SCHOOL RD.
HORESHOE DRIVE
STAPLEFORD CL.
CAVENDISH CL.
KINVER CLOSE
RICHMOND LANE
BROOK LANE
BROOK WAY
CARISBROOKE CT.
DURBAN CL.
RALPH LA.
WOODLEY LANE
WINTERBOURNE RD.
ANSTEY RD.
TAVISTOCK CL.
HALDEN CL.
ABBOTSWOOD CL.
HOGARTH CL.
FAIRVIEW CL.
BARTON CL.
ASHLEY MEADOWS
WINDFIELD DR.
THE CRESCENT
SELSDON AVENUE
VINEY AVENUE
FABER M.
ST. BLAIZE RD.
HAREFIELD CT.
CAMPION WAY
BRIAR WAY
WESTERING
SEWARD
JENNER
HIGH FIRS RD.
KENNETT RD.
MEON CL.
ANTON CL.
AVON CRESCENT
SAXON WAY
HALTERWORTH CL.
HOLYBORNE RD.
ASHDOWN WAY
ACRES
EIGHT ACRES
HILLSIDE AV.
CHAMBERS
NIGHTINGALE CL.
ROSEDALE AV.
OAKLEIGH GS.
FRYERS CL.
QUEEN'S CL.
TADFIELD RD.
SYMES RD.
ALLAN GR.
SENLAC
WESSEX
THE VIKINGS
MONTFORT HEIGHTS
MONTFORT CL.
GROSVENOR CT.
NORTHLANDS
BENEDICT CL.
WHITENAP CL.
WHITENAP LANE
FIVE ELMS DR.
THE COVERT
THE THICKET
SYCAMORE CL.
MAPLE CL.
ASH CL.
TADBURN ROAD
TEMPLE GS.
NURSERY GS.
GRAYS CL.
WILLS WAY
KNYGHT CL.
SYDMANTON RD.
THE TYLEHADES
ST. BARBE CL.
JACOBS CL.
PETTY CL.
KNATCHBULL CL.
BRIDGE RD.
HARRAGE
CRESSEY
LOVE LANE
LINDEN RD.
PEMBROKE
ORCHARD
STATION ROAD
ALBANY RD.
PRINCES
BREWERY
MALTHOUSE CL.
CHURCH ST.
CHURCH LA.
CHURCH PL.
PORTERSBRIDGE
MARKET PLACE
ABBEY
NARROW LA.
NEWTON LANE
BANNING
CHAVY WK.
MIDDLEBRIDGE
PRIESTLANDS
WESTLANDS
Lansdowne Gdns.
Lansdowne Ct.
KINGFISHER WY.
GRAYLING MEAD
ROBERT WHITWORTH DR.
THE CLOISTERS
HORSECROFT
TITHE MEAD
THE MEWS
CANAL WALK
OLD RD.
JUBILEE RD.
MOUNTBATTEN AV.
MITCHELLS CL.

Abbotswood House
Woodley Close Flats
WOODLEY CL.
Ganger Farm
Nursery
Fishery and Fish Farm
South Holmes Copse
Woodley
Woodlands
Ganger Wood
Crampmoor Farm
Oxlease Copse
WINCHESTER HILL
WINCHESTER ROAD STRAIGHT MILE
A3090
CRAMPMOOR LANE
Crampmoor
Halterworth Crossing
Tadburn Lake
Stroud School
Playing Fields
Halterworth Farm
HIGHWOOD LANE
Harefield
Romsey
SO51
Tadburn Meadows Local Nature Reserve
Halterworth Lodge
Highwood Cottage
Halterworth
Highwood Farmhouse
Warren Farm
Luzborough View
Halterworth Primary School
Montfort College
BOTLEY ROAD
Whitenap
Elmtree Gdns.
Luzborough Farm
BOTLEY LANE
Brooklyn
Scrag Hill
ABBEY PARK IND.EST.
THE QUADRANGLE
THE PREMIER CEN.
THE TRITON CENTRE
PREMIER WAY
Depots
Works
PARK COURT
ABBEY ENTERPRISE CENTRE
The Mountbatten School & Language College
Beggarspath Wood
A27
LUZBOROUGH LANE
LUZBOROUGH PLANTATION
NORTH BADDESLEY
Parker's Moor
Keepers Cottage
29
36

31
E
F
G
H
Lower Farm
LOWER FARM LA.
Sports Ground
Club House
AMPFIELD GOLF COURSE
Buddy's Barn
POTTERS HERON CL.
Ampfield Common Piece
Gosport Farm
LANE
POUND
Gosport
Bramble Cottages
Purser's Great Copse
Bluebell Copse
Green Lane Farm
Great High Trees
1
2
Tadburn
Lake
Churchers Common Plantation
Broadgate Plantation
Woodend Copse
Monks Brook
FURTHER COMMON PLANTATION
Green Acres
3
Newlands Copse
Emer Bog
32
Castle Hill
Bucket Corner
BADDESLEY COMMON
4
Elmer Cottage
Lights Copse
Castlehill Farm
ROAD
Ryders Farm
Body Farm
FLEXFORD
Manor House
Manor Farm
POUND ROAD
5
Southampton
Alpine Lodge
Nutburn Cottage
Playground
TEST VALLEY BUSINESS PARK
SO52
DIRTY DRIVE
A27
Nutburn Farm
6
WHITEBEAM WAY
FIRGROVE RD.
CRESCENT RD.
SPENCER GS.
CAMELLIA CL.
STREET END
SANDY LA.
Hall
Nutburn
NUTBURN
MIDDLE
LABURNUM CL.
Rec. Grd.
Great Covert
ROAD
SIX OAKS RD.
Chamberlayne Ct.
Thatched Cottages
MERRY GS.
ST. JOHN'S CEN.
EDWINA CLO.
BADDESLEY
SANDY LANE
37
Gainsborough Ct.
Pav.
ROAD
39
40
41
23
22
21
20

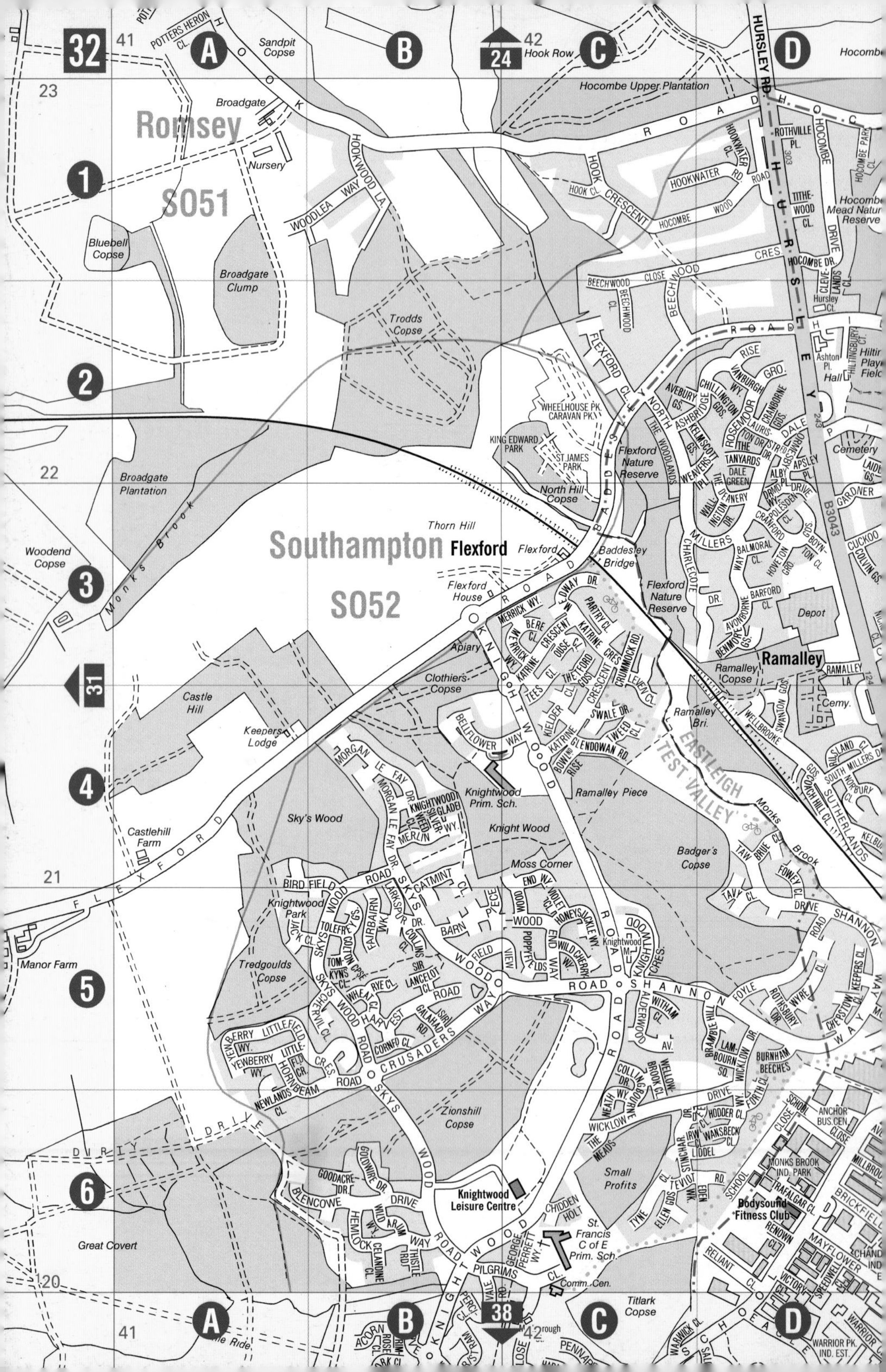

32
24
31
38
Romsey
SO51
Southampton
SO52
Flexford
Ramalley
EASTLEIGH
TEST VALLEY
Sandpit Copse
Hook Row
Hocombe Upper Plantation
Broadgate
Nursery
Bluebell Copse
Broadgate Clump
Trodds Copse
Broadgate Plantation
Woodend Copse
Monks Brook
Thorn Hill
Flexford House
Apiary
Clothiers Copse
Castle Hill
Keepers Lodge
Castlehill Farm
Manor Farm
Great Covert
Sky's Wood
Knightwood Park
Tredgoulds Copse
Knight Wood
Moss Corner
Knightwood Prim. Sch.
Ramalley Piece
Badger's Copse
Zionshill Copse
Knightwood Leisure Centre
Small Profits
St. Francis C of E Prim. Sch.
Comm. Cen.
Titlark Copse
Wheelhouse Pk. Caravan Pk.
King Edward Park
St. James Park
North Hill Copse
Flexford Nature Reserve
Baddesley Bridge
Ramalley Copse
Ramalley Bri.
Depot
Cemy.
Cemetery
Hocombe Mead Nature Reserve
Hursley Ct.
Ashton Pl.
Hall
Monks Brook Ind. Park
Bodysound Fitness Club
Anchor Bus. Cen.
Warrior Pk. Ind. Est.
Hursley Rd.
Hook Road
Hookwood La.
Woodlea Way
Hook Crescent
Hookwater Rd.
Hocombe Wood Road
Beechwood Cres.
Baddesley Road
Flexford Road
Knightwood Road
Shannon Road
Shannon Way
Crusaders Way
Skys Wood Road
Dirty Drive
Wicklow Drive
Blencowe Drive
Pilgrims Cl.
Bird Field Road
Bellflower Way
Millers Way
Avonborne Dr.
B3043

33
25
34
39
Winchester
SO21
SO53
SO50
Hocombe
Hiltingbury
Cuckoo Bushes
CHANDLER'S FORD
Eastleigh
Fryern Hill
Recreation Ground
Chandler's Ford
Boyatt Wood
South Hill
Junction 12
M3 MOTORWAY
M3
CRANBURY PARK
Upper Pond
Lower Pond
The Castle
Castle Copse
Woodend Copse
Little Hessians Copse
Gunville Hill Plantation
Hocombe Bridge
Hocombe Lodge
The Lodge
Home Farm
The Gardens
WESSEX NUFFIELD HEALTH HOSPITAL
Thornden School
Playing Field
Lakeside School
Lincolns Farm
Broom Hill
The Lakes
Sherborne House Sch.
Hiltingbury Inf. Sch.
Hiltingbury Jun. Sch.
Merdon Jun. Sch.
Fryern Arcade
Scantabout Prim. Sch.
Chandler's Ford Inf. Sch.
Fryern Inf. Sch.
Fryern Jun. Sch.
St. Swithun Wells Cath. Prim. Sch.
The Toynbee School
Crestwood Coll. Leis. Centre
Crestwood Coll. for Bus. & Enterprise
THE CENTRAL PRECINCT
REX IND. ESTATE
PEACOCK TRADING ESTATE
OMEGA ENTERPRISE PARK
Monks Brook
Roman Road (Course Of)
WINCHESTER ROAD
BOURNEMOUTH ROAD
KINGSWAY
HURSLEY ROAD
WINCHESTER ROAD
LAKEWOOD ROAD
PARK ROAD
BRAMPTON

Great Moorlands Copse
Little Hessians Copse
Little Hessians Copse
CRANBURY PARK
The Castle
Woodend Copse
HOCOMBE ROAD
M3 MOTORWAY
Otterbourne Hill Common
Resr. (covered)
OTTERBOURNE
Otterbourne C of E Prim. Sch.
Hall
Lodge
MAIN ROAD
HILL
KILN LANE
CRANBOURNE DR.
CRANBURY CL.
COLES MEDE
Otterbourne Ho.
Otterbourne Ho. Gds.
Dell Copse
Otterbourne Hill
ROMAN ROAD (Course of)
Otterbourne Farm
Manor Farm Cottage
Manor House
Bore Hole (Water)
Kingfisher Cott
Kingfisher Lodge
Bram Bri.
Bridge Cott.
Garden Cen. & Miniature Railway
Otterbourne Park Wood & Nature Reserve
Cricket Ground
Stone Ter.
Fleet Ter.
BOYATT LA.
CHAPEL LA.
PARK
Junction 12
WINCHESTER ROAD
WESSEX NUFFIELD HEALTH HOSPITAL
Thornden School
Playing Field
Pitmore Copse
Pitmore Gulley Copse
LINCOLNS RISE
PITMORE CL.
MAYPOLE VILLAS
WINTERS PL.
Lodge
Otterbourne Grange
Lincolns Copse
Lincolns Farm
ALLBROOK WAY A335
PITMORE ROAD
PARK LANE
Depot
Green Pastures
Bugle Farm
WARDLE
High Bridge
HIGHBRIDGE
ALLBROOK
Allbrook School
AVERY FIELDS
Allbrook Farm
Highbridge Farm
ALLBROOK HILL B3335
OSBORNE
Eastleigh
SO50
Little Boyatt Farm
ALLBROOK CT.
OAK FIELDS
PORTCHESTER RISE
CHILHAM CL.
HIGHCLIFFE DR.
WALMER CL.
BROOMHILL WY.
Subway
BIRCH GRO.
LEWES CL.
SADDLERS CL.
AVENUE
Rookwood Centre
Hall Rec. Grd.
WOBURN CL.
PENSHURST
TORRE CL.
ROOKWOOD CL.
TWYFORD ROAD
BROADLANDS
BREAMORE CL.
CHARTWELL CL.
Ham Fm.
SOVEREIGN WY.
WINDSOR GATE
KENILWORTH
ARUNDEL RD.
LOUGHWOOD CL.
Raglan Ct.
CHATSWORTH RD.
ROSEBERY CRESCENT
SHERBORNE CT. DR.
RUFFORD CL.
BUCKLAND CL.
MOUNTBATTEN RD.
HAREWOOD CL.
LYDIARD CL.
HADDON DR.
THE HAVEN
CLANDON DR.
Breach Sling Copse
Breach Farm
Breach Copse
Stoke Lodge
Rec. Grd.
Boyatt Wood
Crestwood Coll. Leisure Cen.
Sports Pitch
Crestwood Coll. for Bus. & Enterprise
BOYATT WOOD SHOP. CEN.
PETWORTH GDS.
LEANDER CL.
HADLEIGH GS.
THORN CL.
OAK TREE WY.
ST. CATHERINE'S
AINSLEY GS.
ROYSTON
SWANLEY CL.
Shakespeare Jun. Sch.
Shakespeare Inf. Sch.
Leslie Loader Ct.
SHAKESPEARE
ADDISON RD.
THE RECESS
RUSKIN ROAD
SURBITON RD.
MILTON RD.
VICTORIA RD.
ALBERT RD.
BRAMBLE CL.
THE NOOK
CONSORT CL.
ELIZABETH CONSORT WAY
Drummond Ct.
Allyn Ct.
The Summit
Bishopstoke Day Services
BREACH LA.
BURROW HILL PL.
CHURCH
Lodge
Bishopstoke Ho.
Gully Copse
Comm. Cen.
EDWARD
Reginald Mitchell Ct.
John Darling Mall
ST. LAWRENCE RD.
Recreation Grd
LAWN
DARWIN RD.
ALEXANDER SQ.
A B C D
1 2 3 4 5 6
23 22 21 20
445 46
26 33 40

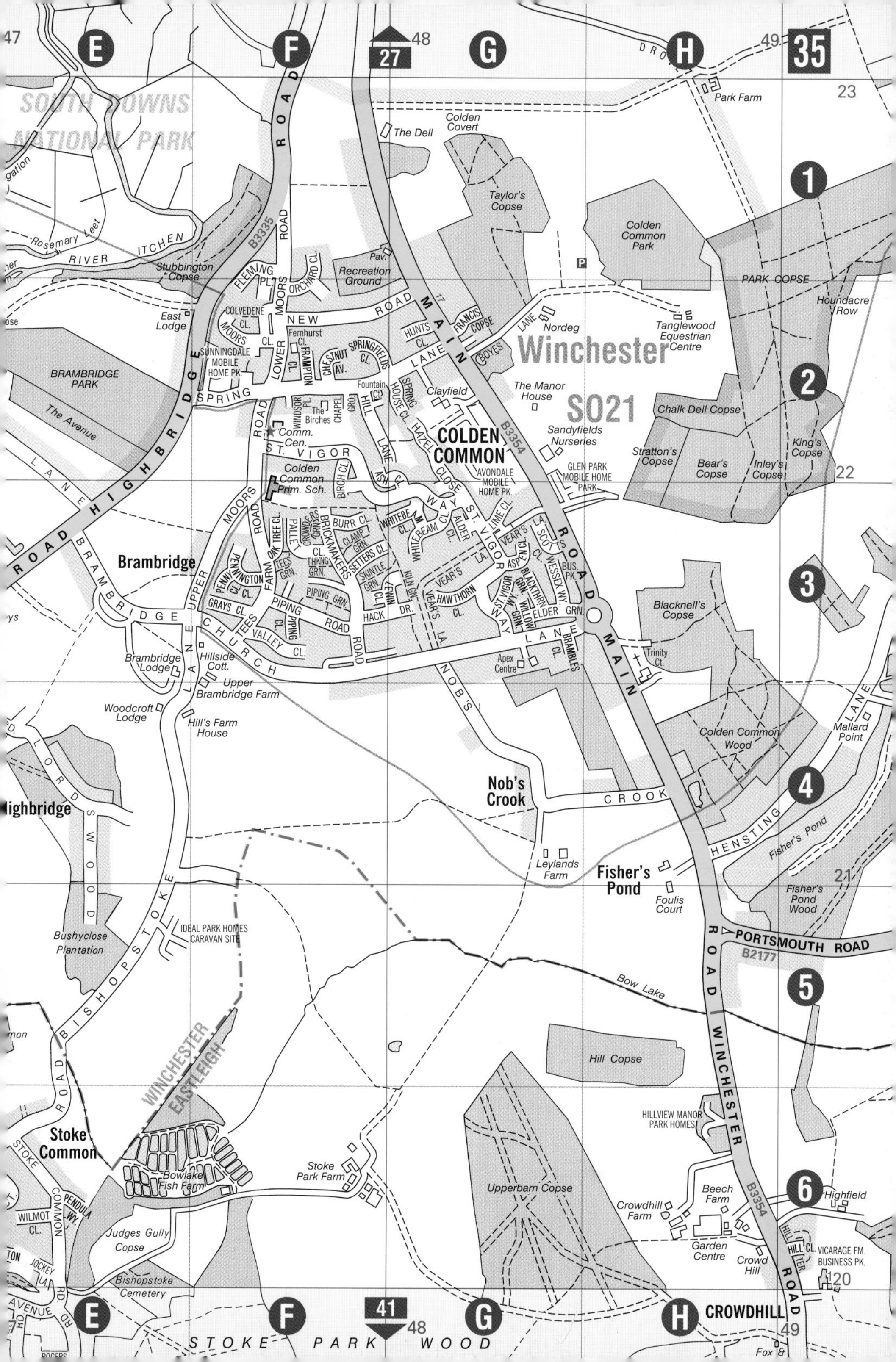
SOUTH DOWNS NATIONAL PARK
River Itchen
Rosemary Leet
Stubbington Copse
East Lodge
Brambridge Park
The Avenue
Highbridge Road
B3335
Colden Covert
The Dell
Taylor's Copse
Colden Common Park
Park Copse
Houndacre Row
Park Farm
Recreation Ground
Tanglewood Equestrian Centre
Nordeg
Winchester
SO21
The Manor House
Chalk Dell Copse
Stratton's Copse
Bear's Copse
Inley's Copse
King's Copse
Sandyfields Nurseries
Glen Park Mobile Home Park
Avondale Mobile Home Pk.
Colden Common
Colden Common Prim. Sch.
Comm. Cen.
Sunningdale Mobile Home Pk.
Main Road
B3354
Brambridge
Brambridge Lodge
Hillside Cott.
Upper Brambridge Farm
Woodcroft Lodge
Hill's Farm House
Blacknell's Copse
Trinity Ct.
Apex Centre
Colden Common Wood
Mallard Point
Nob's Crook
Highbridge
Leylands Farm
Fisher's Pond
Foulis Court
Fisher's Pond Wood
Hensting Lane
Portsmouth Road
B2177
Bow Lake
Ideal Park Homes Caravan Site
Bushyclose Plantation
Bishopstoke Road
Winchester
Eastleigh
Hill Copse
Hillview Manor Park Homes
Stoke Common
Bowlake Fish Farm
Stoke Park Farm
Upperbarn Copse
Crowdhill Farm
Beech Farm
Garden Centre
Crowd Hill
Highfield
Vicarage Fm. Business Pk.
Judges Gully Copse
Bishopstoke Cemetery
Winchester Road
Crowdhill
Stoke Park Wood
27
41

30
LUZBOROUGH LA.
A27
Keepers Cottage
Ashfield Lodge
Ashfield
Parker's Moor
LUZBOROUGH PLANTATION
RINGWOOD DRIVE
AMBERLEY CL.
FORES CL.
WOODLANDS WAY
THE BIRCHES
PINE CL.
NORTHERWOOD CL.
CRESCENT
UPR. CRESCENT RD.
WYNYARDS GAP
ROWNHAMS
FIRGROVE
CERNE CL.
HOLLYWOOD CL.
CORSE CL.
TUTLAND R.
SEYMOUR LA.
HEATHERBRE. GS.
QUEENS RIDE
Hall
Mountbatten Park
FIELDEN CL.
WOODSIDE RD.
TORNAY GRO.
SYLVAN DR.
HULLES WAY
LANGHAM CL.
TOTTEHALE CL.
Playgrd.
Rec. Grd.
LAVINGTON GDNS.
MORTIMER WAY
PROCTOR DR
LAUNCELYN CL.
SYLVAN DRIVE
Hatchet Cottage
Hoe Cottage
Hoe Farm
Hoe Copse
HOE LANE
Ashfield Copse
Upper Ashfield Farm
Romsey
SO51
Sand Pits
Telegraph Wood Fort
TOOT HILL
Toothill
Packridge
Kiln Farm Riding Sch.
Kiln Farm House
Thatched Cottage
Lower Toothill
LEE DROVE
TOOTHILL ROAD
The Yews
Middle Farm
Upper Toothill
PACKRIDGE LANE
A3057
UPPER TOOTHILL ROAD
ROWNHAMS LANE
Greenhill Copse
Greenhill Cottage
Greenhill
GREENHILL
NIGHTINGALE WOOD
ROWNHAMS PARK
Austrey Wood
Subway
ROMSEY GOLF COURSE
Routs Copse
COLDHARBOUR LANE
Grove Farm
M271
ROMSEY ROAD
Aldermoor Copse
Adcock Court
ROUTS WAY
DROVE
Parkers Farm
Club House
UPTON CRES
UPTON CRESCENT
M27
ACORN DR.
St. Johns Home
ROWNHAMS
Grove Lodge Farm
Fir Copse
M271 MOTORWAY
ARMADA CL.
COLTS RD.
VICTORY WY.
WAY
Lymers Copse
HEDGEROW CL.
LOREILLE GS.
HANN RD.
ST. JOHNS CL.
M27 MOTORWAY
UPTON LANE
PRINCE RD.
HURRICANE DR.
BARKER MILL CL.
HORNS
ST. JOHN'S GLEBE
Comm. Cen.
BALMORAL
NUTFIELD RD.
NICHOLSON WK.
ROWNHAMS HOUSE
THE M.
Playing Field
Upton
LYMER LA.
A B C D
1 2 3 4 5 6
36 37 38
120 19 18 17

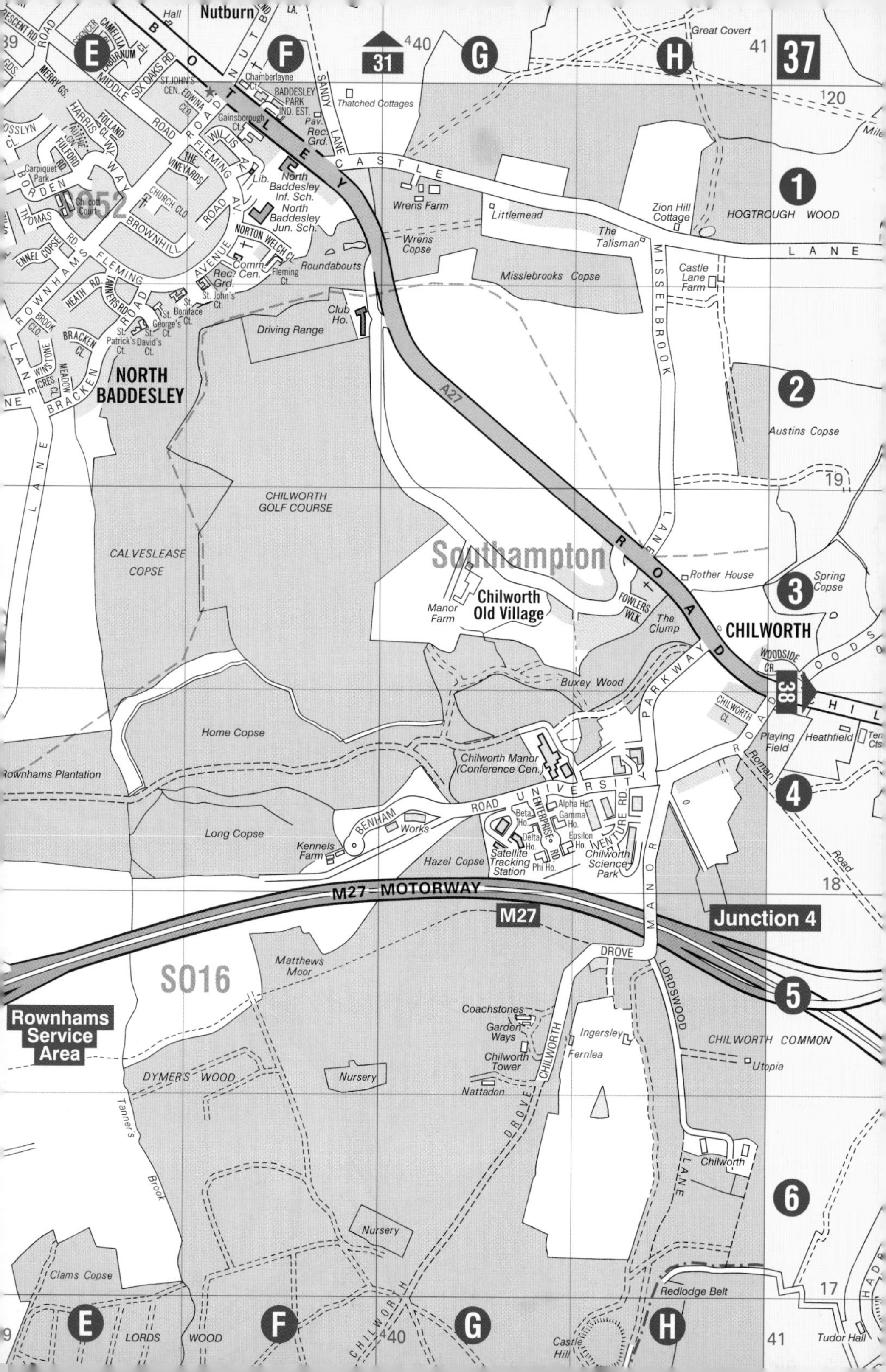

37
31
38
E
F
G
H
1
2
3
4
5
6
440
41
120
19
18
17
Nutburn
Hall
BOTLEY ROAD
NUTBURN RD.
SANDY LANE
CASTLE LANE
Great Covert
Thatched Cottages
Chamberlayne Ct.
BADDESLEY PARK IND. EST.
Pav.
Rec. Grd.
Gainsborough Ct.
ST JOHN'S CEN.
EDWINA CLO.
SIX OAKS RD.
MIDDLE ROAD
CAMELLIA GDNS.
LABURNUM CL.
SPENCER GDNS.
MERRY GS.
HARRIS AVE.
FOLLAND CL.
FULFORD RD.
CRESCENT RD.
WILLIS AV.
FLEMING AV.
THE VINEYARDS
CHURCH CLO.
BROWNHILL WAY
North Baddesley Inf. Sch.
North Baddesley Jun. Sch.
Lib.
NORTON WELCH CL.
Comm. Cen.
Rec. Grd.
Fleming Ct.
St. John's Ct.
St. Boniface Ct.
St. George's Ct.
St. David's Ct.
St. Patrick's Ct.
Carpiquet Park
BORDEN
Chilcott Court
SO52
THOMAS RD.
FENNEL COPSE
ROWNHAMS LANE
HEATH RD.
TANNERS RD.
BROOK CLO.
BRACKEN CL.
WINSTONE CRES.
MEADOW CL.
BRACKEN LANE
NORTH BADDESLEY
Wrens Farm
Wrens Copse
Roundabouts
Littlemead
Zion Hill Cottage
HOGTROUGH WOOD
The Talisman
Misslebrooks Copse
MISSELBROOK LANE
Castle Lane Farm
Club Ho.
Driving Range
A27
Austins Copse
CHILWORTH GOLF COURSE
CALVESLEASE COPSE
Southampton
Chilworth Old Village
Manor Farm
Rother House
Spring Copse
FOWLERS WLK.
The Clump
CHILWORTH
WOODSIDE CR.
CHILWORTH CL.
Playing Field
Heathfield
Roman Road
Buxey Wood
PARKWAY
Home Copse
Chilworth Manor (Conference Cen.)
Rownhams Plantation
UNIVERSITY ROAD
BENHAM
Works
Alpha Ho.
Beta Ho.
Gamma Ho.
Delta Ho.
Epsilon Ho.
ENTERPRISE RD.
VENTURE RD.
Long Copse
Kennels Farm
Hazel Copse
Satellite Tracking Station
Phi Ho.
Chilworth Science Park
MANOR RD.
M27 MOTORWAY
M27
Junction 4
DROVE
Matthews Moor
SO16
LORDSWOOD
Rownhams Service Area
Coachstones
Garden Ways
Chilworth Tower
Nattadon
Ingersley
Fernlea
CHILWORTH DROVE
CHILWORTH COMMON
Utopia
DYMER'S WOOD
Nursery
Tanner's Brook
Chilworth
LANE
Clams Copse
Redlodge Belt
LORDS WOOD
CHILWORTH
Castle Hill
Tudor Hall

38
32
37
A
B
C
D
1
2
3
4
5
6
Great Covert
Mile Ride
HOGTROUGH WOOD
CASTLE LANE
Castle Lane Farm
Austins Copse
The Rough
SO52
Spring Copse
Rother House
Marshalls Rows
BOTLEY RD.
WOODSIDE
CHILWORTH
HUT WOOD
Southampton
Velmore Farm
Velmore Farm Cottages
Roman Road (course of)
TEMPLARS WAY
SCHOOL LANE
EAGLE
HAMPSHIRE CORPORATE PARK
BOURNEMOUTH ROAD
Builders Yard Offices
Hicknor Hill
Hicknor Hill Cottage
Cox's Rough
Titlark Copse
Comm. Cen.
Marlborough Ct.
PILGRIMS CL.
KNIGHTWOOD RD.
SANDRINGHAM
BLENHEIM CL.
RAGLAN CLOSE
PENNARD WAY
TENBY DR.
WOLVESEY PL.
VELMORE
GUILDFORD DRIVE
BURLEY DOWN
DONNINGTON
HIGHCLERE WY.
MONTGOMERY
CONWAY CL.
LULWORTH
TEMPLARS MEDE
WARRIOR PK. IND. EST.
RELIANT CL.
MAYFLOWER
Playing Field
Heathfield
Ten. Cts.
MANOR
Maryland
Hawkridge
Green Acres
Heather Hill
Heather Farm
Nyewoods
GREEN LANE
M27
M27 MOTORWAY
Junction 4
Three Gables
Chilworth Grange
HUTWOOD ROAD
SO16
BIRCH RD.
Willowbend
WINCHESTER
HEATHERLANDS RD.
PINELANDS RD.
ROMAN WAY
CHILWORTH COMMON
Utopia
LORDSWOOD LANE
Chilworth
M3
M3 MOTORWAY
Hut Hill
Smithys Wood
Bracken Hall
Bracken Place
Stoneham House
Hotel
STONEHAM GOLF COURSE
Club House
PINE WALK
LINGWOOD CLOSE
FITZROY CL.
Chilworth Ring
HADRIAN
BASSETT AVENUE
BASSETT GREEN RD.
The Haven
THE SPINNEY
Oak Tree Manor
A27
A33
TEST VALLEY
SOUTHAMPTON
41
42
17
18
19
120

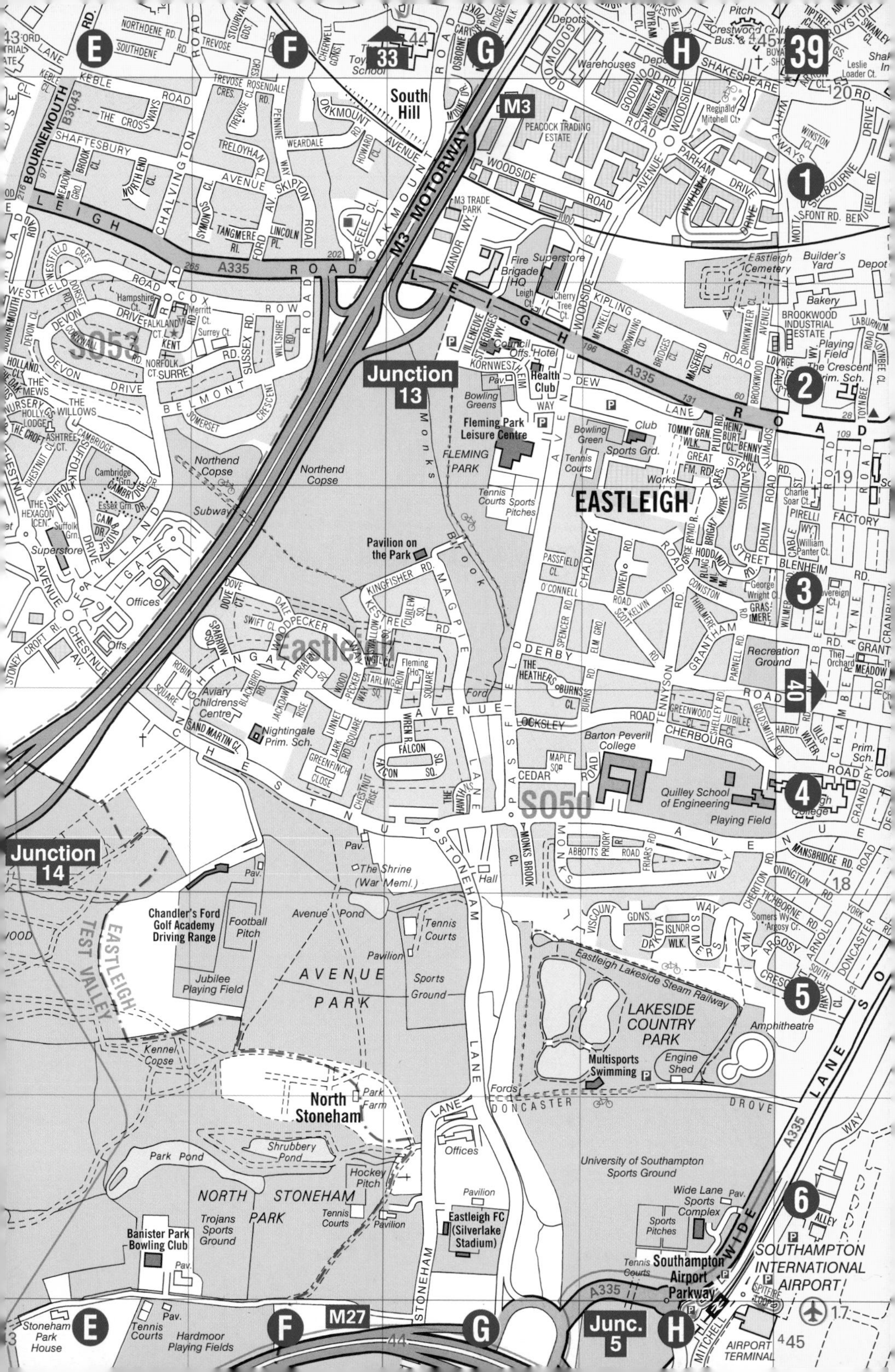
39
EASTLEIGH
Junction 13
Junction 14
Junc. 5
M3 MOTORWAY
M27
A335
SO50
SO53
LAKESIDE COUNTRY PARK
AVENUE PARK
NORTH STONEHAM PARK
North Stoneham
SOUTHAMPTON INTERNATIONAL AIRPORT
Southampton Airport Parkway
Fleming Park Leisure Centre
Barton Peveril College
Quilley School of Engineering
Eastleigh FC (Silverlake Stadium)
Chandler's Ford Golf Academy Driving Range
Banister Park Bowling Club
University of Southampton Sports Ground
Eastleigh Lakeside Steam Railway
South Hill
Northend Copse
PEACOCK TRADING ESTATE
BROOKWOOD INDUSTRIAL ESTATE
Eastleigh Cemetery

40
34
39
A
B
C
D
1
2
3
4
5
6
445
46
EASTLEIGH
Eastleigh
SO50
SO18
SO30
Southampton
SOUTHAMPTON INTERNATIONAL AIRPORT
Control Tower
AIRPORT TERMINAL
Southampton Airport Parkway
Wide Lane Sports Complex
Amphitheatre
Engine Shed
Steam Railway
Quilley School of Engineering
Eastleigh College
Playing Field
Recreation Ground
Eastleigh Cemetery
Builder's Yard
Depot
Bakery
BROOKWOOD INDUSTRIAL ESTATE
The Crescent Prim. Sch.
The Point
The Park Superstore
Superstore Depot
Eastleigh
Team-Sport Indoor Karting
BARTON PARK INDUSTRIAL ESTATE
PHOENIX IND. PK.
DEACON TRAD. EST.
TOWER LANE IND. EST.
Works
Playground
THE SWAN CENTRE
Lib.
Bowl.
Cinema
Mus.
Sch.
Prim. Sch.
Coll.
Shakespeare Jun. Sch.
Shakespeare Inf. Sch.
John Darling Mall
Depot
SHAKESPEARE BUS. CEN.
The Bridge Education Cen.
Gully Copse
Bishopstoke Day Services
The Summit
Bishopstoke Ho.
Comm. Cen.
Playing Field
Football Pitch
Tennis Cts.
The Hub
Collins Ho.
Itchen Ho.
Bishopstoke Manor
Itchen Grange
Rec. Grd.
Play. Fld.
The Itchen Navigation (Disused)
Conegar Lock
Fish House Bay
Sewage Works
Viaduct
Viaduct
RIVER ITCHEN
Decoy Covert
TWYFORD ROAD
BISHOPSTOKE ROAD
SHOPSTOKE ROAD B3037
ROMSEY ROAD A335
LEIGH ROAD
SOUTHAMPTON ROAD A335
WIDE LANE A335
SHAKESPEARE DRIVE
BLENHEIM ROAD
CHESTNUT AVENUE
CHERBOURG ROAD
DERBY ROAD
GRANTHAM ROAD
FACTORY RD.
MARKET STREET
HIGH STREET
DESBOROUGH ROAD
CRANBURY ROAD
CHAMBERLAYNE ROAD
NUTBEEM RD.
CAMPBELL ROAD
CHICKENHALL LANE
BARTON RIVER
TOWER LANE
DOUCASTER DROVE
MITCHELL WY.
TINKER ALLEY
SPITFIRE LOOP
FAIR OAK ROAD
RIVERSIDE
CHURCH RD.
SPRING LA.
HAMILTON RD.
LONGMEAD
EDWARD
BREACH
DUTTON LANE

35
41
42
E
F
G
H
Judges Gully Copse
Bishopstoke Cemetery
Upperbarn Copse
Garden Centre
Crowd Hill
VICARAGE FARM BUSINESS PARK
CROWDHILL
Fox & Hounds
Crowdhill Copse
STOKE PARK WOOD
BISHOPSTOKE
Stoke Pk. Jun. Sch.
Stoke Park Inf. Sch.
DRAYTON
B3037
ALAN DRAYTON WY.
ROAD ALAN
FAIR OAK ROAD
B3354
WINCHESTER ROAD
HARDINGS LANE
STOKE HEIGHTS
FAIR OAK
Rec. Grd.
Squash Club
Halls
Lib.
Stoke Park
The Kings School
Rockford House
Factory
Playground
West Horton Farm
Quobleigh Pond
Lake Farm
Firtree Farm
FIR TREE LANE
ALLINGTON LANE
ALLINGTON MANOR FARM BUS. CEN.
Allington Manor Farm Cottages
Allston
Hearts Row
Hog Wood
Woodlands
Playing Field
1
2
3
4
5
6
48
49
120
19
18
17

42
41
CROWDHILL
Pylehill
FAIR OAK
HORTON HEATH
Eastleigh
SO50
WINCHESTER
EASTLEIGH
WINCHESTER ROAD
B3354
B3037
MORTIMERS LANE
EASTLEIGH RD.
BOTLEY ROAD
KNOWLE LANE
HALL LANDS LANE
DURLEY ROAD
GREENWOOD LANE
FIR TREE LANE
Low Hill Farm
The Cottages
Park Hills Wood
Tippers Copse
Hall Lands Copse
Hall Lands House
Hall Lands Farm
Middle Farm
Warwick House
Stocks Farm
Gore Copse
Hardings Copse
Satellite Teleport
East Horton Cotts.
Deer Park Farm Ind. Est.
Knowlehill Copse
Knowle Hill
Merrol
Knowle Hill Farm
Castlenau
Plantation Copse
Whitetree Farm
Knowle Lodge
Hammerley Farm
The Cockpit Farm
Poultry Houses
Holme Farm
Foxholes Farm
Oakmoor House
Oakmore Park
The Little Dower House
Sunnyside Cottage
Mortimers Farm
Club Ho.
East Horton Farm
East Horton Golf Centre
Driving Range
Durley Copse
Greenwood Farm
Greenwood Lodge
EAST HORTON GOLF COURSE
Church Copse
Church Cott.
Rectory
Vicarage Farm Business Park
Fox & Hounds
Garden Centre
Wyvern Technology College
Wyvern Leisure Centre
Playing Field
Fair Oak Inf. Sch.
Fair Oak Jun. Sch.
Squash Club
Rec. Grd.
Halls
Lib.
The Square
Cemy.
The Kings School
Rockford House
Quobleigh Pond
Comm. Cen.

E
F
G
H
52
53
120
Leal Cottage
Ivy Cottage
Stroudwood Farm
The Laurels
Red House Farm
Popes Farm
POPES LANE
Upham Farm
Slappinrail Copse
SOUTH DOWNS NATIONAL PARK
Tylers Copse
Riddlecotts
Julitta Cottage
New Farm
WINCHESTER
B2177
Lower Upham
UPHAM ST.
UPHAM STREET
Hoyle Close
Broom Croft
1
STROUDWOOD ROAD
Stroudwood Dairy Farm
B3037
LANE
Rec. Grd.
Holly Farm
Merry Orchard Farm
Mount Pleasant
Trurodene
Pond Farm
EASTLEIGH
WINCHESTER
Taylor's Cottages
Torbay Farm
2
Abbotswold
Wold Cottages
Kiln Farm
Down Farm
The Bungalow
19
Woodward Farm
Windrush
Woolstreet Farm
ROAD
Woodley Farm
SCIVIER'S LANE
THE CRESCENT
Compton Cottage Farm
North Lodge
Coombs Farm
Vine Cottage
3
Moplands Copse
Sciviers Farm
Sciviers Cottage
Kimbers Copse
44
Wintershill Hall
Southampton
SO32
ALMA LANE
Oakdale Farm
South Cottage
Winters Hill
4
DURLEY HALL LANE
Giles Farm
Common View Farm
May Bank
South Lodge
Park Cottage
Woodlands
Job's Corner
Durley Hall Farm
18
Green Pastures
Longlands Copse
Noyces Copse
WINTERS HILL
Trullingham Farm
5
Parker's Copse
DURLEY STREET
MANOR ROAD
THE DROVE
Tarrytown
Greenwood Farm
GREENWOOD
Manor Terrace
Moss's Copse
Manor Cottages
Fir Plantation
Elm Tree Farm
Four Winds
6
High Field
Durley Manor Farm
Victoria Ct.
Nettlebed
Mill Down
17
Middle Farm
MANOR LANE
DURLEY
Rec. Grd.
Pav.
KYTES LANE
Perlins Farm
MINCINGFIELD LA.
HATCHLEY LA.

A
B
C
D
53
54
1
2
3
4
5
6
20
19
18
17
43
Upham Farm
Slappinrail Copse
Broom Croft
Little Stakes Cottage
STAKES LANE
Peak Copse
Blackmans Copse
Footpath Copse
The Beeches
PEAK
SOUTH DOWNS
Redlands Copse
Stakes Farm
Stakes Cottages
CROSS LANE
Kiln Farm
Down Farm
The Bungalow
Wal Street Farm
WINCHESTER ROAD
B2177
STAKES
Limmers
Penselwood
Meadowview
North Lodge
Old Farm
Little Ashton Farm
Little Manor
Ashton Cottage
Ashton
Thimble Cottage
Becketts Farm
Yew Cottage
Dell Cottage
Cross Lanes Farm
Southampton
Park Dairy Farm
ROKE
The Cottage
Applegarth
Roke Farm
SO32
Bucklands
Kimbers Copse
Wintershill Hall
Glendale
Papercourt
ASHTON LANE
Ashton Stoke Cottages
Wintershill Farm
Oak Tree Cottage
HILL
Wingham Ho.
Tolgate House Farm
Wintershill
ASHTON CLOSE
CHURCHILL
NORTHFIELD CL.
PINE LEA
The Hawthorns
Park Cottage
Little Paddock
Laurel Farm
Trullingham Farm
Woodlea Nursery
WINTERS
Park View
LANE
MANOR ROAD
THE DROVE
DURLEY STREET
Manor Terrace
Manor Cottages
MANOR
Durley Manor Farm
Albany Farm
ALBANY CT.
ALBANY ROAD
ALBANY DR.
COLE HILL GDS.
MARLOW RD.
HERMITAGE CL.
CUNNINGHAM AV.
KESTREL CL.
SISKIN
HAWK CL.
BATTERY HILL
CLAYLANDS CT.
CLAYLANDS RD. IND. EST.
CLAYLANDS ROAD
POTTERY CL.
Works
MERLIN CL.
BLANCHARD RD.
Cunningham Ho.
GREENS CL.
Highfield Ct.
BLACK
MANS WY.
LANE
PARK RD.
THE AVENUE
Victoria Bldgs.
PRINCES CLOSE
VICTORIA
Priory Ct.
Pilgrims Gate
LEOPOLD DR.
WAY
THE OLD SCH.
ALBERT RD.
THE PRY.
ELIZABETH
MARTIN ST.
Play. Fld.
Newtown
AMBLESIDE
Newtown Farm
MALLARD CL.
Playing Field
Pavilion
Tennis Cts.
Playing Field
BISHOP'S WALTHAM
TANGIER
Tangier Farm
Thicket House

Street End
Street End Farm
Buryfield Farm
Strete End
Ridgedale
Peak Cottage
NATIONAL PARK
Cleverly Cottages
Oatfield Bungalow
Beech Close
Dean
Ashton Farm Cottages
Highfield Farm
Gilbert's Knapp
Claytons
West Dean Farm
Grove Farm
Meadowbank
Ashton Farm
Jarmans Farm
Ashton Place
The Hangers
Hilltop
Galley Down
Primrose Terrace
Elberry Farm
Works
Margaret Cotts.
Metlands Farm
Vernon Hill House
Green Oaks
Bishop's Down Farm
Ivy Cottage
Poultry Houses
Cornhill Hall
Red Hill
Duncombe
Spring Close
Hill House
Northbrook Farm
Beechen Copse
Runny Down Copse
Northbrook
Northbrook Ho.
Northbrook Bower
Wks.
Bishop's Waltham Inf. Sch.
Bishop Waltham Jun. Sch.
Cemetery
Upfield
Y Berllan
Hoe
North Pond
Southbrook M.
Roman Row
Lib.
Malt Hall
St. George's Sq.
Palace M.
(remains of)
Palace Ho.
Play. Fld.
Nursery
Recreation Ground
Yew Tree Villa
South View
Hoe Farm
Little Hoe Farm
Hornbeam House
Coppice Hill
Post Mead
Thickets Farm Cott.
Mill Pond
Chase Mill
The Moors Nature Reserve
Suetts Farm
DEAN LANE
LIMEKILN LANE
LITTLE ASHTON LANE
THE HANGERS
B3035
NEW ROAD
SHIPCOTE LANE
VERNON HILL
VERNON CL.
DUNDRIDGE LANE
LOWER LANE
FREE STREET
BEAUFORT DR.
ANDREWES CL.
GARFIELD RD.
BROOKLANDS RD.
DENEWULF CL.
CHALKY LA.
BUTTS FARM LA.
COLVILLE DR.
RARERIDGE LANE
TENNYSON CL.
WORDSWORTH CL.
BYRON CL.
HAZEL GRO.
OAK RD.
PINE RD.
ELM RD.
WILLOW RD.
SYCAMORE RD.
GUNNERS PK.
HOE ROAD
WEST HOE LANE
JERVIS LA.
COURT LANE
SWANMORE ROAD
BANK STREET
HIGH ST.
HOUCHIN ST.
BASINGWELL ST.
MALVERN CL.
SHORE CR.
LITTLE SHORE LA.
GREEN LANE
PENFORD PADDOCK
CRICKLEMEDE
FOLLY FIELD
STATION RD.
BISHOP'S LANE
BOTLEY ROAD
COPPICE HILL
WINCHESTER ROAD
B2177
HAMBLE SPRINGS
THE GARDENS
PARADISE LANE
SUETTS LANE
MOORLANDS RD.

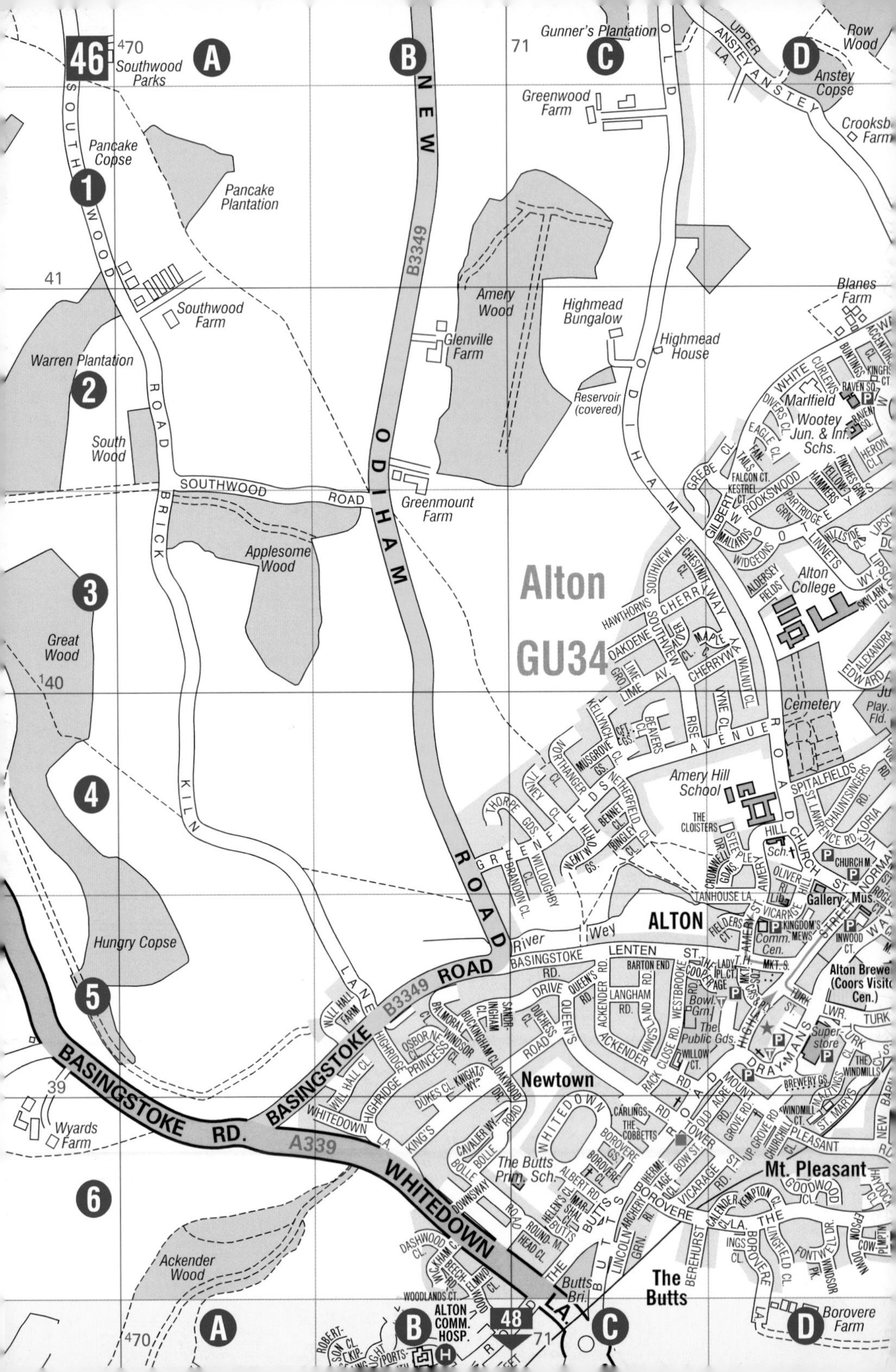
Southwood Parks
Pancake Copse
Pancake Plantation
Warren Plantation
South Wood
Great Wood
Hungry Copse
Wyards Farm
Ackender Wood
Southwood Farm
SOUTHWOOD ROAD
BRICK KILN LANE
Applesome Wood
NEW ODIHAM ROAD
B3349
Amery Wood
Glenville Farm
Greenmount Farm
Gunner's Plantation
Greenwood Farm
Highmead Bungalow
Highmead House
Reservoir (covered)
OLD ODIHAM ROAD
UPPER ANSTEY LA.
ANSTEY
Row Wood
Anstey Copse
Crooksbury Farm
Blanes Farm
Marlfield
Wootey Jun. & Inf. Schs.
Alton College
Alton
GU34
Cemetery
Amery Hill School
ALTON
River Wey
BASINGSTOKE ROAD
BASINGSTOKE RD.
A339
WHITEDOWN LA.
Newtown
The Butts Prim. Sch.
Mt. Pleasant
The Butts
Butts Bri.
Alton Brewery (Coors Visitor Cen.)
Super-store
Gallery
Mus.
Comm. Cen.
The Public Gds.
Bowl. Grn.
ALTON COMM. HOSP.
Borovere Farm
LENTEN ST.
HIGH ST.
CHURCH ST.
DRAYMANS WY.
VICARAGE RD.
BOROVERE LA.
48
470
71
41
40
39

Cannon's Copse
Cuckoo's Corner
Sports Field
Manor Farm
Field Cottage
Howards Farm
Holybourne
Cadnam Farm
Playing Fields
Treloar College
Andrews' C of E Prim. Sch.
Eggar's School
Playing Field
Thtre.
Alton Convent School
Anstey Park
Alton Town FC
Anstey
Tennis Courts
Neatham Mill Cottage
Neatham Mill
Neatham
Neatham Manor
Upper Neatham Mill Farm
Depot
Mill
Warehouse
Copt Hill
Lynch Hill
Sports Grd.
Lynch Hill Cottage
Golden Chair Hill
Golden Chair Farm
Sewage Works
Alton
King's Pond Nature Reserve
Spitalhatch
Neatham Down
Monk Wood
Factory
Wilsom
Hurdles
Wixes
Club House
Driving Range
WORLDHAM GOLF COURSE
Cox's Copse
Little Caker Bri.
MONTECCHIO WY.
MILL LANE
WILSOM ROAD
CAKERS LANE
LONDON ROAD
A31
B3004
HOLYBOURNE
E F G H
1 2 3 4 5 6
72 73 74
41 40 39

46
Dark Wick's Wood
Ackender Wood
Alexandra Wood
ALTON COMMUNITY HOSPITAL
Chawton Park Indoor Bowls Club
Alton Sports Centre
Mounter's Farm
Stonehill Farm
The Butts
Butts Bridge
Borovere Farm
Lumbry Farm
Little Eastfield Farm
SELBORNE RD.
A339
A31
B3006
WHITEDOWN LANE
WINCHESTER RD.
MOUNTERS LANE
WOLF'S LANE
Jubilee Playing Fields
Pavilion
(MID HANTS RAILWAY)
WATERCRESS LINE
NORTHFIELD LA.
CHAWTON PARK
New Cottages
Chalk Dell Cottages
CHAWTON
Jane Austen's House Museum
Pound Farm
Eastfield Farm
Mingledown Plantation
Diamond Jubilee Clump
Eastfield Plantation
Chawton C of E Prim. Sch.
Cricket Grd.
Pav.
Silver Wedding Clump
Adela Copse
FERNEY CL.
Chawton Glebe
Home Farm
Knickerknocker Copse
Peck Copse
Chawton House Library & Study Centre
GOSPORT ROAD
A32
Imbook Copse
Hulvers Row
SOUTH DOWNS NATIONAL PARK
Broadlands Row
Three Acres Copse
Crocklands Copse
Southfield Farm
Tennis Court
Holm Wood
Comp
Alton
GU34
Park Cottage
Noar Copse
New Close Plantation
Montlings Plantation
Jubilee Clump
Berryhill Plantation
WOODSIDE LANE
WOODSIDE LA.
Manor House Farm
Upper Farringdon
GASTON LANE
MOUNTSOM'S LA.
CHURCH ROAD
CROWS LA.
Crows Farm
Stapley's Fa

49
E
F
G
H
1
2
3
4
5
6
466
67
36
135
34
Bowling Green
High Wood
CHAWTON PARK WOOD
Roe Downs Farm
Roedowns Cottage
Roe Downs House
South Town Farm
South Town
Redhill Copse
Redhill Farm
Eighteen Acre Plantation
Fourteen Acre Plantation
Red Bushes
Five Ash Pond
Beverley Court
Estevan Farm
Common Farm
Soldridge Nursery
Alton
GU34
Woodlea Farm
WOODLEA PARK
MANSFIELD PARK
Medstead and Four Marks
LYMINGTON BARN
Factories
Oakgreen Pde.
Winchester M.
Charters Cl.
FOUR MARKS
Nursery
Hall
Garden Centre
Greenways Farm
Bowl. Grn.
Pav.
Tennis Courts
Play. Fld.
Pavilion
Playing Field
Cemy.
Depot
Pine Court
Hawthorn Farm
Hawthorn
Hawthorn Cottage Farm
Cob Farm
Kitfield Farm
Four Marks C of E Primary School
Homestead Farm
Beech Farm
SO24
Old Down Wood
HOMESTEAD RD.
SOUTH TOWN LANE
ROAD
PAICE
KNAPP LANE
ROE DOWNS ROAD
RED HILL
THE CRESCENT
WINDSOR RD.
RED BUSHES CL.
BOYNESWOOD CL.
BRACENBURY GDS.
THORNYBUSH GDS.
BLUE-BELL GDNS.
FRIARS OAK
BOYNESWOOD ROAD
FIVE ASH ROAD
STONEY LANE
BEECHLANDS ROAD
BOYNESWOOD LANE
SOLDRIDGE ROAD
LYMINGTON BOTTOM
WATERCRESS WY.
CHAWTON END CL.
HANDYSIDE PL.
THE SHRAVE
WINCHESTER ROAD
A31
STATION APPROACH
STATION RISE
STATION APP.
WINDMILL FIELDS
FAIRLIGHT GDNS.
FAIRFIELD GREEN
TELEGRAPH LANE
BADGER CLOSE
MULBERRY CT.
BLACKBERRY CL.
PINE RD.
BELMONT DR.
BLENHEIM CL.
SPENCER CL.
CHURCH CL.
CROWN WOOD
WINSTON RISE
HAZEL ROAD
BRIAR LA.
THORN CL.
THORN CT.
THORN DR.
THORN CR.
LYMINGTON CL.
TAWNY GRO.
WATERCRESS LINE (MID HANTS RAILWAY)
WAY
KIRTLE DR.
LELANT DR.
MINDEN PL.
RIVER CL.
BANK CT.
BOGMOOR CL.
MERLIN RD.
Merlin Ct.
PENROSE WAY
READ'S FIELD
CHALK RI.
BRAMBLES CL.
GLOUCESTER CL.
ST. FAITH CL.
LYMINGTON RI.
YARNHAMS CL.
KINGSWOOD
DRUMMOND CL.
LAPWING WAY
ST. AUBINS CL.
BERNARD AV.
BISHOP'S WY.
GOLDCREST WY.
VECTIS CL.
TIMBERCROFT CL.
PHEASANT CL.
CHAFFINCH RD.
UPLANDS LANE
BLACKBERRY LANE
SOKE-HILL
BARN LANE
GREEN LA.
GRADWELL LANE
BRISLANDS
LYMINGTON BOTTOM
ALTON LANE
WILLIS LANE
HAWTHORN ROAD
KITWOOD ROAD
KITWOOD LA.

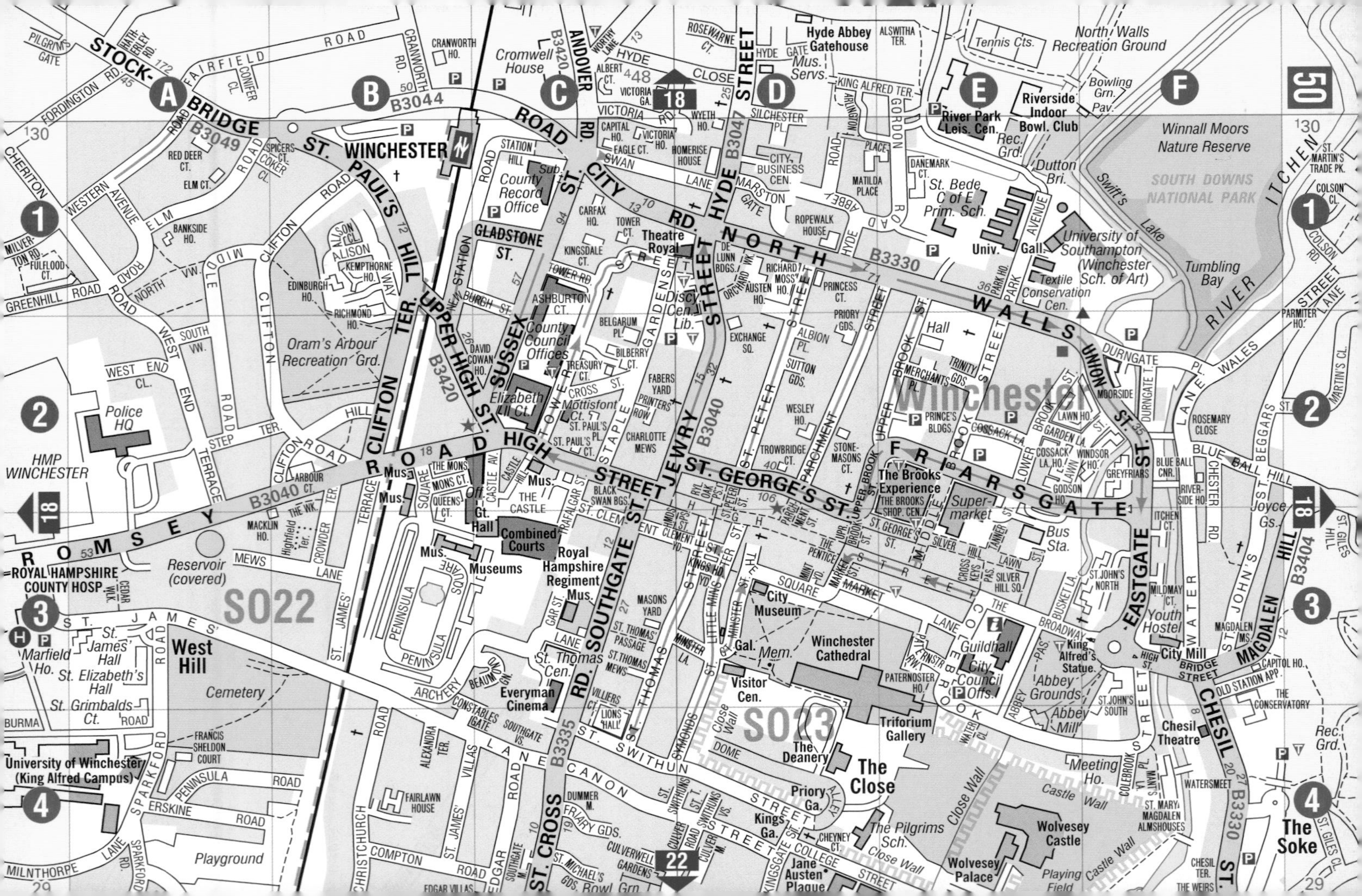
Winchester
North Walls Recreation Ground
Winnall Moors Nature Reserve
SOUTH DOWNS NATIONAL PARK
RIVER ITCHEN
Tumbling Bay
Swift's Lake
Hyde Abbey Gatehouse
Mus. Servs.
River Park Leis. Cen.
Riverside Indoor Bowl. Club
University of Southampton (Winchester Sch. of Art)
Textile Conservation Cen.
St. Bede C of E Prim. Sch.
Univ.
Gall.
WINCHESTER
County Record Office
Cromwell House
Theatre Royal
Disc. Cen.
Lib.
County Council Offices
Elizabeth II Ct.
The Brooks Experience
Super-market
Bus Sta.
Youth Hostel
City Mill
King Alfred's Statue
Abbey Grounds
Abbey Mill
Guildhall
City Council Offs.
Winchester Cathedral
Triforium Gallery
Visitor Cen.
City Museum
The Deanery
The Close
Wolvesey Castle
Wolvesey Palace
The Pilgrims Sch.
Jane Austen Plaque
Chesil Theatre
The Soke
Combined Courts
Gt. Hall
Royal Hampshire Regiment Mus.
Museums
Everyman Cinema
St. Thomas Cen.
Oram's Arbour Recreation Grd.
Police HQ
HMP WINCHESTER
Reservoir (covered)
ROYAL HAMPSHIRE COUNTY HOSP.
West Hill
Cemetery
University of Winchester (King Alfred Campus)
Playground
SO22
SO23
STOCK-BRIDGE ROAD
ANDOVER RD.
CITY RD.
NORTH WALLS
HYDE STREET
JEWRY ST.
ST. GEORGE'S ST.
FRIARSGATE
EASTGATE ST.
HIGH ST.
UPPER HIGH ST.
SOUTHGATE ST.
ST. CROSS RD.
ROMSEY ROAD
CLIFTON TER.
ST. PAUL'S HILL
SUSSEX ST.
GLADSTONE ST.
MAGDALEN HILL
CHESIL ST.
UNION ST.
B3044 B3049 B3420 B3047 B3330 B3040 B3335 B3404
18 22

INDEX

Including Streets, Places & Areas, Hospitals etc., Industrial Estates, Selected Flats & Walkways, Service Areas, Stations and Selected Places of Interest.

HOW TO USE THIS INDEX

1. Each street name is followed by its Postcode District, then by its Locality abbreviation(s) and then by its map reference; e.g. **Ashton La.** SO32: Bis W . . . .4C **44** is in the SO32 Postcode District and the Bishop's Waltham Locality and is to be found in square 4C on page **44**. The page number is shown in bold type.
2. A strict alphabetical order is followed in which Av., Rd., St., etc. (though abbreviated) are read in full and as part of the street name; e.g. **Fair Field** appears after **Fairfax Cl.** but before **Fairfield Grn.**
3. Streets and a selection of flats and walkways that cannot be shown on the mapping, appear in the index with the thoroughfare to which they are connected shown in brackets; e.g. **Abbey Wlk.** *SO51: Rom . . . .4E **29** (off Church St.)*
4. Addresses that are in more than one part are referred to as not continuous.
5. Places and areas are shown in the index in **BLUE TYPE** and the map reference is to the actual map square in which the town centre or area is located and not to the place name shown on the map; e.g. **ALTON 5D 46**
6. An example of a selected place of interest is **Jane Austen's House Mus. 2B 48**
7. An example of a station is **Alton Station (Rail)** . . . .**4E 47**, also included is **Park & Ride**. e.g. **East Winchester (Barfield) (Park & Ride) 1D 22**
8. Service Areas are shown in the index in **BOLD CAPITAL TYPE**; e.g. **ROWNHAMS SERVICE AREA 5D 36**
9. An example of a Hospital, Hospice or selected Healthcare facility is **ALTON COMMUNITY HOSPITAL 1B 48**
10. Map references for entries that appear on large scale page **50** are shown first, with small scale map references shown in brackets; e.g. **Andover Rd.** SO23: Winche 1C **50** (2A **18**)

GENERAL ABBREVIATIONS

All. : Alley
App. : Approach
Arc. : Arcade
Av. : Avenue
Bldgs. : Buildings
Bungs. : Bungalows
Bus. : Business
Cen. : Centre
Cl. : Close
Comn. : Common
Cnr. : Corner
Cotts. : Cottages
Ct. : Court
Cres. : Crescent
Cft. : Croft
Dr. : Drive
E. : East
Est. : Estate
Fld. : Field
Flds. : Fields
Gdns. : Gardens
Ga. : Gate
Gt. : Great
Grn. : Green
Gro. : Grove
Hgts. : Heights
Ho. : House
Ind. : Industrial
Info. : Information
La. : Lane
Lit. : Little
Lwr. : Lower
Mnr. : Manor
Mkt. : Market
Mdw. : Meadow
Mdws. : Meadows
M. : Mews
Mt. : Mount
Mus. : Museum
Nth. : North
Pde. : Parade
Pk. : Park
Pas. : Passage
Pl. : Place
Ri. : Rise
Rd. : Road
Shop. : Shopping
Sth. : South
Sq. : Square
St. : Street
Ter. : Terrace
Trad. : Trading
Up. : Upper
Vw. : View
Vs. : Villas
Vis. : Visitors
Wlk. : Walk
W. : West
Yd. : Yard

LOCALITY ABBREVIATIONS

Abb W : **Abbots Worthy**
Alt : **Alton**
Ampf : **Ampfield**
A'field : **Ashfield**
Avin : **Avington**
Bass : **Bassett**
Bee : **Beech**
Bis S : **Bishop's Sutton**
B'stke : **Bishopstoke**
Bis W : **Bishop's Waltham**
Brai : **Braishfeld**
B'dge : **Brambridge**
Cha F : **Chandler's Ford**
Chilc : **Chilcomb**
Chilw : **Chilworth**
Col C : **Colden Common**
Comp : **Compton**
Cram : **Crampmoor**
Craw : **Crawley**
Durl : **Durley**
E Wel : **East Wellow**
E Wor : **East Worldham**
E'leigh : **Eastleigh**
E'ton : **Easton**
Fair O : **Fair Oak**
Fis P : **Fisher's Pond**
Fob : **Fobdown**
Four M : **Four Marks**
Hens : **Hensting**
Highb : **Highbridge**
Holy : **Holybourne**
Hor H : **Horton Heath**
Hunt : **Hunton**
Hurs : **Hursley**
Itc A : **Itchen Abbas**
Itc S : **Itchen Stoke**
Kin W : **Kings Worthy**
Lee : **Lee**
Lit : **Littleton**
Lwr B : **Lower Bullington**
Lwr Farr : **Lower Farringdon**
Lwr U : **Lower Upham**
Mar W : **Martyr Worthy**
Meds : **Medstead**
More : **Morestead**
Neat : **Neatham**
New A : **New Alresford**
N Bad : **North Baddesley**
Nur : **Nursling**
Old A : **Old Alresford**
Oli B : **Oliver's Battery**
Ott : **Otterbourne**
Ovin : **Ovington**
Pitt : **Pitt**
Rom : **Romsey**
Rop : **Ropley**
Rown : **Rownhams**
Shal : **Shalden**
Shaw : **Shawford**
South : **Southampton**
S'ton A : **Southampton International Airport**
Sth W : **South Wonston**
Spar : **Sparsholt**
Stoke C : **Stoke Charity**
Sut S : **Sutton Scotney**
Swanm : **Swanmore**
S'ing : **Swaythling**
Tich : **Tichborne**
Toot : **Toothill**
Twyf : **Twyford**
Uph : **Upham**
Up B : **Upper Bullington**
Up Farr : **Upper Farringdon**
Wal C : **Waltham Chase**
Winche : **Winchester**
Wons : **Wonston**
Wor D : **Worthy Down**

A

Abbas Bus. Cen. SO21: Itc A . . .5F **13**
Abbey, The SO51: Rom 4E **29**
Abbey Enterprise Cen. SO51: Rom 6B **30**
Abbey Hill Cl. SO23: Winche . . .3C **18**
Abbey Hill Rd. SO23: Winche 3B **18**
Abbey Pk. Ind. Est. SO51: Rom 5B **30**
Abbey Pas. SO23: Winche 4E **50** (6C **18**)
Abbey Wlk. *SO51: Rom . . . . . . .4E **29** (off Church St.)*
Abbey Water SO51: Rom 4E **29**
Abbotsbury Rd. SO50: B'stke . . .3F **41**
Abbotstone Rd. SO24: Fob 1C **14**
Abbotswood Cl. SO51: Rom . . .2A **30**
ABBOTS WORTHY 5F **11**
Abbotts Ann Rd. SO22: Winche 2H **17**
ABBOTTS BARTON 3C **18**
Abbotts Cl. SO23: Winche 3C **18**
Abbotts Ct. SO23: Winche 3B **18**
Abbotts Rd. SO23: Winche 3C **18**
SO50: E'leigh 4G **39**
Accentors Cl. GU34: Alt 2D **46**
Ackender Rd. GU34: Alt 5C **46**
Acorn Cl. SO22: Winche 3H **17**
Acorn Dr. SO16: Rown 6C **36**
SO53: Cha F 3E **33**
Acorn Gro. SO53: Cha F 1B **38**
Adams Ho. GU34: Alt 4E **47**
Adamson Cl. SO53: Cha F 3F **33**
Adams Way GU34: Alt 4E **47**
Adcock Ct. SO16: Rown 6C **36**
Addison Cl. SO22: Winche 2G **21**
SO51: Rom 2H **29**
Addison Rd. SO50: E'leigh 6B **34**
AGC Museum, The . . .2B **50** (5B **18**)
Ainsley Gdns. SO50: E'leigh 6A **34**
Aintree Cl. SO50: Hor H 6B **42**
Airlie Cnr. SO22: Winche 1A **22**
Airlie La. SO22: Winche 1A **22**
Airlie Rd. SO22: Winche 1A **22**
Alan Drayton Way SO50: B'stke . . . . .3E **41** (not continuous)
Albany Ct. SO32: Bis W 5C **44**
Albany Dr. SO32: Bis W 5C **44**
Albany Rd. SO32: Bis W 5C **44**
SO51: Rom 4F **29**
Albert Ct. SO23: Winche 1C **50** (4B **18**)
Albert Rd. GU34: Alt 6C **46**
SO32: Bis W 6D **44**
SO50: E'leigh 6B **34**
Albion Pl. SO23: Winche 2D **50** (5C **18**)
Albury Pl. SO53: Cha F 2D **32**
Alder Cl. GU34: Alt 3C **46**
SO21: Col C 3G **35**
SO51: Rom 5B **30**
Alders Ct. SO24: New A 3F **15**
Aldersey Flds. GU34: Alt 3D **46**
Alderwood Av. SO53: Cha F 5C **32**
Alexander Sq. SO50: E'leigh . . .1B **40**
Alexandra Rd. GU34: Alt 3D **46**
SO53: Cha F 3G **33**
Alexandra Ter. SO23: Winche 4B **50** (6B **18**)
Alexandria Rd. SO21: Sut S 2D **4**
Alison Way SO22: Winche 1B **50** (5B **18**)
Allan Gro. SO51: Rom 4H **29**
ALLBROOK 4B **34**
Allbrook Hill SO50: E'leigh 4B **34**

Allbrook Knoll SO50: E'leigh . . .4A 34
Allbrook Way SO50: E'leigh 3A 34
Allen Cl. GU34: Alt 3E 47
Allen Gallery 5D 46
Allington La. SO50: Fair O 6F 41
Allington Mnr. Farm Bus. Cen.
SO50: Fair O 6E 41
Allyn Ct. SO50: E'leigh 6B 34
Alma La. SO32: Lwr U 4F 43
Alma Rd. SO51: Rom 4F 29
Alpha Ho. SO16: Chilw 4G 37
Alresford Drove
SO21: Kin W, Mar W, Sth W
. . . . .4E 7
Alresford Golf Course 6E 15
Alresford Rd. SO21: Winche . . .6D 18
SO23: Winche 6D 18
SO24: New A, Ovin 6A 14
Alresford Station
Watercress Line
(Mid-Hants Railway) 4F 15
Alswitha Ter.
SO23: Winche 1E 50 (4C 18)
ALTON 5D 46
Alton Brewery (Coors Visitor Cen.)
. . . . .5D 46
Alton Bus. Cen. GU34: Alt 5F 47
Alton Cl. SO50: Fair O 3H 41
ALTON COMMUNITY HOSPITAL
. . . . .1B 48
Alton Ct. SO23: Winche 3C 18
(off Northlands Dr.)
Alton La. GU34: Four M 6G 49
Alton Sports Cen. 1B 48
Alton Station (Rail) 4E 47
Alwyn Hall SO22: Winche 6A 18
Amberley Cl. SO52: N Bad 6C 30
Amberley M. GU34: Alt 4D 46
(off Amery Hill)
Ambleside SO32: Bis W 5C 44
Amery Hill GU34: Alt 4D 46
Amery St. GU34: Alt 5D 46
AMF Bowling
Eastleigh 3B 40
Ampfield Golf Course 1G 31
Amport Cl. SO22: Winche 2G 17
Anchor Bus. Cen.
SO53: Cha F 6D 32
Anderson Cl. SO51: Rom 1A 30
Anders Rd. SO21: Sth W 5E 7
Andover Rd.
SO22: Winche 2A 18
SO23: Winche 1C 50 (2A 18)
Andover Rd. Nth.
SO22: Winche 6H 9
Andover Rd. Retail Pk.
SO23: Winche 4B 18
Andrewes Cl. SO32: Bis W 5E 45
Anfield Cl. SO50: Fair O 4A 42
Anfield Ct. SO50: Fair O 4H 41
Angelica Gdns. SO50: Hor H . . .6A 42
Anson Rd. SO50: Hor H 6A 42
ANSTEY 3F 47
Anstey La. GU34: Alt 1D 46
Anstey Mill Cl. GU34: Alt 3F 47
Anstey Mill La. GU34: Alt 3F 47
Anstey Rd. GU34: Alt 4E 47
SO51: Rom 2H 29
Anton Cl. SO51: Rom 4A 30
Apex Cen. SO21: Col C 3G 35
Apollo Rd. SO53: Cha F 4H 33
Appledown Cl. SO24: New A . . .5F 15
Appledown La. SO24: Tich 6G 15
Appleshaw Cl.
SO22: Winche 1H 17
Apsley Pl. SO53: Cha F 2D 32
Arbour Ct. SO22: Winche 2B 50
Archers Rd. SO50: E'leigh 1A 40
Archery La.
SO23: Winche 3B 50 (6B 18)
Archery Ri. GU34: Alt 6C 46
Argosy Cres. SO50: E'leigh 5H 39
Argyll Ct. SO23: Winche 3A 22
Arlebury Pk. SO24: New A 3D 14
Arle Cl. SO24: New A 3E 15
Arle Gdns. SO24: New A 3F 15
Arlington Pl. SO23: Winche . . .1D 50
Armada Cl. SO16: Rown 6C 36
Armstrong Cl. SO21: Sth W 5E 7
Arnold Rd. SO50: E'leigh 5A 40
Arrow Cl. SO50: E'leigh 6A 34
Arthur Rd. SO23: Winche 4C 18
SO50: E'leigh 1A 40
Arundel Cl. SO24: New A 5E 15
Arundel Rd. SO50: E'leigh 5A 34
Ascot Cl. GU34: Alt 6E 47
Ascot Rd. SO50: Hor H 6B 42
Asford Gro. SO50: B'stke 1C 40
Ashbarn Cres.
SO22: Winche 2H 21
Ashbourne Ct.
SO22: Winche 3B 18
(off Winton Cl.)
Ashbridge Ri. SO53: Cha F 2C 32
Ashburton Cl. SO24: New A 4E 15
Ashburton Ct. SO23: Winche . . .1C 50
Ashburton Rd.
SO24: New A 4E 15
Ash Cl. SO21: Col C 2F 35
SO51: Rom 5A 30
SO52: N Bad 6D 30
Ashcroft Ct. SO53: Cha F 5F 33
Ashdell Rd. GU34: Alt 5E 47
Ashdown Cl. SO53: Cha F 1E 33
Ashdown Dr. SO53: Cha F 1E 33
Ashdown Rd. SO53: Cha F 1E 33
Ashdown Way SO51: Rom 4H 29
Ashen Cl. SO53: Cha F 3E 33
ASHFIELD 1A 36
Ashfield Vw. SO52: N Bad 6E 31
Ashlea Cl. SO50: Fair O 3B 42
Ashley Cl. SO22: Winche 2G 17
Ashley Gdns. SO53: Cha F 6G 33
Ashley Ho. SO51: Rom 5E 29
Ashley Mdws. SO51: Rom 3G 29
Ashmore Rd. SO22: Winche . . .4G 17
ASHTON 3D 44
Ashton Cl. SO32: Bis W 4C 44
Ashton La. SO32: Bis W 4C 44
Ashton Pl. SO53: Cha F 2D 32
Ashtree Ct. SO53: Cha F 2E 39
Ashurst Cl. SO22: Winche 2H 17
Ash Wlk. SO24: New A 4F 15
Ashwood Ct. SO22: Winche 4H 17
Aspen Cl. SO21: Col C 3G 35
Athelstan Rd. SO23: Winche . . .4B 18
Athena Cl. SO50: Fair O 2G 41
Attwoods Drove
SO21: Comp 1C 26
Audley Pl. SO50: B'stke 3F 41
Augustus Cl. SO53: Cha F 4G 33
Augustus Way SO53: Cha F 4G 33
Austen Av. SO22: Oli B 3F 21
Austen Cl. SO23: Winche 3C 18
Austen Ho. SO23: Winche 1D 50
Authie Grn. SO52: N Bad 1E 37
Avebury Gdns.
SO53: Cha F 2C 32
Avenger Cl. SO53: Cha F 6D 32
Avens Cl. SO50: Hor H 6A 42
Avenue, The SO21: Sut S 4C 4
SO21: Twyf 3G 27
SO24: New A 4D 14
SO32: Bis W 5D 44
Avenue Rd.
SO22: Winche 1A 50 (5A 18)
Avery Flds. SO50: E'leigh 4B 34
AVINGTON 6E 13
Avington Cl. SO50: B'stke 6E 35
Avington La.
SO21: Avin, Itc A 5F 13
Avington Park Golf Course 6F 13
Avlan Ct. SO23: Winche 2B 22
Avonborne Way
SO53: Cha F 3D 32
Avon Cres. SO51: Rom 4A 30
Avondale Mobile Home Pk.
SO21: Col C 2G 35
Avon Grn. SO53: Cha F 6F 33

B

Back St. SO23: Winche 3B 22
Baddesley Cl. SO52: N Bad 6D 30
Baddesley Pk. Ind. Est.
SO52: N Bad 1F 37
Baddesley Rd. SO52: N Bad . . .3C 32
SO53: Cha F 3C 32
Baden Powell Ho.
SO51: Rom 4F 29
(off Baden Powell Way)
Baden Powell Way
SO51: Rom 4F 29
Badger Cl. GU34: Four M 3H 49
SO50: B'stke 3F 41
Badger Ct. SO50: B'stke 3F 41
BADGER FARM 3G 21
Badger Farm Rd.
SO22: Winche 2F 21
SO23: Winche 2F 21
(not continuous)
Baigent Cl. SO23: Winche 5E 19
Bailey Cl. SO22: Winche 1H 21
Bailey Ho. SO24: New A 3F 15
(off Station App.)
Bakehouse Yd. SO24: New A . . .3F 15
(off The Dean)
Balfour Museum of Red Cross
. . . . .4E 19
Balldown Caravan & Camping Pk.
SO21: Spar 5A 8
Balmoral Cl. GU34: Alt 5B 46
SO53: Cha F 3D 32
Balmoral Way SO16: Rown 6B 36
Bampton Ct. SO53: Cha F 5E 33
Banister Park Bowling Club . . .6E 39
Bankside Ho.
SO22: Winche 1A 50 (5A 18)
Bank St. SO32: Bis W 5E 45
Banning St. SO51: Rom 5E 29
BAR END 1D 22
Bar End Ind. Est.
SO23: Winche 2D 22
Bar End Rd. SO23: Winche 1D 22
(not continuous)
Barfield Cl. SO23: Winche 1D 22
Barford Cl. SO53: Cha F 3D 32
Baring Cl. SO21: Itc A 4G 13
Baring Rd. SO23: Winche 6D 18
Barker Mill Cl. SO16: Rown . . .6C 36
Bark Mill M. SO51: Rom 5E 29
Barley Down Dr.
SO22: Winche 3H 21
Barlow M. GU34: Alt 3E 47
Barnes Cl. SO23: Winche 2A 22
Barn La. GU34: Four M 5E 49
Barn Piece SO53: Cha F 5B 32
Barrington Cl. SO50: E'leigh . . .6H 33
Bartholomew Cl.
SO23: Winche 4C 18
Barton Cl. SO51: Rom 3H 29
Barton Drove SO21: Sut S 1A 4
Barton End GU34: Alt 5C 46
Barton Pk. Ind. Est.
SO50: E'leigh 3B 40
Barton Rd. SO50: E'leigh 2C 40
Basing M. SO32: Bis W 6E 45
(off Basingwell St.)
Basingstoke Rd.
GU34: Alt, Bee 5A 46
SO21: Kin W, Mar W 5F 11
SO23: Kin W 5F 11
Basing Way SO53: Cha F 1C 38
Basingwell St. SO32: Bis W . . .6E 45
Bassett Av. SO16: Bass 6B 38
Bassett Dale SO16: Bass 6B 38
Bassett Grn. Rd.
SO16: Bass, S'ing 6C 38
Bassett Heath Av.
SO16: Bass 6B 38
Bath Pl. SO22: Winche 6H 17
Battery Hill SO22: Winche 1G 21
SO32: Bis W 5D 44
Baverstocks GU34: Alt 2E 47
Bay Tree Yd. SO24: New A 3F 15
Beacon Cl. SO16: Rown 6B 36
Beaufort Dr. SO32: Bis W 5E 45
Beaufort Rd. SO23: Winche 1B 22
Beaulieu Cl. SO22: Winche 1H 17
Beaulieu Rd. SO50: E'leigh 1A 40
Beaumaris Cl. SO53: Cha F 1C 38
Beaumond Grn.
SO23: Winche 3C 50 (6B 18)
Beaver Dr. SO50: B'stke 3G 41
Beavers Cl. GU34: Alt 4C 46
Bedfield La. SO23: Winche 6D 10
Beech Cl. SO22: Oli B 4F 21
SO51: Rom 5A 30
SO53: Cha F 2F 33
Beech Copse SO22: Winche 4F 17
Beechcroft SO21: Twyf 2H 27
Beechcroft Cl. SO53: Cha F 5F 33
Beechcroft Way SO53: Cha F . . .5F 33
Beeches, The SO50: Fair O 4B 42
Beeches Hill SO32: Bis W 1F 45
Beech Glade SO22: Winche 1A 22
Beechlands Rd.
GU34: Meds 2G 49
Beech Rd. SO24: New A 4F 15
SO53: Cha F 3F 33
Beechwood Cl. SO53: Cha F . . .2C 32
Beechwood Cres.
SO53: Cha F 2C 32
Beechwood Rd. GU34: Alt 6B 46
Beggars Drove SO21: Sut S 4D 4
Beggars La.
SO23: Winche 2F 50 (5D 18)
Belgarum Pl. SO23: Winche . . .2C 50
Bell Ct. SO51: Rom 4E 29
Bellevue Rd. SO50: E'leigh 2A 40
Bellflower Way SO53: Cha F . . .4B 32
Bell St. SO51: Rom 4E 29
Belmont Dr. GU34: Four M 3G 49
Belmont Rd. SO53: Cha F 2E 39
Benedict Cl. SO51: Rom 4A 30
Benenden Grn. SO24: New A . . .5F 15
Benham Rd. SO16: Chilw 4F 37
Benmore Gdns. SO53: Cha F . . .3D 32
Bennet Cl. GU34: Alt 4C 46
Benny Hill Cl. SO50: E'leigh . . .2H 39
Bentley Cl. SO23: Kin W 5D 10
Bercote Cl. SO22: Lit 6F 9
Bere Cl. SO22: Winche 3H 17
SO53: Cha F 3C 32
Berehurst GU34: Alt 6C 46
Beresford Cl. SO53: Cha F 6G 33
Beresford Gdns.
SO53: Cha F 6G 33
Beresford Rd. SO53: Cha F 6G 33
Bereweeke Av.
SO22: Winche 2A 18
Bereweeke Cl.
SO22: Winche 4A 18
Bereweeke M.
SO22: Winche 3A 18
Bereweeke Rd.
SO22: Winche 4A 18
Bereweeke Way
SO22: Winche 3A 18
Bernard Av. GU34: Four M 4G 49
Bernie Tunstall Pl.
SO50: E'leigh 2B 40
(off Romsey Rd.)
Berry La. SO21: Twyf 2F 27
Berthon Ho. SO51: Rom 5E 29
Beta Ho. SO16: Chilw 4G 37
Beverley Gdns. SO51: Rom 2H 29
Beyne Rd. SO22: Oli B 4F 21
Bilberry Ct.
SO23: Winche 2C 50 (5B 18)
Bingley Cl. GU34: Alt 4C 46
Birch Cl. SO21: Col C 3F 35
SO51: Rom 5B 30
Birch Ct. SO22: Winche 1G 21
Birches, The SO21: Col C 2F 35
Birches Close, The
SO52: N Bad 6D 30
Birch Gro. SO50: E'leigh 5H 33
Birch Rd. SO16: Chilw 5B 38
Bird Fld. SO53: Cha F 4A 32
Birinus Rd. SO23: Winche 4C 18
Bishops Ct. SO50: B'stke 6D 34
Bishop's La. SO32: Bis W 6E 45
Bishops Sutton Rd.
SO24: New A 3G 15
BISHOPSTOKE 2D 40
Bishopstoke La.
SO50: B'dge 5E 35
Bishopstoke Mnr.
SO50: E'leigh 2C 40
Bishopstoke Rd.
SO50: E'leigh 2B 40
Bishop's Vw. GU34: Four M 4E 49
BISHOP'S WALTHAM 6E 45
Bishop's Waltham Palace & Museum
. . . . .6E 45
(off Brook St.)
Blackberry Cl.
GU34: Four M 3H 49
Blackberry Dr. SO50: Fair O . . .4H 41
Blackberry La.
GU34: Four M 5G 49
Blackbird Rd. SO50: E'leigh 4F 39
Blackmans Way
SO32: Bis W 5D 44
Black Swan Bldgs.
SO23: Winche 2C 50
Blackthorn Cl. SO21: Sth W 5C 6
Blackthorn Grn. SO21: Col C . . .3G 35
Blackwell Rd. SO21: Wor D 6C 6
Blanchard Rd. SO32: Bis W . . .5D 44
Blencowe Dr. SO53: Cha F 6A 32
Blenheim Cl. GU34: Alt 5E 47
GU34: Four M 3G 49
SO53: Cha F 1B 38

Blenheim Ho. SO50: E'leigh . . .3B **40**
SO51: Rom 4H 29
(off Chambers Av.)
Blenheim Rd. SO50: E'leigh . . .3A **40**
Blue Ball Cnr. SO23: Winche . . .2F **50**
Blue Ball Hill
SO23: Winche 2F **50** (5D **18**)
Bluebell Gdns. GU34: Meds . . .2H **49**
Bodmin Rd. SO50: B'stke 2E **41**
Bodycoats Rd. SO53: Cha F 5F **33**
Bodysound Fitness Club 6D **32**
Bogmoor Cl. GU34: Four M 4G **49**
Bolderwood Cl. SO50: B'stke . . .3F **41**
Bolle Rd. GU34: Alt 6B **46**
Bonhams Cl. GU34: Holy 1H **47**
Borden Way SO52: N Bad 1E **37**
Borman Way SO21: Sth W 5E **7**
Borovere Cl. GU34: Alt 6C **46**
Borovere Gdns. GU34: Alt 6C **46**
Borovere La. GU34: Alt 6C **46**
Boscobel Rd. SO22: Winche . . .4B **18**
Bostock Cl. SO21: Spar 2B **16**
Boston Ct. SO53: Cha F 4F **33**
Bosville SO50: E'leigh 5H **33**
Botley Rd. SO16: Chilw 5B **30**
SO32: Bis W 6E **45**
SO50: Fair O, Hor H 4B **42**
SO51: Rom 4G **29**
SO52: N Bad 5B **30**
Bourne Cl. SO21: Ott 5C **26**
Bournefields SO21: Twyf 2H **27**
Bourne La. SO21: Twyf 2G **27**
Bournemouth Rd.
SO53: Cha F 3D **38**
Bowland Ri. SO53: Cha F 4C **32**
Bow St. GU34: Alt 6C **46**
Boyatt Cres. SO50: E'leigh 3A **34**
Boyatt La. SO21: Ott 2A **34**
SO50: E'leigh 3A **34**
BOYATT WOOD 6A **34**
Boyatt Wood Shop. Cen.
SO50: E'leigh 6A **34**
Boyes La. SO21: Col C 2G **35**
Boyne Mead Rd.
SO23: Kin W 4D **10**
Boyne Ri. SO23: Kin W 3D **10**
Boyneswood Cl.
GU34: Meds 2H **49**
Boyneswood La.
GU34: Meds 2G **49**
Boyneswood Rd.
GU34: Meds 2H **49**
Boynton Cl. SO53: Cha F 3D **32**
Bracenbury Gdns.
GU34: Meds 2H **49**
Bracken Cl. SO52: N Bad 2E **37**
Bracken Cres. SO50: B'stke 3F **41**
Bracken Hall SO16: Chilw 5D **38**
Bracken Pl. SO16: Chilw 6C **38**
Bracken Rd. SO52: N Bad 2E **37**
Brackenway Rd.
SO53: Cha F 3E **33**
Brackley Av. SO50: Fair O 2H **41**
Bradley Peak SO22: Winche . . .4G **17**
Bradley Rd. SO22: Winche 2G **17**
Bradshaw Cl. SO50: Fair O 3C **42**
Braeside Cl. SO22: Oli B 3F **21**
Braishfield Rd.
SO51: Brai, Rom 2A **30**
Bramble Cl. SO50: E'leigh 6B **34**
Bramble Dr. SO51: Rom 2A **30**
Bramblegate SO50: Fair O 4B **42**
Bramble Hill SO24: New A 4F **15**
SO53: Cha F 5D **32**
Brambles Cl. GU34: Four M . . .4G **49**
SO21: Col C 3G **35**
BRAMBRIDGE 3F **35**
Brambridge SO50: B'dge 3E **35**
Brambridge Park 2E **35**
Bramley Cl. GU34: Alt 5E **47**
Bramley Gdns. SO50: Hor H . . .6A **42**
Bramshaw Cl.
SO22: Winche 2G **17**
Brandon Cl. GU34: Alt 4C **46**
Brandy Mt. SO24: New A 3F **15**
Branksome Cl.
SO22: Winche 1F **21**
Bransley Cl. SO51: Rom 2H **29**
Brasher Cl. SO50: B'stke 3G **41**
Brassey Rd. SO22: Winche 4B **18**
Braxton Ho. SO23: Winche 4E **19**
Breach La. SO50: B'stke 6D **34**
Breamore Cl. SO50: E'leigh 5A **34**
Brecon Cl. SO53: Cha F 2D **38**
Brewers La. SO21: Twyf 4F **27**
Brewery Gdns. GU34: Alt 5D **46**
Brewery La. SO51: Rom 3E **29**
Brewhouse Yd. *SO24: New A . . .3F 15*
(off West St.)
Briar La. GU34: Four M 3H **49**
Briar Way SO51: Rom 2A **30**
Brickfield La. SO53: Cha F 6D **32**
Brickfield Trad. Est.
SO53: Cha F 6E **33**
Brick Kiln La. GU34: Alt 3A **46**
Brickmakers Rd.
SO21: Col C 3F **35**
Brickwoods Cl. SO51: Rom 3H **29**
Bridge Ct. SO51: Rom 5E **29**
Bridge La. SO21: Shaw 2E **27**
Bridge Rd. SO24: New A 4D **14**
SO51: Rom 4G **29**
Bridges Cl. SO50: E'leigh 2H **39**
Bridge St.
SO23: Winche 3F **50** (6D **18**)
Bridge Ter. SO21: Shaw 3E **27**
Bridgetts La. SO21: Mar W 1H **11**
Bright Wire Cres.
SO50: E'leigh 3H **39**
Brill Cl. SO24: New A 4E **15**
Brislands La.
GU34: Four M, Rop 6E **49**
SO24: Rop 6E **49**
Broad Chalke Down
SO22: Winche 3G **21**
Broadlands 6E **29**
Broadlands Av.
SO50: E'leigh 5A **34**
Broad La. SO52: N Bad 6C **30**
Broad St. SO24: New A 3F **15**
Broadview Cl. SO23: Kin W 4E **11**
Broad Vw. La. SO22: Oli B 4E **21**
Broadwater Rd. SO51: Rom . . .5E **29**
Broadway, The
SO23: Winche 3E **50** (6C **18**)
Brockham Hill La.
GU34: Holy 1F **47**
Brook, The SO24: Old A 1F **15**
Brook Cl. SO52: N Bad 2E **37**
SO53: Cha F 1E **39**
Brooke Cl. SO23: Kin W 3D **10**
Brookfield Rd. SO50: Fair O . . .3H **41**
Brooklands Rd. SO32: Bis W . . .5E **45**
Brooklyn Cl. SO21: Ott 6C **26**
Brooklyn Ct. *SO21: Ott 6C 26*
(off Main Rd.)
Brook Rd. SO50: Fair O 3A **42**
Brooks Experience, The 2E **50**
Brooks Shop. Centre, The
SO23: Winche 2E **50** (5C **18**)
Brook St. SO32: Bis W 6E **45**
Brooks Way SO21: Hurs 5D **24**
Brook Way SO51: Rom 2G **29**
Brookwood Av.
SO50: E'leigh 2H **39**
Brookwood Ind. Est.
SO50: E'leigh 2A **40**
Broomhill Way
SO50: E'leigh 4A **34**
Brownhill Cl. SO53: Cha F 4E **33**
Brownhill Gdns.
SO53: Cha F 4E **33**
Brownhill Rd. SO52: N Bad 1E **37**
(not continuous)
SO53: Cha F 4E **33**
Browning Cl. SO50: E'leigh 2H **39**
Browning Dr. SO22: Winche . . .5H **17**
Browsholme Cl.
SO50: E'leigh 5A **34**
Broxburn Cl. SO53: Cha F 2G **33**
Brue Cl. SO53: Cha F 4D **32**
Brunswick Cl. SO50: Fair O 2H **41**
Brunswick Rd. SO50: Fair O . . .2H **41**
Bryony Gdns. SO50: Hor H 6A **42**
BUCKET CORNER 4G **31**
Buckingham Cl. GU34: Alt 5B **46**
Buckland Cl. SO50: E'leigh 5A **34**
Buddlesgate SO21: Sut S 4D **4**
Budds La. SO51: Rom 2E **29**
Budds La. Ind. Est.
SO51: Rom 2E **29**
Bullington La.
SO21: Sut S, Up B 1C **4**
BUNSTEAD 3F **25**
Bunstead La. SO21: Hurs 3F **25**
Buntings GU34: Alt 2D **46**
Buriton Rd. SO22: Winche 1H **17**
Burley Cl. SO53: Cha F 1D **38**
Burley Down SO53: Cha F 1D **38**
Burley Rd. SO22: Winche 1H **17**
Burma Rd.
SO22: Winche 4A **50** (6A **18**)
SO51: Rom 5F **29**
Burne Cl. SO21: Wor D 1H **9**
Burnett Cl. SO22: Winche 3G **17**
Burnetts Flds. SO50: Hor H 6A **42**
Burnetts Gdns.
SO50: Hor H 6A **42**
Burnetts La. SO50: Hor H 6A **42**
Burnham Beeches
SO53: Cha F 5D **32**
Burnham Rd. GU34: Alt 1A **48**
Burns Cl. SO21: Sth W 5E **7**
SO50: E'leigh 4G **39**
Burns Rd. SO50: E'leigh 4H **39**
Burrage M. SO24: New A 3F **15**
Burr Cl. SO21: Col C 3F **35**
Burrow Hill Pl. SO50: B'stke . . .1D **40**
Burrow Rd. SO21: Spar 5A **16**
Busket La.
SO23: Winche 3E **50** (6C **18**)
Buttermere Gdns.
SO24: New A 5F **15**
BUTTS, THE 6C **46**
Butts, The GU34: Alt 6C **46**
Butts Cl. SO22: Winche 4H **17**
Butts Farm La. SO32: Bis W . . .5F **45**
Butts M. GU34: Alt 6C **46**
Butts Rd. GU34: Alt 1C **48**
By-Pass Rd. SO21: Sut S 3B **4**
Byron Av. SO22: Winche 5H **17**
Byron Cl. SO32: Bis W 5G **45**
Byron Rd. SO50: E'leigh 1B **40**

C

Cable St. SO50: E'leigh 3A **40**
Caernarvon Gdns.
SO53: Cha F 1C **38**
Cakers La. GU34: E Wor 6G **47**
Caker Stream Rd. GU34: Alt . . .4F **47**
Calender Cl. GU34: Alt 6D **46**
Calshot Dr. SO53: Cha F 2C **38**
Camborne Cl. SO50: B'stke 3E **41**
Cambridge Dr. SO53: Cha F 2E **39**
(not continuous)
Cambridge Grn.
SO53: Cha F 2E **39**
Camelia Gro. SO50: Fair O 3C **42**
Camellia Cl. SO52: N Bad 6E **31**
Campbell Ct. GU34: Holy 2G **47**
Campbell Rd. SO50: E'leigh 4B **40**
Campbell Way SO50: Fair O . . .3A **42**
Campion Dr. SO51: Rom 2A **30**
Campion Way SO23: Kin W 5E **11**
Canal Cl. SO51: Rom 2G **29**
Canal Wlk. SO51: Rom 3F **29**
Canon Ct. SO50: Fair O 3B **42**
Canon St.
SO23: Winche 4C **50** (6B **18**)
Canute Rd. SO23: Winche 1D **22**
Capital Ho. SO23: Winche 1C **50**
Capitol Ho.
SO23: Winche 3F **50** (6D **18**)
Carfax Ho. SO23: Winche 1C **50**
Carisbrooke Cl.
SO24: New A 5F **15**
Carisbrooke Ct. SO51: Rom . . .2G **29**
Carisbrooke Cres.
SO53: Cha F 6G **33**
Carlings GU34: Alt 6C **46**
Carlyn Dr. SO53: Cha F 4F **33**
Carmans La. SO21: Comp 1D **26**
Carne Cl. SO53: Cha F 3E **33**
Carpenters SO24: New A 4F **15**
Carpenters Cl. GU34: Holy 2H **47**
Carpiquet Pk. SO52: N Bad 1E **37**
Carrol Cl. SO50: Fair O 4B **42**
Carthage Cl. SO53: Cha F 4H **33**
Carthagena SO21: Sut S 3D **4**
Castle, The
SO23: Winche 2C **50** (6B **18**)
Castle Av.
SO23: Winche 2C **50** (5B **18**)
Castle Hill
SO23: Winche 2C **50** (5B **18**)
Castle La.
SO52: Cha F, N Bad 1F **37**
SO53: Cha F 1C **38**
Castle Ri. SO23: Kin W 2E **11**
Castlewood SO53: Cha F 1D **38**
Cathedral Vw.
SO23: Winche 1D **22**
Catmint Cl. SO53: Cha F 4B **32**
Catways SO21: Hurs 2D **24**
Causeway SO51: Rom 5D **28**
Causton Gdns. SO50: E'leigh . . .2A **40**
Cavalier Way GU34: Alt 6B **46**
Cavendish Cl. SO51: Rom 1H **29**
Cavendish Gro.
SO23: Winche 2D **18**
Cedar Cl. SO23: Kin W 3D **10**
Cedar Ct. SO32: Bis W 5F **45**
Cedar Cres. SO52: N Bad 6D **30**
Cedar Lawn SO51: Rom 2A **30**
Cedar Rd. SO50: E'leigh 4G **39**
Cedar Wlk.
SO22: Winche 3A **50** (6A **18**)
Cedarwood SO23: Kin W 4E **11**
Cedar Wood Cl.
SO50: Fair O 3C **42**
Celandine Cl. SO53: Cha F 6B **32**
Centaury Gdns. SO50: Hor H . . .6A **42**
Central Precinct, The
SO53: Cha F 6E **33**
Cerne Cl. SO52: N Bad 1D **36**
Chadwick Rd. SO50: E'leigh . . .3H **39**
Chaffinch Rd. GU34: Four M . . .5E **49**
Chalcrafts GU34: Alt 3E **47**
Chalk Cl. GU34: Four M 4G **49**
Chalk Ridge SO23: Winche 6E **19**
Chalky La. SO32: Bis W 5F **45**
Chalvington Rd.
SO53: Cha F 6E **33**
Chamberlayne Ct.
SO52: N Bad 6F **31**
Chamberlayne Rd.
SO50: E'leigh 4A **40**
Chambers Av. SO51: Rom 4H **29**
CHANDLER'S FORD 4G **33**
Chandler's Ford Golf Academy Driving Range 5E **39**
Chandler's Ford Ind. Est.
SO53: Cha F 6D **32**
Chandler's Ford Station (Rail) 5E **33**
Chandlers Gate SO53: Cha F . . .5E **33**
Chapel Drove SO50: Hor H 6A **42**
Chapel Fld. SO21: E'ton 1H **19**
Chapel Gro. SO21: Col C 2F **35**
Chapel La.
SO21: E'ton . . . . .6A **12** & 1H **19**
SO21: Ott 2B **34**
Charden Rd. SO50: B'stke 3G **41**
Charfield Cl. SO22: Winche 2A **22**
Charlecote Dr. SO53: Cha F 3C **32**
Charles Cl. SO23: Winche 3D **18**
Charlie Soar Ct.
SO50: E'leigh 3A **40**
Charlotte Ct. SO53: Cha F 4G **33**
Charlotte M. SO23: Winche 2C **50**
Charnwood Cl. SO53: Cha F . . .1E **33**
Charnwood Cres.
SO53: Cha F 1E **33**
Charnwood Gdns.
SO53: Cha F 1E **33**
Charters Cl. GU34: Meds 2H **49**
Chartwell Cl. SO50: E'leigh 5B **34**
Chatham Rd. SO22: Winche . . .2G **21**
Chatsworth Rd.
SO50: E'leigh 5B **34**
Chaucer Cl. SO21: Sth W 4E **7**
Chaundler Rd. SO23: Winche . . .3C **18**
Chauntsingers Rd.
GU34: Alt 4D **46**
Chavywater SO51: Rom 5E **29**
CHAWTON 2C **48**
Chawton Cl. SO22: Winche 1H **17**
Chawton End Cl.
GU34: Four M 2H **49**
Chawton House Library & Study Cen. 4B **48**
Chawton Park Indoor Bowls Club 1B **48**
Chawton Pk. Rd. GU34: Alt 2A **48**
Chelmarsh Gdns.
SO50: Fair O 5B **42**
Chepstow Cl. SO53: Cha F 5D **32**
Cherbourg Rd. SO50: E'leigh . . .4H **39**
Cheriton Cl. SO22: Winche 4H **17**
Cheriton Rd.
SO22: Winche 1A **50** (4H **17**)
SO50: E'leigh 5H **39**
Cherry Cl. SO21: Sth W 5D **6**
Cherry Gdns. SO32: Bis W 6F **45**

Cherry Tree Ct. SO50: E'leigh 2G **39**
Cherry Way GU34: Alt 3C **46**
Cherrywood Gdns. SO50: B'stke 3H **41**
Chervil Cl. SO53: Cha F 5B **32**
Cherville Ct. SO51: Rom 4E **29**
Cherville M. SO51: Rom 3E **29**
Cherville St. SO51: Rom 4E **29**
Cherwell Gdns. SO53: Cha F 6F **33**
Chesil St. SO23: Winche 4F **50** (6D **18**)
Chesil Ter. SO23: Winche 4F **50** (6D **18**)
Chesil Theatre 4F **50** (6D **18**)
Chesil Wood SO23: Winche 6E **19**
Chester Rd. SO23: Winche 2F **50** (5D **18**)
Chestnut Av. SO21: Col C 2F **35**
SO22: Lit 1F **17**
SO50: E'leigh 4F **39**
SO53: Cha F 2E **39**
Chestnut Cl. GU34: Alt 3C **46**
SO51: Rom 5B **30**
SO53: Cha F 2E **39**
Chestnut Mead SO23: Winche 2B **22**
Chestnut Ri. SO50: E'leigh 4F **39**
Chestnut Wlk. SO24: New A 4F **15**
Cheyney Ct. SO23: Winche 4D **50**
Chickenhall La. SO50: E'leigh 2C **40**
Chidden Holt SO53: Cha F 6C **32**
Chilbolton Av. SO22: Winche 5G **17**
CHILCOMB 2H **23**
Chilcombe Hgts. *SO23: Winche 6D 18 (off Quarry Rd.)*
Chilcomb La. SO21: Chilc 2F **23**
SO23: Winche 2D **22**
Chilcott Ct. SO52: N Bad 1E **37**
Chilham Cl. SO50: E'leigh 4A **34**
CHILLAND 5C **12**
Chillandham La. SO21: Itc A, Mar W 1C **12**
Chilland La. SO21: Mar W 5C **12**
Chillington Gdns. SO53: Cha F 2D **32**
Chiltern Ct. SO24: New A 4F **15**
CHILWORTH 4A **38**
Chilworth Cl. SO16: Chilw 4H **37**
Chilworth Drove SO16: Chilw, South 6F **37**
Chilworth Golf Course 2F **37**
Chilworth Grange SO16: Chilw 5C **38**
CHILWORTH OLD VILLAGE 3G **37**
Chilworth Rd. SO16: Bass, Chilw 4A **38**
Chirk Pl. SO51: Rom 4G **29**
Christchurch Gdns. SO23: Winche 2B **22**
Christchurch Rd. SO23: Winche 4B **50** (2A **22**)
Christmas Hill SO21: Sth W, Sut S 2B **6**
Church Cl. SO50: B'stke 1D **40**
SO52: N Bad 1E **37**
Churchfields SO21: Twyf 3G **27**
Churchfields Rd. SO21: Twyf 3F **27**
Church Grn. Cl. SO23: Kin W 6E **11**
Churchill Av. SO32: Bis W 4C **44**
Churchill Cl. GU34: Alt 6D **46**
GU34: Four M 3G **49**
SO23: Kin W 2D **10**
Church La. GU34: Holy 1G **47**
SO21: Col C 3F **35**
SO21: E'ton 6H **11**
SO21: Mar W 5B **12**
SO21: Spar 2A **16**
SO21: Twyf 2G **27**
SO22: Lit 5E **9**
SO23: Kin W 5E **11**
SO32: Durl 6D **42**
SO51: Rom 4E **29**
Church M. GU34: Alt 4D **46**
Church Pl. SO51: Rom 4E **29**
Church Rd. GU34: Up Farr 6C **48**
SO50: B'stke 2D **40**
SO51: Rom 4E **29**
Church St. GU34: Alt 4D **46**
SO51: Rom 4E **29**
Church Vw. SO50: E'leigh 4A **40**
Churchyard Cotts. SO24: New A 3F **15**
City Bus. Cen. SO23: Winche 1D **50** (5C **18**)
City Mill 3F **50** (6D **18**)
City Mus. 3D **50** (6C **18**)
City Rd. SO23: Winche 1C **50** (5B **18**)
Clamp Grn. SO21: Col C 3F **35**
Clandon Dr. SO50: E'leigh 5H **33**
Clanfield Cl. SO53: Cha F 5F **33**
Clanfield Dr. SO53: Cha F 5F **33**
Clanfield Way SO53: Cha F 5F **33**
Claremont Cl. SO50: E'leigh 5A **34**
Clarendon Cl. SO51: Rom 2H **29**
Clarendon Way SO22: Winche 5E **17**
Claudius Cl. SO53: Cha F 4H **33**
Claudius Gdns. SO53: Cha F 4H **33**
Clausentum Cl. SO53: Cha F 4G **33**
Clausentum Rd. SO23: Winche 2B **22**
Claylands Ct. SO32: Bis W 5D **44**
Claylands Rd. SO32: Bis W 5D **44**
Claylands Rd. Ind. Est. SO32: Bis W 5D **44**
Clease Way SO21: Comp 2C **26**
Clement Ct. GU34: Alt 2B **48**
Clevelands Cl. SO53: Cha F 2D **32**
Clifford Pl. SO50: Fair O 3A **42**
Cliff Way SO21: Comp 3D **26**
Clifton Hill SO22: Winche 2B **50** (5B **18**)
Clifton Rd. SO22: Winche 1B **50** (5A **18**)
Clifton Ter. SO22: Winche 2B **50** (5B **18**)
Cloisters, The GU34: Alt 4C **46**
SO51: Rom 2E **29**
CLOSE, THE 4D **50** (6C **18**)
Close, The SO50: B'dge 2D **34**
Cloudbank SO21: Sth W 5C **6**
Cloverbank SO23: Kin W 1D **10**
Clover Way SO51: Rom 3A **30**
Coach Hill Cl. SO53: Cha F 4D **32**
Coachmakers M. SO51: Rom 4E **29**
Coate Dr. SO21: Wor D 1G **9**
Cobbett Cl. SO22: Winche 2G **21**
Cobbetts, The GU34: Alt 6C **46**
Cobbles Cl. SO21: Sut S 3C **4**
Cocket's Mead SO21: E'ton 1H **19**
Coker Cl. SO22: Winche 1A **50** (5B **18**)
Colbourne Ct. SO23: Winche 3C **18**
Colchester Av. SO50: B'stke 1E **41**
COLDEN COMMON 3G **35**
Colden La. SO24: Old A 1G **15**
Coldharbour La. SO16: Nur 5A **36**
Colebrook Pl. SO23: Winche 4F **50** (6D **18**)
Colebrook St. SO23: Winche 3E **50** (6C **18**)
Colehill Gdns. SO32: Bis W 5C **44**
Coles Cl. SO21: Twyf 2G **27**
SO50: E'leigh 2B **40**
Coles Mede SO21: Ott 6B **26** (not continuous)
College St. SO23: Winche 4D **50** (6C **18**)
College Wlk. SO23: Winche 1C **22**
Colley Cl. SO23: Winche 2C **18**
Collingbourne Dr. SO53: Cha F 5C **32**
Collins Cl. SO53: Cha F 5B **32**
Collins Ho. SO50: E'leigh 2C **40**
SO53: Cha F 5F **33**
Collins La. SO21: Hurs 2D **24**
Colson Cl. SO23: Winche 1F **50** (5D **18**)
Colson Rd. SO23: Winche 1F **50** (5D **18**)
Colton Copse SO53: Cha F 5B **32**
Coltsfoot Wlk. SO51: Rom 2A **30**
Colts Rd. SO16: Rown 6C **36**
Colvedene Cl. SO21: Col C 2F **35**
Colville Dr. SO32: Bis W 5F **45**
Colvin Gdns. SO53: Cha F 3D **32**
Combined Court Winchester 3C **50** (6B **18**)
Comfrey Cl. SO51: Rom 2A **30**
Common Cl. SO53: Cha F 3E **33**
Common Gdns. SO53: Cha F 3E **33**
Common Rd. SO53: Cha F 3E **33**
Complins GU34: Holy 2G **47**
COMPTON 1D **26**
Compton Cl. SO22: Oli B 4F **21**
SO50: E'leigh 5H **33**
Compton Rd. SO23: Winche 4B **50** (6B **18**)
Compton St. SO21: Comp 1C **26**
Compton Way SO22: Oli B 4F **21**
Coney Grn. SO23: Winche 3C **18**
Conifer Cl. SO22: Winche 1A **50** (4A **18**)
Coniston Gro. SO24: New A 5F **15**
Coniston Rd. SO50: E'leigh 3H **39**
Connaught Rd. SO21: Wor D 1G **9**
Connaught Way GU34: Alt 1B **48**
Conservatory, The SO23: Winche 3F **50** (6D **18**)
Consort Cl. SO50: E'leigh 6B **34**
Consort Rd. SO50: E'leigh 6B **34**
Constables Ga. SO23: Winche 3B **50**
Constantine Av. SO53: Cha F 5G **33**
Constantine Cl. SO53: Cha F 5H **33**
Conway Cl. SO53: Cha F 2D **38**
Cooperage, The GU34: Alt 5C **46**
Coopers Cl. SO21: Wor D 1H **9**
Coppice Cl. SO22: Winche 4G **17**
Coppice Hill SO32: Bis W 6E **45**
Copse, The SO51: Rom 2A **30**
SO53: Cha F 6G **33**
Copse Cl. SO21: Ott 5C **26**
SO52: N Bad 1D **36**
Copse La. SO16: Chilw 4B **38**
Coram Cl. SO23: Winche 3C **18**
Corfe Cl. SO24: New A 5E **15**
Corinthian Rd. SO53: Cha F 4G **33**
Cornerways SO23: Kin W 5E **11**
Cornes Cl. SO22: Winche 6H **17**
Cornfield Cl. SO53: Cha F 5B **32**
Cornmarket SO51: Rom 4E **29**
Cornwall Rd. SO53: Cha F 2E **39**
Cosford Cl. SO50: B'stke 3G **41**
Cossack La. SO23: Winche 2E **50** (5C **18**)
Cossack La. Ho. SO23: Winche 2E **50**
Cotsalls SO50: Fair O 4A **42**
Cotton Cl. SO50: B'stke 2E **41**
COUCH GREEN 4C **12**
Couch Grn. SO21: Mar W 4C **12**
Coultas Rd. SO53: Cha F 1G **33**
Courtenay Rd. SO23: Winche 3C **18**
Court Rd. SO23: Kin W 6E **11**
Courtyard, The SO22: Lit 6F **9**
Coventry Ct. SO23: Winche 3C **18**
Covert, The SO51: Rom 5H **29**
Covey Way SO24: New A 5D **14**
Cowdray Cl. SO50: B'stke 3F **41**
Cowdray Pk. GU34: Alt 6D **46**
Cowley Dr. SO21: Wor D 1H **9**
Cowslip Way SO51: Rom 2A **30**
Cox Row SO53: Cha F 2E **39**
Cox's Hill SO21: Twyf 1G **27**
Crab Wood (Nature Reserve) 5B **16**
Craddock Ho. SO23: Winche 4E **19**
CRAMPMOOR 2C **30**
Crampmoor La. SO51: Cram 2B **30**
Cranborne Gdns. SO53: Cha F 2D **32**
Cranbourne Dr. SO21: Ott 6B **26**
Cranbury Cl. SO21: Ott 1B **34**
Cranbury Rd. SO50: E'leigh 4A **40** (not continuous)
Cranford Dr. GU34: Holy 2G **47**
Cranford Gdns. SO53: Cha F 3D **32**
Cranworth Ho. SO22: Winche 1B **50**
Cranworth Rd. SO22: Winche 1B **50** (4B **18**)
Craven Rd. SO53: Cha F 5F **33**
CRAWLEY 1A **8**
Crescent, The GU34: Meds 2G **49**
SO21: Twyf 3G **27**
SO32: Lwr U 3G **43**
SO50: E'leigh 1A **40**
SO51: Rom 3H **29**
Crescent Cl. SO22: Oli B 3F **21**
Crescent Rd. SO52: N Bad 6D **30**
Cressey Rd. SO51: Rom 4F **29**
Crestwood College Leisure Cen. 6H **33**
Crestwood Vw. SO50: E'leigh 6H **33**
Cricklemede SO32: Bis W 6F **45**
Cricklewood Cl. SO32: Bis W 6F **45**
Cripstead La. SO23: Winche 2B **22**
Crispin Cl. SO50: Hor H 6A **42**
Croft, The SO50: E'leigh 3A **40**
SO53: Cha F 2E **39**
Croft Gdns. GU34: Alt 4C **46**
Cromwell Gdns. GU34: Alt 4D **46**
Cromwell Rd. SO22: Winche 2H **21**
Cross & Pillory La. GU34: Alt 5D **46**
Cross Keys Pas. SO23: Winche 3E **50**
Cross La. SO32: Bis W 2B **44**
Cross St. SO23: Winche 2C **50** (5B **18**)
SO32: Bis W 5E **45**
Cross Way SO21: Shaw 4D **26**
Crossways, The SO53: Cha F 1E **39**
Croucher's Cft. SO22: Winche 3G **17**
Crowders Grn. SO21: Col C 3F **35**
Crowder Ter. SO22: Winche 3B **50** (6B **18**)
CROWDHILL 6H **35**
Crowley Dr. GU34: Alt 5E **47**
Crown Cl. M. GU34: Alt 5D **46**
Crown Wood GU34: Meds 3F **49**
Crows La. GU34: Up Farr 6C **48**
Crummock Rd. SO53: Cha F 3C **32**
Crusaders Way SO53: Cha F 5B **32**
CUCKOO BUSHES 3E **33**
Cuckoo Bushes La. SO53: Cha F 3D **32**
CUCKOO'S CORNER 1H **47**
Culley Vw. SO24: New A 5F **15**
Culver M. SO23: Winche 4D **50** (6C **18**)
Culver Rd. SO23: Winche 4D **50** (1B **22**)
Culverwell Gdns. SO23: Winche 4C **50** (6B **18**)
Cumberland Av. SO53: Cha F 5G **33**
Cumberland Cl. SO53: Cha F 5G **33**
Cundell Way SO23: Kin W 2D **10**
Cunningham Av. SO32: Bis W 5C **44**
Cunningham Ho. SO32: Bis W 5D **44**
CUPERNHAM 2H **29**
Cupernham Cl. SO51: Rom 2G **29**
Cupernham La. SO51: Rom 1G **29**
Curlews GU34: Alt 2D **46**
Curlew Sq. SO50: E'leigh 3G **39**
Curtis Museum, The 5D **46**
Curtis Rd. GU34: Alt 6E **47**
Cypress Gro. SO53: Cha F 3E **33**

D

Daisy Flds. SO50: Fair O 5B **42**
Dakota Way SO50: E'leigh 5H **39**
Dale Cl. SO22: Lit 6E **9**
Dale Grn. SO53: Cha F 2D **32**
Damson Cres. SO50: Fair O 4G **41**
Danebury Gdns. SO53: Cha F 1C **38**
Danemark Ct. SO23: Winche 1E **50** (5C **18**)
Danes Rd. SO23: Winche 4C **18**
Dartington Rd. SO50: B'stke 6D **34**
Darwin Rd. SO50: E'leigh 1B **40**
Dashwood Cl. GU34: Alt 6B **46**
David Ct. SO51: Rom 5G **29**
David Cowan Ho. SO23: Winche 2C **50**
Dawn Gdns. SO22: Winche 1G **21**
Deacon Trad. Est. SO50: E'leigh 3C **40**
Deakin Ct. SO53: Cha F 6E **33**
DEAN
SO21 2C **16**
SO32 2H **45**
Dean, The SO24: New A 3E **15**
Dean Cl. SO22: Winche 3G **17**

Deane Down Drove
SO22: Lit 1F 17
Deanery, The 4D 50 (6C 18)
Deanery, The SO53: Cha F 2D 32
Dean La. SO21: Spar 2B 16
SO22: Spar, Winche 3F 17
SO32: Bis W 1G 45
Dean Pl. SO53: Cha F 5E 33
Dean Rd. SO50: Fair O 4H 41
Deansfield Cl. SO51: Rom 3H 29
Dee Cl. SO53: Cha F 6D 32
Deer Pk. Farm Ind. Est.
SO50: Fair O 4C 42
Dell Cl. SO50: Fair O 4A 42
Dell Rd. SO23: Winche 1E 23
Delta Bus. Pk. GU34: Alt 5F 47
Delta Ho. SO16: Chilw 4G 37
De-Lucy Av. SO24: New A 4D 14
De Lunn Bldgs.
SO23: Winche 1D 50
Denbigh Cl. SO50: E'leigh 6H 33
Dene Cl. SO16: Chilw 6B 38
Denewulf Cl. SO32: Bis W 5E 45
Denham Cl. SO23: Winche 3B 18
Denham Ct. SO23: Winche 3C 18
Denham Flds. SO50: Fair O 2A 42
Dennett Ho. SO23: Winche 4F 19
Derby Rd. SO50: E'leigh 3G 39
Derwent Gdns. SO24: New A . . .5F 15
Desborough Rd.
SO50: E'leigh 4A 40
Devenish Rd. SO22: Winche . . .2H 17
Devine Gdns. SO50: B'stke 3E 41
Devon Cl. SO53: Cha F 2E 39
Devon Dr. SO53: Cha F 2E 39
Dew La. SO50: E'leigh 2H 39
Dibben Wlk. SO51: Rom 2A 30
Dibble Dr. SO52: N Bad 2D 36
Dickenson Wlk.
SO24: New A 5F 15
Dicker's La. GU34: Alt 4E 47
Dirty Dr. SO52: N Bad 6H 31
Divers Cl. GU34: Alt 2D 46
Dolphin Cl. SO50: B'stke 3F 41
Dolphin Hill SO21: Twyf 3G 27
Dome All.
SO23: Winche 4D 50 (6C 18)
Domum Rd. SO23: Winche 1D 22
Doncaster Drove
SO50: E'leigh 6G 39
Doncaster Rd. SO50: E'leigh . . .5A 40
Donnington Ct.
SO23: Winche 4C 18
Donnington Dr. SO53: Cha F . . .2C 38
Dorian Gro. SO24: New A 5D 14
Doric Cl. SO53: Cha F 4H 33
Dorset Rd. SO53: Cha F 2E 39
Dove Ct. GU34: Alt 2E 47
Dove Dale SO50: E'leigh 3F 39
Dover Cl. SO24: New A 5F 15
Dowden Gro. GU34: Alt 3D 46
Down Farm La.
SO22: Winche 3G 9
SO23: Winche 3G 9
Down Ga. SO24: New A 5E 15
Downlands Rd. SO22: Oli B 3F 21
Downlands Way SO21: Sth W . . .5C 6
(not continuous)
Down La. SO51: Rom 3H 29
Downside Rd. SO22: Winche . . .3F 17
Downs Rd. SO21: Sth W 5C 6
Downs Vw. GU34: Holy 1H 47
Downsway GU34: Alt 6B 46
Drake Rd. SO50: B'stke 1E 41
Draymans Way GU34: Alt 5D 46
Drayton St. SO22: Winche 1G 21
Drinkwater Cl. SO50: E'leigh . . .2H 39
Drove, The SO21: Twyf 4F 27
SO32: Durl 5H 43
SO50: Hor H 6B 42
Drove Cl. SO21: Twyf 4F 27
Drove La.
SO24: New A, Old A 3C 14
Drummond Cl.
GU34: Four M 4E 49
SO22: Winche 2A 22
Drummond Ct. SO50: E'leigh . . .6B 34
Drummond Way
SO53: Cha F 3D 32
Drum Rd. SO50: E'leigh 3H 39
Duchess Cl. GU34: Alt 5C 46
Dukes Cl. GU34: Alt 6B 46
Dukes Ct. *SO32: Bis W 5E 45*
(off St Bonnet Dr.)
Duke's Dr.
SO21: Avin, Winche 6D 12
Dukes Mill Cen. SO51: Rom . . .4E 29
Dummer M. SO23: Winche 4C 50
Dumpers Drove
SO50: Hor H 6B 42
Dundridge La. SO32: Bis W 4F 45
Dunnings La. SO52: N Bad 6C 30
Durban Cl. SO51: Rom 2G 29
Durley Hall La. SO32: Durl 4F 43
Durley Rd. SO50: Hor H 5B 42
DURLEY STREET 5H 43
Durley St. SO32: Durl 6F 43
Durngate Pl.
SO23: Winche 2F 50 (5D 18)
Durngate Ter.
SO23: Winche 2F 50 (5D 18)
Dutton La. SO50: E'leigh 1B 40
Duttons Rd. SO51: Rom 3E 29
Dyram Cl. SO50: E'leigh 6H 33
Dyson Dr. SO23: Winche 3C 18

E

Eagle Cl. GU34: Alt 2D 46
SO53: Cha F 1D 38
Eagle Ct. SO23: Winche 1C 50
Earle Ho. SO23: Winche 5F 19
Earls Cl. SO50: B'stke 3G 41
Eastacre SO22: Winche 4A 18
Eastbrooke Rd. GU34: Alt 4E 47
East Dr. SO50: B'stke 1D 40
Eastgate St.
SO23: Winche 3F 50 (6D 18)
East Hill SO23: Winche 1D 22
East Horton Golf Cen. 4D 42
East Horton Golf Course 4D 42
East La. SO24: Ovin 5A 14
EASTLEIGH 3B 40
Eastleigh FC 6G 39
Eastleigh Lakeside Steam Railway
. . . . .5H 39
Eastleigh Mus. 3A 40
Eastleigh Rd. SO50: Fair O 4A 42
Eastleigh Station (Rail) 2B 40
EASTON 6A 12
Easton La.
SO21: E'ton, Mar W, Winche
. . . . .5A 12
SO21: E'ton, Winche 3F 19
SO23: Winche 5D 18
Easton La. Bus. Pk.
SO23: Winche 5D 18
East St. SO24: New A 3F 15
Eastville Rd. SO50: Fair O 4A 42
Eastways SO32: Bis W 6E 45
East Winchester (Barfield)
(Park & Ride) 1D 22
East Winchester (St Catherine's)
(Park & Ride) 2D 22
Eastwood Ct. SO51: Rom 4E 29
E. Woodhay Rd.
SO22: Winche 1H 17
Ebden Rd. SO23: Winche 5D 18
Eden Wlk. SO53: Cha F 6D 32
Edgar Rd.
SO23: Winche 4C 50 (2B 22)
Edgar Vs.
SO23: Winche 4B 50 (6B 18)
Edinburgh Ho.
SO22: Winche 1B 50 (5B 18)
Edinburgh Rd. SO23: Kin W . . .2D 10
Edington Cl. SO32: Bis W 5D 44
Edington Rd. SO23: Winche . . .3C 18
Edward Av. SO50: B'stke 1D 40
Edward Rd. GU34: Alt 3D 46
SO23: Winche 2A 22
Edwards Cl. SO23: Kin W 6E 11
Edward Ter. SO24: New A 4F 15
Edwina Cl. SO52: N Bad 1F 37
Edwina Mountbatten Ho.
SO51: Rom 4E 29
(off Broadwater Rd.)
Egbert Rd. SO23: Winche 4C 18
Eggars Cl. GU34: Alt 4F 47
EGYPT 2D 4
Eight Acres SO51: Rom 4G 29
Elan Ct. SO23: Kin W 2D 10
Elderberry Cl. SO50: Fair O 3G 41
Elder Cl. SO22: Winche 3G 21
Elder Ct. SO22: Winche 3G 21
Elder Grn. SO21: Col C 3G 35
Eldridge Gdns. SO51: Rom 3F 29
Electron Way SO53: Cha F 5E 33
Eling Cl. SO22: Winche 2H 17
Elizabeth Cl. SO23: Kin W 2D 10
Elizabeth Ct. SO50: E'leigh 1A 40
Elizabeth Way SO32: Bis W 6D 44
SO50: E'leigh 6B 34
Elkins Sq. SO50: B'stke 3G 41
Elland Cl. SO50: Fair O 4A 42
Ellen Gdns. SO53: Cha F 6C 32
Ellingham Cl. SO24: New A 4F 15
Elm Cl. SO32: Bis W 5E 45
Elm Ct.
SO22: Winche 1A 50 (5A 18)
Elm Gro. SO50: E'leigh 3H 39
Elm Rd.
SO22: Winche 1A 50 (5A 18)
SO24: New A 4F 15
SO32: Bis W 5G 45
Elmtree Gdns. SO51: Rom 5A 30
Elmwood Cl. GU34: Alt 6B 46
Emer Cl. SO52: N Bad 6E 31
Enmill La. SO22: Pitt 1A 20
Ennel Copse SO52: N Bad 1E 37
Ennerdale Gdns.
SO24: New A 5F 15
Enterprise Rd. SO16: Chilw 4G 37
Epsilon Ho. SO16: Chilw 4H 37
Epsom Cl. SO50: Hor H 6B 42
Epsom Down GU34: Alt 6D 46
Erasmus Pk. SO23: Winche 4E 19
Erskine Rd.
SO22: Winche 4A 50 (6A 18)
Escombe Rd. SO50: B'stke 2D 40
Essex Grn. SO53: Cha F 3E 39
Evelyn M. SO24: New A 3F 15
Eversley Pl. SO22: Winche 2H 21
Everyman Cinema 3C 50 (6B 18)
Exbury Cl. SO50: B'stke 3F 41
Exchange Sq.
SO23: Winche 2D 50
Exeter Cl. SO50: E'leigh 6H 33
Exmouth Gdns. SO50: Hor H . . .6A 42

F

Faber M. SO51: Rom 3H 29
Fabers Yd.
SO23: Winche 2C 50 (5B 18)
Factory Rd. SO50: E'leigh 3A 40
Fairbairn Wlk. SO53: Cha F 5B 32
Fairclose Dr. SO22: Lit 6F 9
FAIRDOWN 6E 19
Fairdown Cl. SO23: Winche 6E 19
Fairfax Cl. SO22: Winche 2F 21
Fair Field SO51: Rom 2G 29
Fairfield Grn. GU34: Four M . . .3H 49
Fairfield Rd. SO21: Shaw 4D 26
SO22: Winche 1A 50 (4A 18)
Fairholme Ct. SO50: E'leigh . . .2A 40
Fair La. SO21: Winche 5H 19
Fairlawn Ho.
SO23: Winche 4B 50 (6B 18)
Fairlight Gdns.
GU34: Four M 3H 49
FAIR OAK 3H 41
Fair Oak Ct. SO50: Fair O 3A 42
Fair Oak Rd.
SO50: B'stke, Fair O 2D 40
Fair Oak Squash Club 3A 42
Fair Vw. SO24: New A 5E 15
Fairview Cl. SO51: Rom 2H 29
Fairview Dr. SO51: Rom 2H 29
Fairway Dr. SO22: Oli B 4E 21
Falcon Ct. GU34: Alt 2D 46
Falcon Sq. SO50: E'leigh 4G 39
Falcon Vw. SO22: Winche 3G 21
Falkland Ct. SO53: Cha F 2E 39
Falkland Rd. SO53: Cha F 3E 39
Fallow Fld. SO22: Winche 3G 21
Fantails GU34: Alt 2D 46
Faringdon Ct. SO23: Winche . . .3C 18
Farley Cl. SO22: Oli B 3F 21
SO50: Fair O 4B 42
Farley Mount Country Pk. 5A 16
Fawley La. SO21: More 6H 23
Felmer Dr. SO23: Kin W 4E 11
Feltham Cl. SO51: Rom 3A 30
Ferndown Ct. GU34: Alt 4E 47
Ferney Cl. GU34: Alt 3B 48
Fernhill SO53: Cha F 5G 33
Fernhurst Cl. SO21: Col C 2F 35
Fernside Wlk. SO50: Fair O 3B 42
Fernside Way SO50: Fair O 3B 42
Field Cl. SO21: Comp 3C 26
SO51: Rom 4G 29
Fielden Cl. SO52: N Bad 1D 36
Field End SO23: Kin W 4E 11
Fielders Ct. GU34: Alt 5D 46
Field Vw. SO53: Cha F 5B 32
Field Way SO21: Comp 3C 26
Finches Grn. GU34: Alt 2D 46
Finches La. SO21: Twyf 3F 27
Fiona Cl. SO23: Winche 5E 19
Fircroft Dr. SO53: Cha F 6F 33
Firgrove Cl. SO52: N Bad 1D 36
Firgrove Rd. SO52: N Bad 1D 36
Firmstone Rd.
SO23: Winche 5D 18
Firs, The SO22: Winche 4A 18
Firs Cres. SO23: Kin W 3D 10
Fir Tree Cl. SO50: Hor H 6A 42
Fir Tree La. SO50: Hor H 5G 41
Firwood Cl. SO53: Cha F 3E 33
FISHER'S POND 4H 35
Fishlake Mdws. SO51: Rom . . .2E 29
Fitzroy Cl. SO16: Bass 6B 38
Five Ash Rd. GU34: Meds 2F 49
Five Bridges Rd.
SO23: Winche 4A 22
Five Elms Dr. SO51: Rom 5H 29
Fivefields Cl. SO23: Winche . . .6E 19
Fivefields Rd. SO23: Winche . . .6E 19
Fleet Ter. SO21: Ott 2A 34
Fleming Av. SO52: N Bad 1F 37
Fleming Ct. SO52: N Bad 1F 37
Fleming Ho. SO50: E'leigh 3G 39
Fleming Park Leisure Cen. . . .2G 39
Fleming Pl. SO21: Col C 2F 35
SO51: Rom 3F 29
Fleming Rd. SO22: Winche 2G 17
FLEXFORD 3C 32
Flexford Cl. SO53: Cha F 2C 32
Flexford Nature Reserve 2C 32
Flexford Rd. SO52: N Bad 5G 31
Florence Way GU34: Alt 1B 48
Flowerdown Barrows 1G 17
Flowerdown Mobile Home Pk.
SO22: Lit 6G 9
FOBDOWN 1C 14
Folland Cl. SO52: N Bad 1E 37
Folly Fld. SO32: Bis W 6F 45
Fontwell Dr. GU34: Alt 6D 46
Fontwell Gdns. SO50: Hor H . . .6B 42
Footner Cl. SO51: Rom 1A 30
Forbes Rd. SO23: Kin W 3D 10
Ford Av. SO53: Cha F 1F 39
Fordington Av.
SO22: Winche 5H 17
Fordington Rd.
SO22: Winche 1A 50 (5A 18)
Fordington Vs. SO53: Cha F . . .5E 33
Forest Cl. SO52: N Bad 6C 30
SO53: Cha F 3E 33
Forest Edge Pk.
SO51: E Wel 5A 28
Forest Rd. SO53: Cha F 3F 33
Forth Cl. SO53: Cha F 6D 32
Fortune Ct. SO53: Cha F 5E 33
Fountain Ct. SO21: Col C 2F 35
FOUR MARKS 3H 49
Fowey Cl. SO53: Cha F 4D 32
Fowlers Wlk. SO16: Chilw 3H 37
Fox Cl. SO50: B'stke 3F 41
Fox La. SO22: Winche 2G 21
Foyle Rd. SO53: Cha F 5D 32
Frampton Cl. SO21: Col C 2F 35
Frampton Way SO23: Kin W . . .4E 11
Francis Copse SO21: Col C 2G 35
Francis Gdns.
SO23: Winche 3D 18
Francis Sheldon Ct.
SO22: Winche 4A 50
Franklin Rd. SO21: Twyf 2G 27
Fraser Gdns. SO22: Winche . . .6G 17
Fraser Rd. SO23: Kin W 3D 10
Fratton Way SO50: Fair O 4A 42
Freda Routh Gdns.
SO50: Fair O 3B 42
Free St. SO32: Bis W 5F 45
Freshwater Ct.
SO53: Cha F 2G 33
Friarsgate
SO23: Winche 2E 50 (5C 18)
Friars Oak GU34: Meds 2H 49
Friars Rd. SO50: E'leigh 4H 39
Friary Gdns.
SO23: Winche 4C 50 (6B 18)

Frobisher Ind. Cen.
SO51: Rom 2E 29
Fromond Rd. SO22: Winche 2G 17
Froxfield Cl. SO22: Winche 1H 17
Fryern Arc. SO53: Cha F 4F 33
Fryern Cl. SO53: Cha F 5G 33
FRYERN HILL 5F 33
Fryers Cl. SO23: Kin W 3E 11
SO51: Rom 4G 29
FULFLOOD 4A 18
Fulflood Ct.
SO22: Winche 1A 50 (5A 18)
Fulford Rd. SO52: N Bad 1E 37
Furley Cl. SO23: Winche 5D 18
Fyfield Way SO22: Lit 6F 9

G

Gables, The SO22: Winche 4H 17
Gainsborough Ct.
SO52: N Bad 1F 37
Gamma Ho. SO16: Chilw 4G 37
Ganger Farm La.
SO51: Rom 1A 30
Ganger Rd. SO51: Rom 1A 30
Garbett Rd. SO23: Winche 5E 19
Gardeners Cl.
SO22: Winche 3H 17
Gardeners La. SO51: E Wel 5A 28
Garden La.
SO23: Winche 2E 50 (5C 18)
Gardens, The SO32: Bis W 6G 45
Gardner Way SO53: Cha F 3D 32
Garfield Cl. SO32: Bis W 5E 45
Garfield Rd. SO32: Bis W 5E 45
Garnier Rd. SO23: Winche 2B 22
Garstons Track SO21: Spar 6A 8
Gar St.
SO23: Winche 3C 50 (6B 18)
Garth, The GU34: Alt 4E 47
Gaskell Cl. GU34: Holy 2G 47
Gaston Gdns. SO51: Rom 3F 29
Gaston La. GU34: Up Farr 6C 48
Gatekeeper Cl.
SO23: Winche 5E 19
Gauvain Cl. GU34: Alt 6E 47
Geale's Ct. GU34: Alt 3E 47
Geale's Cres. GU34: Alt 3E 47
General Johnson Ct.
SO22: Winche 1G 21
George Eyston Dr.
SO22: Winche 1H 21
George Perrett Way
SO53: Cha F 1B 38
George Raymond Rd.
SO50: E'leigh 3H 39
George St. SO50: E'leigh 2B 40
Georges Way SO50: E'leigh 2G 39
George Wright Cl.
SO50: E'leigh 3H 39
George Yard, The
SO24: New A 3F 15
Gerald Sq. GU34: Alt 2E 47
Gilbert White Way GU34: Alt 3D 46
Gillingham Cl. SO23: Kin W 4E 11
Gilmour Gdns. GU34: Alt 2E 47
Glade, The SO53: Cha F 2H 33
Gladstone St.
SO23: Winche 1C 50 (5B 18)
Glebe Ct. SO50: Fair O 3B 42
Glen, The *SO50: E'leigh 3A 40*
(off Grantham Rd.)
Glendeep Cl. SO23: Kin W 5D 10
Glendowan Rd. SO53: Cha F 4C 32
Glen Pk. Mobile Home Pk.
SO21: Col C 2G 35
Glenwood Ct. SO50: Fair O 3C 42
Gloucester Cl. GU34: Four M 4F 49
Godfrey Olson Ho.
SO50: E'leigh 2B 40
Godfrey Pink Way
SO32: Bis W 6F 45
Godson Ho. SO23: Winche 2E 50
Godwin Cl. SO22: Winche 2G 17
Godwins Fld. SO21: Comp 1C 26
Goldcrest Way
GU34: Four M 4F 49
Goldfinch Way SO21: Sth W 4E 7
Goldsmith Rd. SO50: E'leigh 4H 39
Goldwire Dr. SO53: Cha F 6B 32
Goodacre Dr. SO53: Cha F 6B 32
Goodison Cl. SO50: Fair O 4H 41
Goodwood Cl. GU34: Alt 6D 46
Goodwood Ct. SO50: Hor H 6B 42
Goodwood Rd.
SO50: E'leigh 6G 33
Goodwyns Grn. GU34: Alt 2E 47
Goodyers GU34: Alt 5E 47
Gordon Av. SO23: Winche 1E 23
Gordon Rd.
SO23: Winche 1E 50 (5C 18)
SO53: Cha F 2F 33
Gordon Watson Ho.
SO23: Winche 2B 22
Goring Fld. SO22: Winche 4G 17
Gosport Rd. GU34: Alt 4B 48
Gradwell La.
GU34: Four M 6F 49
Grafton Rd. SO23: Winche 1B 22
Grange Cl. SO23: Winche 3A 22
SO24: New A 4E 15
Grange M. SO51: Rom 2A 30
Grange Rd. SO23: Winche 4A 22
SO24: New A 4E 15
Grangewood Ct.
SO50: Fair O 3H 41
Grangewood Gdns.
SO50: Fair O 3H 41
Grantham Rd. SO50: E'leigh 3H 39
Granville Pl. SO23: Winche 1D 22
Grasmere SO50: E'leigh 3H 39
Gratton Cl. SO21: Sut S 3D 4
Grayling Mead SO51: Rom 2F 29
Grays Cl. SO21: Col C 3F 35
SO51: Rom 4G 29
Grayshott Cl. SO22: Winche 1H 17
Greatbridge Rd. SO51: Rom 1E 29
Gt. Farm Rd. SO50: E'leigh 2H 39
Greatfield Rd.
SO22: Winche 2H 17
Gt. Minster St.
SO23: Winche 3D 50 (6C 18)
Great Weir SO24: New A 2F 15
Gt. Well Dr. SO51: Rom 3G 29
Grebe Cl. GU34: Alt 2C 46
Green, The SO22: Pitt 4D 20
SO51: Rom 2A 30
Greenacres Dr. SO21: Ott 6C 26
Green Cl. SO21: Sth W 5E 7
SO23: Winche 6C 10
SO24: Old A 1F 15
Greendale Cl. SO53: Cha F 5G 33
Greenfields Av. GU34: Alt 4B 46
Greenfinch Cl. SO50: E'leigh 4F 39
Greenhill Av. SO22: Winche 5A 18
Greenhill Cl. SO22: Winche 5H 17
Greenhill La. SO16: Rown 5C 36
Greenhill Rd.
SO22: Winche 1A 50 (5H 17)
Greenhill Ter. SO22: Winche 5A 18
SO51: Rom 5D 28
Greenhill Vw. SO51: Rom 4D 28
Green Jacket Cl.
SO22: Winche 2A 22
Green La. GU34: Four M 5E 49
SO16: Chilw 4B 38
SO32: Bis W 6F 45
SO51: Ampf, Rom 3C 30
Green Pk. Cl. SO23: Winche 3D 18
Greens Cl. SO32: Bis W 5D 44
SO50: B'stke 4G 41
Greenways SO53: Cha F 5G 33
Greenwood Cl.
SO50: E'leigh 4H 39
SO51: Rom 3G 29
Greenwood La. SO32: Durl 6D 42
Greyfriars SO23: Winche 2F 50
Griffen Cl. SO50: B'stke 3E 41
Grosvenor Ct. SO51: Rom 4A 30
Grosvenor Dr. SO23: Winche 3D 18
Grosvenor Rd. SO53: Cha F 2G 33
Grovelands Rd.
SO22: Winche 4F 17
Grovely Way SO51: Cram 2C 30
Grove Pk. Ind. Est.
GU34: Alt 4F 47
Grove Pl. SO22: Winche 2A 18
Grove Rd. GU34: Alt 6D 46
SO21: Shaw 4C 26
Groves Cl. SO21: Sth W 5C 6
Guardroom Museum, The 2B 50 (5B 18)
Guest Rd. SO50: B'stke 2D 40
Guildford Dr. SO53: Cha F 2D 38
Gunners M. SO32: Bis W 5F 45
Gunners Pk. SO32: Bis W 5G 45
Gurdons GU34: Alt 1B 48
Gurkha Museum, The 3B 50 (6B 18)

H

Hack Dr. SO21: Col C 3F 35
Haddon Dr. SO50: E'leigh 6A 34
Hadleigh Gdns.
SO50: E'leigh 6A 34
Hadrians Cl. SO53: Cha F 4G 33
Hadrian Way SO16: Chilw 6A 38
Haig Rd. SO24: New A 3F 15
SO50: B'stke 3G 41
Halden Cl. SO51: Rom 2H 29
Hall Cl. SO32: Bis W 5F 45
Hall Lands La.
SO50: Fair O 3B 42
Hall Rd. GU34: Alt 2E 47
Halls Farm Cl.
SO22: Winche 2A 18
Hall Way, The SO22: Lit 6F 9
HALTERWORTH 4A 30
Halterworth Cl. SO51: Rom 4H 29
Halterworth La.
SO51: Cram, Rom 4A 30
Hamble Ct. SO53: Cha F 6F 33
Hambledon Cl.
SO22: Winche 1H 17
Hamble Springs
SO32: Bis W 6F 45
Hamilton Rd. SO50: B'stke 2D 40
Hammond's Pas.
SO23: Winche 3C 50
Hampshire Corporate Pk.
SO53: Cha F 2D 38
Hampshire Ct. SO53: Cha F 2E 39
Hampton La. SO22: Winche 4G 17
Handyside Pl.
GU34: Four M 2H 49
Handy Vs. *SO23: Winche 1E 50*
(off Park Av.)
Hangers, The SO32: Bis W 4F 45
Hann Rd. SO16: Rown 6C 36
Hanns Way SO50: E'leigh 2A 40
Hanover Cl. SO51: Rom 4E 29
Hanover Lodge
SO23: Winche 1B 22
Hardings La. SO50: Fair O 2H 41
Hardwick Rd. SO53: Cha F 5F 33
Hardy Rd. SO50: E'leigh 4A 40
HAREFIELD 3A 30
Harefield Ct. SO51: Rom 3H 29
Hare La. SO21: Twyf 5G 27
HARESTOCK 2G 17
Harestock Cl. SO22: Winche 6H 9
Harestock Rd.
SO22: Winche 2G 17
Harewood Cl. SO50: E'leigh 5A 34
Harlaxton Cl. SO50: E'leigh 6H 33
Harlech Dr. SO53: Cha F 1C 38
Harold Gdns. GU34: Alt 3E 47
Harrage, The SO51: Rom 4F 29
Harris Way SO52: N Bad 1E 37
Harrow Down SO22: Winche 3H 21
Hartley Cl. SO50: B'stke 4G 41
Hartley Rd. SO50: B'stke 4G 41
Harvest Cl. SO22: Winche 3H 21
Harvest Rd. SO53: Cha F 5B 32
Harvey Rd. SO50: B'stke 2E 41
Harwood Pl. SO23: Kin W 3E 11
Hasted Dr. SO24: New A 5E 15
Hatchley La. SO32: Lwr U 1G 43
Hathaway Cl. SO50: E'leigh 1B 40
Hatherley Rd.
SO22: Winche 1A 50 (4A 18)
Haven, The SO16: Bass 6C 38
SO50: E'leigh 5B 34
Hawkins Ct. SO24: New A 3F 15
HAWTHORN 6H 49
Hawthorn Cl. SO21: Col C 3G 35
SO24: New A 4F 15
SO50: Fair O 3A 42
Hawthorn Rd. GU34: Four M 6G 49
Hawthorns GU34: Alt 3C 46
Hawthorns, The
SO32: Bis W 4C 44
SO50: E'leigh 4G 39
Haydn Cl. SO23: Kin W 3D 10
Haydock Cl. GU34: Alt 6D 46
Hayter Gdns. SO51: Rom 3G 29
Hazel Cl. SO21: Col C 2G 35
SO53: Cha F 1E 33
Hazel Ct. SO22: Winche 3G 17
Hazeldene Gdns.
SO21: Itc A 4E 13
Hazeley Enterprise Pk.
SO21: Twyf 2H 27
Hazeley Rd.
SO21: More, Twyf 3G 27
Hazel Gro. SO22: Winche 2H 21
SO32: Bis W 5G 45
Hazel Rd. GU34: Four M 3H 49
HEADBOURNE WORTHY 5C 10
Headbourne Worthy Ho.
SO23: Winche 6D 10
Headley Cl. SO24: New A 5F 15
Heath Cl. SO50: Fair O 4B 42
Heathcote Pl. SO21: Hurs 2D 24
Heathcote Rd. SO53: Cha F 5F 33
Heatherbrae Gdns.
SO52: N Bad 1D 36
Heather Chase SO50: B'stke 3G 41
Heatherdene Rd.
SO53: Cha F 2G 33
Heatherlands Rd.
SO16: Chilw 5B 38
Heathers, The SO50: E'leigh 3G 39
Heatherview Cl.
SO52: N Bad 6D 30
Heathfield Cl. SO53: Cha F 1E 33
Heathfield Rd. SO53: Cha F 1E 33
Heathlands Cl. SO53: Cha F 3E 33
Heathlands Rd. SO53: Cha F 3E 33
Heath Rd. SO52: N Bad 2E 37
Hedgerow Cl. SO16: Rown 6C 36
Hedges, The *SO50: E'leigh 3A 40*
(off Grantham Rd.)
Heinz Burt Cl. SO50: E'leigh 2H 39
Helen's Cl. GU34: Alt 6C 46
Hemlock Way SO53: Cha F 6B 32
Henry Rd. SO50: B'stke 1D 40
Hensting La.
SO50: Fis P, Hens 4H 35
Herdman Ho. *GU34: Alt 4E 47*
(off York M.)
Hereward Cl. SO51: Rom 4H 29
Hermitage Cl. GU34: Alt 6C 46
SO32: Bis W 5C 44
Heron Cl. GU34: Alt 2D 46
Heron Sq. SO50: E'leigh 3G 39
Hestia Cl. SO51: Rom 3A 30
Hexagon Centre, The
SO53: Cha F 3E 39
Hickory Dr. SO22: Winche 1H 17
HIGHBRIDGE 4E 35
Highbridge Rd. SO21: Twyf 3E 35
SO50: B'dge, Highb 4C 34
Highbury Cl. SO50: Fair O 4A 42
Highclere Way SO53: Cha F 2C 38
HIGHCLIFFE 1E 23
Highcliffe Dr. SO50: E'leigh 4A 34
Highcliffe Rd.
SO23: Winche 1D 22
Highcroft Rd. SO22: Winche 6G 17
Highfield SO21: Twyf 4G 27
Highfield Av. SO21: Twyf 4G 27
Highfield Cl. SO53: Cha F 5G 33
Highfield Ct. SO32: Bis W 5C 44
Highfield Rd. SO53: Cha F 5G 33
Highfield Ter.
SO22: Winche 3B 50 (6A 18)
High Firs Gdns. SO51: Rom 4A 30
High Firs Rd. SO51: Rom 3A 30
Highlands Cl. SO52: N Bad 6C 30
Highmount Cl.
SO23: Winche 6D 18
Highridge GU34: Alt 5B 46
High St. GU34: Alt 5D 46
SO21: Twyf 4G 27
SO23: Winche 3F 50 (6D 18)
(Bridge St.)
SO23: Winche 2C 50 (5B 18)
(Tower St., not continuous)
SO32: Bis W 6E 45
SO50: E'leigh 4A 40
(Desborough Rd., not continuous)
SO50: E'leigh 3A 40
(Wells Pl.)
High Trees SO50: Fair O 3C 42
High Trees Dr.
SO22: Winche 3A 18
Highways Rd. SO21: Comp 4C 26
Highwood La. SO51: Rom 3A 30
Hilden Way SO22: Lit 6E 9
Hill Barn La.
SO21: Lwr B, Sut S 1A 4
Hill Cl. SO50: Fair O 6H 35

Hillcrest Av. SO53: Cha F 5F 33
Hillcrest Cl. SO52: N Bad 6D 30
Hillcrest Dr. SO53: Cha F 5F 33
Hillier Way SO23: Winche 3C 18
Hill La. SO21: Col C 2F 35
Hill Ri. SO21: Twyf 3G 27
Hillside SO22: Lit 6F 9
Hillside Av. SO51: Rom 4G 29
Hillside Cl. GU34: Alt 3D 46
SO22: Winche 3G 17
SO53: Cha F 5F 33
Hillside Rd. SO21: Spar 1A 16
SO22: Winche 4G 17
Hill Ter. SO24: New A 3F 15
SO50: Fair O 6H 35
Hilltop SO22: Lit 6G 9
Hillview Manor Pk. Homes
SO50: Fair O 6H 35
Hillway, The SO53: Cha F 4F 33
HILTINGBURY 2F 33
Hiltingbury Cl. SO53: Cha F 2F 33
Hiltingbury Ct. SO53: Cha F . . .2D 32
Hiltingbury Rd. SO53: Cha F . . .2D 32
Hinton Flds. SO23: Kin W 5E 11
Hinton Ho. Dr. SO23: Kin W . . .5E 11
HMP Winchester
SO22: Winche 2A 50 (5A 18)
Hobbs Ct. SO50: Fair O 2H 41
Hockley Golf Course 6C 22
Hockley Link SO21: Winche . . .5A 22
HOCOMBE 1D 32
Hocombe Dr. SO53: Cha F 1D 32
Hocombe Mead Nature Reserve
. . . . .1D 32
Hocombe Pk. Cl.
SO53: Cha F 1D 32
Hocombe Rd. SO53: Cha F 1D 32
Hocombe Wood Rd.
SO53: Cha F 1C 32
Hodder Cl. SO53: Cha F 6D 32
Hoddinott Rd. SO50: E'leigh . . .3H 39
HOE 6H 45
Hoe La. SO51: Toot 3A 36
SO52: N Bad 2B 36
Hoe Rd. SO32: Bis W 5F 45
Hogarth Cl. SO51: Rom 2H 29
Holdaway Cl. SO23: Kin W 4E 11
Holland Cl. SO53: Cha F 2E 39
Hollands Cl. SO22: Lit 6F 9
Hollman Dr. SO51: Rom 3D 28
Holly Lodge SO53: Cha F 2E 39
Holly Mdws. SO22: Winche 3G 17
Holly Tree Pk. SO21: Sut S 3C 4
Hollywood Cl. SO52: N Bad . . .1D 36
Holm Oak Cl. SO22: Lit 6E 9
Holt Vw. SO50: B'stke 3F 41
Holyborne Rd. SO51: Rom 4H 29
HOLYBOURNE 1H 47
Holybourne Theatre 2G 47
Homefield SO51: Rom 2G 29
Home La. SO21: Spar 2A 16
Homemead Ho. SO51: Rom . . .5E 29
Homerise Ho.
SO23: Winche 1D 50
Homestead Rd. GU34: Meds . . .1E 49
Honeysuckle Cl.
SO22: Winche 3H 21
Honeysuckle Ct.
SO22: Winche 2G 17
Honeysuckle Way
SO53: Cha F 5C 32
Hook Cl. SO51: Ampf 1C 32
Hook Cres. SO51: Ampf 1C 32
Hookpit Farm La.
SO23: Kin W 3D 10
Hook Rd. SO51: Ampf 6A 24
Hookwater Cl. SO53: Cha F 1D 32
Hookwater Rd. SO53: Cha F . . .1C 32
Hookwood La. SO51: Ampf 1B 32
Hornbeam Cl. SO21: Sth W 5E 7
Hornbeam Rd. SO53: Cha F . . .5A 32
Horns Drove SO16: Rown 6C 36
Horsecroft SO51: Rom 3F 29
Horsefair, The SO51: Rom 4E 29
Horsefair Ct. SO51: Rom 4E 29
Horsefair M. SO51: Rom 4E 29
HorsePower - The Museum of the
King's Royal Hussars
. . . . .3B 50 (6B 18)
Horseshoe Dr. SO51: Rom 1H 29
HORTON HEATH 6B 42
Horton Way SO50: B'stke 3F 41
Houchin St. SO32: Bis W 6E 45
Hoveton Gro. SO53: Cha F 3D 32
Howard Cl. SO50: Fair O 3A 42
SO53: Cha F 1F 39
Howards La. GU34: Holy 1F 47
Hoyle Cl. SO32: Lwr U 1H 43
Hub, The
Eastleigh 2C 40
Hubert Rd. SO23: Winche 3A 22
Hulles Way SO52: N Bad 1D 36
Hundred, The SO51: Rom 4E 29
Hunt Cl. SO21: Sth W 5E 7
Hunters Cres. SO51: Rom 1A 30
Hunter's Ride SO21: Hurs 5A 24
Hunters Way SO50: B'stke 3G 41
Huntingdon Gdns.
SO50: Hor H 6B 42
HUNTON 3G 5
Hunton Down La.
SO21: Hunt, Sut S 3G 5
Hunton La.
SO21: Hunt, Wons 3E 5
Hunts Cl. SO21: Col C 2G 35
Huntsmead GU34: Alt 5E 47
Hurdle Way SO21: Comp 1C 26
Hurricane Dr. SO16: Rown 6C 36
HURSLEY 2D 24
Hursley Ct. SO53: Cha F 2D 32
Hursley Pk. SO21: Hurs 2C 24
Hursley Pk. Rd. SO21: Hurs 2B 24
Hursley Rd. SO21: Hurs 6D 24
SO53: Cha F 1D 32
Hurst Cl. SO53: Cha F 1C 38
Hussey Cl. SO23: Winche 3C 18
Hut Farm Pl. SO53: Cha F 6E 33
Hutwood Rd. SO16: Chilw 5C 38
HYDE 4C 18
Hyde Abbey Gatehouse 1D 50
Hyde Abbey Rd.
SO23: Winche 1D 50 (5C 18)
Hyde Church La.
SO23: Winche 4C 18
Hyde Church Path
SO23: Winche 4C 18
(off Hyde St.)
Hyde Cl.
SO23: Winche 1C 50 (4B 18)
Hyde Gate
SO23: Winche 1D 50 (4C 18)
Hyde Ho. Gdns.
SO23: Winche 4C 18
Hyde Lodge SO23: Winche 4B 18
Hyde St.
SO23: Winche 1D 50 (5C 18)

I

Ideal Pk. Homes Caravan Site
SO50: B'dge 5E 35
Ilex Cl. SO23: Kin W 3D 10
Imber Rd. SO23: Winche 5E 19
Inglewood Gdns.
SO50: Fair O 2A 42
Ings Cl. GU34: Alt 6D 46
Inhams Rd. GU34: Holy 2H 47
Inwood Ct. GU34: Alt 5D 46
Ionic Cl. SO53: Cha F 4H 33
Irwell Cl. SO53: Cha F 6C 32
Islander Wlk. SO50: E'leigh . . .5H 39
ITCHEN ABBAS 4E 13
Itchen Av. SO50: B'stke 3F 41
Itchen Ct. SO23: Winche 3F 50
Itchen Grange SO50: E'leigh . . .2D 40
ITCHEN STOKE 3A 14
Itchen Vw. SO24: Itc S 4A 14
Ivy Cl. SO22: Winche 2A 22

J

Jack Cl. SO53: Cha F 5A 32
Jackdaw Ri. SO50: E'leigh 4F 39
Jacklyns Cl. SO24: New A 5E 15
Jacklyns La. SO24: New A 5E 15
JACKSPLACE HOSPICE 4B 4
Jacobs Cl. SO51: Rom 4G 29
James Ct. SO21: Sut S 3C 4
SO51: Rom 5G 29
Jane Austen Plaque 4D 50
Jane Austen's House Mus. . . .2B 48
Jenner Way GU34: Alt 2E 47
SO51: Rom 3A 30
Jervis Ct. La.
SO32: Bis W, Swanm 5H 45
Jesty Rd. SO24: New A 5D 14
Jewry St.
SO23: Winche 2C 50 (5C 18)
JOB'S CORNER 4F 43
Jockey La. SO50: B'stke 6E 35
John Arlott Ct.
SO24: New A 4E 15
John Darling Mall
SO50: E'leigh 1A 40
John Eggar's Sq. GU34: Alt 3F 47
Jubilee Cl. SO50: E'leigh 4H 39
Jubilee Rd. SO51: Rom 3E 29
Judd Cl. SO50: E'leigh 1G 39
Julian Cl. SO16: Chilw 6A 38
Julius Cl. SO53: Cha F 5G 33
Juniper Cl. SO22: Winche 2H 21
SO52: N Bad 6D 30
Justinian Cl. SO53: Cha F 4H 33

K

Katrine Cres. SO53: Cha F 3C 32
Keats Cl. SO21: Sth W 5D 6
SO22: Oli B 3G 21
Keble Cl. SO21: Hurs 2D 24
SO53: Cha F 6E 33
Keble Rd. SO53: Cha F 1E 39
Keble St. SO22: Winche 1G 21
Keepers Cl. SO53: Cha F 5D 32
Kelburn Cl. SO53: Cha F 4D 32
Kellynch Cl. GU34: Alt 4C 46
Kelmscott Gdns.
SO53: Cha F 2D 32
Kelvin Rd. SO50: E'leigh 3H 39
Kempthorne Ho.
SO22: Winche 1B 50
Kempton Cl. GU34: Alt 6D 46
Kendal Cl. SO53: Cha F 4G 33
Kenilworth Ct.
SO23: Winche 3C 18
(off Northlands Dr.)
Kenilworth Dr. SO50: E'leigh . . .5A 34
Kennel La. SO22: Lit 1F 17
Kennett Cl. SO51: Rom 3A 30
Kennett Rd. SO51: Rom 3A 30
Kensington Ct. SO50: B'stke . . .6D 34
Kent Rd. SO53: Cha F 2E 39
Kerrfield SO22: Winche 6H 17
Kerrfield M. SO22: Winche 6H 17
Kerridge Ind. Est. GU34: Alt . . .4E 47
Kerry Cl. SO53: Cha F 5E 33
Kestrel Cl. SO22: Winche 3H 21
SO32: Bis W 5C 44
Kestrel Ct. GU34: Alt 3D 46
Kestrel Rd. SO50: E'leigh 3F 39
Kielder Cl. SO53: Cha F 4C 32
Kilham La. SO22: Winche 6E 17
Kiln Grn. SO21: Col C 3G 35
Kiln La. SO21: Ott 1B 34
SO24: Old A 1F 15
SO50: B'dge 2D 34
Kilns, The GU34: Alt 5F 47
Kimberley Cl. SO50: Fair O 3B 42
King Alfred Pl.
SO23: Winche 4C 18
King Alfred's Statue 3E 50
King Alfred Ter.
SO23: Winche 1D 50 (4C 18)
Kingdom's M. GU34: Alt 5D 46
King Edward Pk.
SO52: N Bad 2B 32
Kingfisher Ct. GU34: Alt 2D 46
Kingfisher Rd. SO50: E'leigh . . .3F 39
Kingfisher Way SO51: Rom 3F 29
King Harold Ct.
SO23: Winche 1A 22
King John's House & Heritage Cen.
. . . . .4E 29
Kings Av. SO22: Winche 2A 22
Kings Cl. SO21: Twyf 2G 27
SO23: Kin W 2D 10
SO53: Cha F 4F 33
Kings Cres. SO22: Winche 1H 21
Kingsdale Ct.
SO23: Winche 1C 50 (5B 18)
Kings Gate 4D 50 (6C 18)
Kingsgate Rd.
SO23: Winche 2B 22
Kingsgate St.
SO23: Winche 4D 50 (1C 22)
Kings Head Yd.
SO23: Winche 3D 50 (6C 18)
Kingsland Rd. GU34: Alt 5C 46
Kings La. SO21: Chilc 6G 19
Kingsley Bungs.
SO24: New A 5D 14
Kingsley Pl. SO22: Winche 2A 22
Kings Lodge *SO22: Winche 6H 17*
(off Highcroft Rd.)
Kingsmead GU34: Alt 5E 47
Kingsmead Ct.
SO23: Winche 1B 22
King's Pond Nature Reserve . . .5E 47
Kings Rd. GU34: Alt 6B 46
SO22: Winche 1G 21
SO53: Cha F 5E 33
Kings Vw. GU34: Alt 5E 47
Kingsway SO53: Cha F 4F 33
Kingsway Ct. SO53: Cha F 3G 33
Kingsway Gdns.
SO53: Cha F 3G 33
Kingswood Ri.
GU34: Four M 4E 49
KINGS WORTHY 6E 11
Kingsworthy Ct.
SO23: Kin W 6E 11
Kinver Cl. SO51: Rom 2H 29
Kipling Rd. GU34: Alt 1B 48
SO50: E'leigh 2H 39
Kirtle Dr. GU34: Four M 4F 49
Kirtling Pl. SO22: Winche 4H 17
Kitwood La. SO24: Rop 6H 49
Kitwood Rd. GU34: Four M 6G 49
Knapp La. GU34: Meds 2E 49
Knatchbull Cl. SO51: Rom 4F 29
Knight Cl. SO23: Winche 3C 18
Knights Lodge
SO22: Winche 1H 21
Knights Way GU34: Alt 5B 46
Knightwood Cres.
SO53: Cha F 5C 32
Knightwood Glade
SO53: Cha F 4B 32
Knightwood Leisure Cen. 6B 32
Knightwood M. SO53: Cha F . . .5C 32
Knightwood Rd.
SO53: Cha F 3B 32
Knightwood Vw.
SO53: Cha F 6E 33
Knowle Hill SO50: E'leigh 4B 34
Knowle La. SO50: Hor H 6B 42
Knox Ter. *GU34: Alt 4E 47*
(off Orchard La.)
Knyght Cl. SO51: Rom 5G 29
Kornwestheim Way
SO50: E'leigh 2G 39
Kynegils Rd. SO22: Winche . . .3H 17
Kytes La. SO32: Durl 6G 43

L

Laburnum Cl. SO52: N Bad 6E 31
Laburnum Dr. SO23: Kin W 3D 10
Laburnum Gro.
SO50: E'leigh 2A 40
LADWELL 5D 24
Ladycroft SO24: New A 5C 14
Lady Pl. Ct. GU34: Alt 5D 46
Ladywell La. SO24: New A 2F 15
Ladywood SO50: E'leigh 5H 33
La Frenaye Pl. SO21: Sth W 4E 7
Laidlaw Gdns. SO53: Cha F 2D 32
Lainston Cl. SO22: Winche 3G 17
Lake Ct. SO21: Hurs 6B 24
Lake Dr. SO22: Oli B 4F 21
Lake Rd. SO53: Cha F 3G 33
Lakeside Country Pk. 5H 39
Lakewood Cl. SO53: Cha F 3F 33
Lakewood Rd. SO53: Cha F 4F 33
Lambourne Cl. SO21: Spar 2A 16
Lambourn Sq. SO53: Cha F 5D 32
Lamports, The GU34: Alt 4E 47
Langham Cl. SO52: N Bad 1D 36
Langham Rd. GU34: Alt 5C 46
Langton Cl. SO22: Winche 4A 18
Langton Rd. SO32: Bis W 5D 44
Langtons Ct. SO24: New A 4G 15
Lanham La. SO22: Winche 6B 16
Lankhills Rd. SO23: Winche . . .3B 18
Lansdowne Av.
SO23: Winche 2B 22
Lansdowne Cl. SO51: Rom 3E 29
Lansdowne Ct.
SO23: Winche 2B 22
SO51: Rom 3E 29
Lansdowne Gdns.
SO51: Rom 3E 29

Lansdowne Rd. GU34: Alt 3E 47
Lantern Ct. SO23: Winche 1A 22
Lapwing Way GU34: Four M . . .4F 49
Larch Cl. SO23: Kin W 2D 10
Larg Dr. SO22: Winche 1G 17
Lark Hill Ri. SO22: Winche 3H 21
Lark Rd. SO50: E'leigh 4F 39
Larkspur Dr. SO53: Cha F 5B 32
La Sagesse Convent 4D 28
Latham Cl. SO50: Fair O 3H 41
Latham Rd. SO50: Fair O 3H 41
SO51: Rom 3F 29
Latimer St. SO51: Rom 4E 29
Latimer Wlk. SO51: Rom 4E 29
Launcelyn Cl. SO52: N Bad 2D 36
Launceston Dr.
SO50: E'leigh 6H 33
Laura Cl. SO21: Comp 4C 26
Laurence Ct. SO50: Fair O 3A 42
Laurence M. SO51: Rom 3F 29
Lauriston Dr. SO53: Cha F 2D 32
Lavant Fld. GU34: Alt 2C 48
Lavington Gdns.
SO52: N Bad 2D 36
Lawn, The GU34: Holy 2H 47
Lawn Ho. SO23: Winche 2E 50
Lawn Rd. SO22: Lit 6G 9
SO50: E'leigh 1B 40
Lawn St.
SO23: Winche 3E 50 (6C 18)
(not continuous)
Lawnswood SO50: Fair O 4B 42
Lawrence Way
SO23: Winche 3C 18
(off Worthy Rd.)
Lawrence Wright Pas.
SO24: New A 3F 15
(off West St.)
Leander Cl. SO50: E'leigh 6A 34
Lee Drove SO51: Lee 4A 36
Legion La. SO23: Kin W 4E 11
Leicester Way
SO23: Winche 4E 19
Leigh Ct. SO50: E'leigh 2G 39
LEIGH HOUSE 5G 19
Leigh Rd. SO50: E'leigh 2G 39
SO53: Cha F 1E 39
Lelant Dr. GU34: Four M 4F 49
Lennox Cl. SO53: Cha F 3G 33
Lenten St. GU34: Alt 5C 46
Lent Hill Ct. SO22: Winche 1H 21
Leopold Dr. SO32: Bis W 5D 44
Leslie Loader Ct.
SO50: E'leigh 6A 34
Leven Cl. SO53: Cha F 3C 32
Lewes Cl. SO50: E'leigh 5A 34
Lewin Cl. SO21: Col C 3F 35
Liddel Way SO53: Cha F 6D 32
Light Infantry Museum, The
. . . . .2B 50 (5B 18)
Lillies, The SO50: Hor H 6A 42
Lime Av. GU34: Alt 4C 46
Lime Cl. SO21: Col C 3G 35
Lime Gro. GU34: Alt 3C 46
Limekiln La. SO32: Bis W 1H 45
Lime Rd. SO24: New A 4F 15
Limetree Wlk.
SO23: Winche 5F 19
Lincoln Cl. SO51: Rom 2H 29
Lincoln Grn. GU34: Alt 6C 46
Lincoln Pl. SO53: Cha F 1F 39
Lincolns Ri. SO50: E'leigh 2B 34
Linden Ct. SO51: Rom 4E 29
Linden Gdns. SO51: Rom 4F 29
Linden Gro. SO53: Cha F 3E 33
Linden Rd. SO51: Rom 4F 29
Linden Wlk. SO52: N Bad 6D 30
Lindley Gdns. SO24: New A 5F 15
Linford Ct. SO50: Fair O 3A 42
Lingdale SO16: Chilw 6B 38
Lingfield Cl. GU34: Alt 6D 46
Lingwood Cl. SO16: Bass 6B 38
Lingwood Wlk. SO16: Bass 6B 38
Link Gallery, The *6H 17*
(off Romsey Rd.)
Link Rd. GU34: Alt 2E 47
Links Rd. SO22: Winche 4H 17
Links Vw. Way SO16: Bass 6B 38
Linnet Sq. SO50: E'leigh 4F 39
Linnets Rd. SO24: New A 5E 15
Linnets Way GU34: Alt 3D 46
Lions Hall
SO23: Winche 4C 50 (6B 18)
Lipscombe Ri. GU34: Alt 3D 46
Lisle Cl. SO22: Oli B 4E 21
Lisle Ct. SO22: Winche 1A 22
Litchfield Rd. SO22: Winche . . .1H 17
Lit. Ashton La. SO32: Bis W . . .2F 45
Littlefield Cres. SO53: Cha F . . .5A 32
Littlefield Rd. GU34: Alt 4E 47
Lit. Hayes La. SO21: Itc A 5F 13
Little Meads SO51: Rom 4D 28
Lit. Minster St.
SO23: Winche 3D 50 (6C 18)
Lit. Shore La. SO32: Bis W 6F 45
LITTLETON 6F 9
Littleton La. SO21: Spar 1E 17
SO22: Lit 1E 17
Littleton Rd. SO22: Lit 1F 17
Loader Cl. SO23: Kin W 4E 11
Lock's La. SO21: Spar 2A 16
Locksley Rd. SO50: E'leigh 4G 39
Lofting Cl. SO50: B'stke 3E 41
London Rd. GU34: Holy 3F 47
SO23: Kin W, Winche 1D 18
Long Barrow Cl. SO21: Sth W . . .5E 7
Longfield Rd. SO23: Winche . . .5E 19
SO50: Fair O 4B 42
Longhouse Grn.
SO23: Winche 5E 19
Longmead Av. SO50: B'stke . . .1D 40
LONG PARK 4C 8
Long Wlk.
SO21: E'ton, Winche 6F 11
Lordswood SO50: Highb 4E 35
Lordswood La. SO16: Chilw 5H 37
Loreille Gdns. SO16: Rown 6C 36
Lortemore Pl. SO51: Rom 4E 29
Loughwood Cl.
SO50: E'leigh 5A 34
Lovedon La. SO23: Kin W 2D 10
Love La. SO21: Twyf 4H 27
SO51: Rom 4E 29
Lovell Cl. SO21: Sth W 5E 7
Lovells Wlk. SO24: New A 4E 15
Loveridge Way SO50: E'leigh . . .2A 40
Lovett Wlk. SO22: Winche 2G 17
Lovington La. SO21: Avin 6H 13
SO24: Ovin 5A 14
Lowden Cl. SO22: Winche 3H 21
Lwr. Brook St.
SO23: Winche 2E 50 (5C 18)
Lwr. Farm La. SO51: Ampf 1F 31
Lower La. SO32: Bis W 5E 45
Lwr. Moors Rd. SO21: Col C . . .2F 35
Lwr. Neatham Mill La.
GU34: Holy, Neat 1H 47
(not continuous)
Lower Rd. SO21: Sth W 5C 6
Lwr. Stanmore La.
SO23: Winche 2A 22
Lwr. Turk St. GU34: Alt 5D 46
LOWER UPHAM 1G 43
Loyd Lindsay Sq.
SO22: Winche 3H 17
Lulworth Cl. SO53: Cha F 2D 38
Lupin Gdns. SO22: Winche 3F 17
Luzborough La.
SO51: A'field, Rom
. . . . .6H 29 & 1A 36
Lydiard Cl. SO50: E'leigh 6A 34
Lyme Cl. SO50: E'leigh 6H 33
Lymer La. SO16: Nur 6A 36
Lymington Barn GU34: Meds . . .3F 49
Lymington Bottom
GU34: Four M 4G 49
Lymington Bottom Rd.
GU34: Four M, Meds 2F 49
Lymington Cl. GU34: Four M . . .4G 49
Lymington Ri.
GU34: Four M 4G 49
Lynch Cl. SO22: Winche 3A 18
Lyndhurst Cl. SO22: Winche . . .1H 17
Lynford Av. SO22: Winche 3A 18
Lynford Way SO22: Winche 3A 18
Lynn Way SO23: Kin W 5E 11
Lynwood Ct. SO22: Winche 3B 18
Lynx Cl. SO50: B'stke 3F 41

M

M3 Trade Pk. SO50: E'leigh 1G 39
Macklin Ho. SO22: Winche 3A 50
Magdalen Hill
SO23: Winche 3F 50 (6D 18)
Magdalen M. SO23: Winche . . .3F 50
Magnolia Gro. SO50: Fair O . . .3C 42
Magpie La. SO50: E'leigh 3G 39
Main Rd. SO21: Col C 2G 35
SO21: Ott 1B 34
SO22: Lit 5E 9
SO50: Fis P 3H 35
Mainstone SO51: Rom 6D 28
Mainstream Ct.
SO50: B'stke 2D 40
Makins Ct. SO24: New A 4E 15
Malcolm Cl. SO53: Cha F 2G 33
Malcolm Rd. SO53: Cha F 2G 33
Maldon Cl. SO50: B'stke 2D 40
Malibres Rd. SO53: Cha F 3H 33
Mall, The SO53: Cha F 4G 33
Mallard Cl. SO24: New A 3F 15
SO32: Bis W 5C 44
SO51: Rom 3F 29
Mallards GU34: Alt 3D 46
Malmesbury Cl.
SO50: Fair O 3A 42
Malmesbury Gdns.
SO22: Winche 3H 17
Malmesbury Rd.
SO51: Rom 3E 29
Malpass Rd. SO21: Wor D 1G 9
Malthouse, The SO51: Rom . . .3E 29
Malthouse Cl. SO21: E'ton 6H 11
SO51: Rom 3E 29
Malthouse M. GU34: Holy 2G 47
Maltings Cl. GU34: Alt 6D 46
Malt La. SO32: Bis W 6E 45
Malvern Cl. SO32: Bis W 6F 45
Manningford Cl.
SO23: Winche 2C 18
Manor Cl. GU34: Alt 2E 47
SO23: Winche 5D 18
Mnr. Farm Cl. SO50: B'stke 3E 41
Mnr. Farm Cotts. SO21: Sut S . . .5B 4
Mnr. Farm Grn. SO21: Twyf 4F 27
Mnr. Farm Gro. SO50: B'stke . . .3E 41
Manor Pk. Cotts. *GU34: Alt 5E 47*
(off Kingsmead)
Manor Rd. GU34: Alt 2E 47
SO16: Chilw 5H 37
SO21: Twyf 4F 27
SO32: Durl 5H 43
SO50: B'stke 3E 41
Manor Way SO50: E'leigh 1G 39
Mansbridge Rd.
SO50: E'leigh 4A 40
Mansfield Pk. GU34: Meds 3G 49
Mant's La.
SO23: Winche 4F 50 (6D 18)
Maple Cl. GU34: Alt 3D 46
SO24: New A 5E 15
SO51: Rom 5A 30
Maple Dr. SO23: Kin W 3D 10
Maples, The SO53: Cha F 3E 33
Maple Sq. SO50: E'leigh 4G 39
Marathon Pl. SO50: B'stke 3H 41
Marcus Cl. SO50: B'stke 3H 41
Market La.
SO23: Winche 3D 50 (6C 18)
Market Pl. SO51: Rom 4E 29
Market Sq. GU34: Alt 5D 46
Market St. GU34: Alt 5D 46
SO23: Winche 3D 50 (6C 18)
SO50: E'leigh 4B 40
(not continuous)
Markson Rd. SO21: Sth W 5C 6
Marlborough Ct.
SO53: Cha F 1C 38
Marlborough Rd.
SO53: Cha F 2G 33
Marlow Rd. SO32: Bis W 5C 44
Marnhull Ri. SO22: Winche 6G 17
Marshal Cl. GU34: Alt 6C 46
Marston Ga.
SO23: Winche 1D 50 (5C 18)
Martins, The SO50: Fair O 4B 42
Martins Cl. GU34: Alt 3E 47
Martins Flds. SO21: Comp 1C 26
Martin St. SO32: Bis W 6D 44
MARTYR WORTHY 5B 12
Mary Rose M. GU34: Alt 3E 47
Masefield Cl. SO50: E'leigh . . .2H 39
Masons Yd. SO23: Winche 3C 50
Matilda Pl.
SO23: Winche 1D 50 (5C 18)
Mayflower Cl. SO53: Cha F 6D 32
Maypole Vs. SO50: E'leigh 3B 34
May Tree Cl. SO22: Winche . . .3G 21
Maytree Cl. SO50: Fair O 3B 42
Maytree Rd. SO53: Cha F 1E 33
Meadbrook Gdns.
SO53: Cha F 5E 33
Mead Cl. SO51: Rom 4H 29
Mead Ct. *SO53: Cha F 5E 33*
(off Meadbrook Gdns.)
Meadow Cl. SO24: New A 4F 15
SO52: N Bad 2E 37
Meadowcroft Cl. SO21: Ott 6C 26
Meadow Gro. SO53: Cha F 1E 39
Meadowland SO23: Kin W 4D 10
Meadow La. SO50: E'leigh 3A 40
Meadow Rise SO22: Lit 1F 17
Meadows, The SO51: Rom 2F 29
Meadowsweet Way
SO50: Hor H 6A 42
Meadow Way SO22: Winche . . .3G 21
Mead Rd. SO23: Winche 3A 22
SO53: Cha F 5E 33
Meads, The SO51: Rom 4D 28
SO53: Cha F 6C 32
Mears Rd. SO50: Fair O 4B 42
Measures Ga. SO21: Stoke C . . .4H 5
Medina Cl. SO53: Cha F 6G 33
Medstead and Four Marks Station
Watercress Line
(Mid-Hants Railway) 3G 49
Medway Dr. SO53: Cha F 3C 32
Melrose Ct. SO23: Winche 1B 22
Meon Cl. SO51: Rom 4A 30
Meon Cres. SO53: Cha F 5F 33
Meon Rd. SO51: Rom 4A 30
Mercer Way SO51: Rom 3G 29
Merchants Pl.
SO23: Winche 2E 50 (5C 18)
Merdon Av. SO53: Cha F 3E 33
Merdon Cl. SO53: Cha F 3F 33
Meredun Cl. SO21: Hurs 2D 24
Meriden Ct. *SO23: Winche 3C 18*
(off Northlands Dr.)
Merlin Cl. SO32: Bis W 5D 44
Merlin Ct. GU34: Four M 4G 49
Merlin Mews *SO32: Bis W 6E 45*
(off Houchin St.)
Merlin Rd. GU34: Four M 4G 49
Merlin Way SO53: Cha F 4B 32
Merrick Way SO53: Cha F 3C 32
Merrieleas Cl. SO53: Cha F 4E 33
Merrieleas Dr. SO53: Cha F 4E 33
Merritt Ct. SO53: Cha F 2F 39
Merry Gdns. SO52: N Bad 6E 31
Meryon Rd. SO24: New A 5E 15
Mews, The SO16: Rown 6D 36
SO53: Cha F 2E 39
Mews Ct. SO21: Ott 6B 26
Mews La.
SO22: Winche 3A 50 (6B 18)
Meynell Cl. SO50: E'leigh 2H 39
Michaels Way SO50: Fair O 3B 42
Middlebridge St.
SO51: Rom 5E 29
Middlebrook SO32: Bis W 5E 45
Middle Brook St.
SO23: Winche 3E 50 (6C 18)
(not continuous)
Middle Rd.
SO22: Winche 1A 50 (5A 18)
SO52: N Bad 6E 31
Midhurst Ct. SO53: Cha F 6E 33
Mildmay Ct. SO23: Winche 3F 50
Mildmay St. SO22: Winche 2H 21
Milesdown Pl.
SO23: Winche 6D 18
Milford Gdns. SO53: Cha F 5G 33
Milford Ho. SO23: Winche 2B 22
Milland Rd. SO23: Winche 1D 22
Millbrook Cl. SO53: Cha F 6D 32
Millcourt SO50: Fair O 3B 42
Millers La. SO22: Pitt 4C 20
Millers Yd. SO21: Sut S 3C 4
Mill Hill SO24: New A 3F 15
Mill La. GU34: Alt 4F 47
SO21: Abb W 5F 11
SO51: Rom 4D 28
Mill La. Ind. Est. GU34: Alt 4F 47
Millstream Ri. SO51: Rom 4D 28
Mill St. SO50: E'leigh 1B 40
Milner Pl. SO22: Winche 1A 22
Milnthorpe La.
SO22: Winche 4A 50 (6A 18)
Milton Rd. SO50: E'leigh 6B 34
Milverton Rd.
SO22: Winche 1A 50 (5H 17)
Mimosa Dr. SO50: Fair O 3C 42
Mincingfield La. SO32: Durl . . .6H 43

Minden Ho. *SO51: Rom* *4G* ***29***
(off Chambers Av.)
Minden Pl. GU34: Four M 4G **49**
Minden Way SO22: Winche . . . 2G **21**
Minstead Cl. SO22: Winche . . . 1H **17**
Minster Gallery *3D 50*
(off Gt. Minster St.)
Minster La.
SO23: Winche . . . 3D **50** (6C **18**)
Mintern Cl. SO50: B'stke 6D **34**
Minters Ct. *SO23: Winche* *2C* ***50***
(off Cross St.)
Mint Yd. SO23: Winche 3D **50**
Misselbrook La.
SO52: N Bad 1H **37**
Mitchell Dr. SO50: Fair O 2A **42**
Mitchell Rd. SO50: E'leigh . . . 3B **40**
Mitchells Cl. SO51: Rom 4F **29**
Mitchell Way SO18: S'ton A . . . 6H **39**
Mitford Rd. SO24: New A 4D **14**
Mitre Copse SO50: B'stke 3F **41**
Momford Rd. SO22: Oli B 4F **21**
Monarch Way SO22: Winche . . . 1G **21**
Monks Brook Cl.
SO50: E'leigh 4G **39**
Monks Brook Ind. Pk.
SO53: Cha F 6D **32**
Monks Rd. SO23: Winche 4C **18**
Monks Way SO50: E'leigh 4G **39**
Monmouth Cl. SO53: Cha F 5D **32**
Monmouth Sq.
SO22: Winche 1F **21**
Mons, The SO23: Winche 2B **50**
Mons Ct.
SO23: Winche . . . 2B **50** (5B **18**)
Montague Rd. SO50: B'stke . . . 2D **40**
Montecchio Way
GU34: Holy 2G **47**
Montfort Cl. SO51: Rom 4A **30**
Montfort College
SO51: Rom 4A **30**
Montfort Hgts. SO51: Rom 4A **30**
Montfort Rd. SO51: Rom 5A **30**
Montgomery Cl.
SO22: Winche 2G **21**
Montgomery Way
SO53: Cha F 2D **38**
Moor Ct. La. SO21: Spar 2A **16**
Moorcroft Cl. SO21: Sut S 4D **4**
Moorlands Rd.
SO32: Swanm 6H **45**
Moors Cl. SO21: Col C 2F **35**
Moorside SO23: Winche 2F **50**
Moorside Rd. SO23: Winche . . . 4E **19**
Moors Nature Reserve, The . . . 6G **45**
Moreland Cl. GU34: Alt 6E **47**
Morestead Rd.
SO21: Chilc, More, Winche
. . . . 2D **22**
(not continuous)
Morgan Le Fay Dr.
SO53: Cha F 4B **32**
Morley Dr. SO32: Bis W 5E **45**
Morley Gdns. SO53: Cha F 3E **33**
Mornington Dr.
SO22: Winche 3G **17**
Mortimer Cl. SO23: Kin W 5D **10**
Mortimers Dr. SO50: Fair O 3B **42**
Mortimers La. SO32: Lwr U . . . 3B **42**
SO50: Fair O 3B **42**
Mortimer Way SO52: N Bad . . . 2D **36**
Moss Rd. SO23: Winche 5D **18**
Mottisfont Lodge
SO51: Rom 4F **29**
Mottisfont Rd. SO50: E'leigh . . . 1A **40**
Mountbatten Av. SO51: Rom . . . 4F **29**
Mountbatten Ct.
SO22: Winche 2A **18**
Mountbatten Pl.
SO23: Kin W 3E **11**
Mountbatten Rd.
SO50: E'leigh 6A **34**
Mount Cl. SO22: Winche 2A **18**
Mount Dr. SO53: Cha F 1G **39**
Mounters La. GU34: Alt 1B **48**
MOUNT PLEASANT 6D **46**
Mt. Pleasant SO23: Kin W 5D **10**
SO51: Rom 5E **29**
Mt. Pleasant Rd. GU34: Alt 5D **46**
Mountsom's La.
GU34: Up Farr 6D **48**
Mount Temple SO51: Rom 4G **29**
Mount Vw. SO50: E'leigh 1B **40**
Mount Vw. Cl. SO22: Oli B 3F **21**
Mount Vw. Rd. SO22: Oli B 3F **21**
Mulberry Cnr. SO53: Cha F 1C **38**
Mulberry Ct. GU34: Four M 3H **49**
Multisports Swimming 5H **39**
Musgrove Gdns. GU34: Alt 4C **46**

N

NAOMI HOUSE HOSPICE 4B **4**
Narrow La. SO51: Rom 4E **29**
Nations Hill SO23: Kin W 4D **10**
NEATHAM 2H **47**
Neath Way SO53: Cha F 6C **32**
Neilson Cl. SO53: Cha F 4E **33**
Nelson Cl. SO51: Rom 3F **29**
Nelson Rd. SO23: Winche 6E **19**
SO50: B'stke 1D **40**
Nerquis Cl. SO51: Rom 3H **29**
Netherfield Cl. GU34: Alt 4C **46**
Nether St. GU34: Alt 4D **46**
Netley Cl. SO53: Cha F 2D **38**
Neville Dr. SO51: Rom 2F **29**
NEW ALRESFORD 3F **15**
New Barn Cotts. SO21: Craw 1C **8**
New Barn La. GU34: Alt 6D **46**
SO21: Craw . . . . 1B **8** & 6A **6**
Newburgh St.
SO23: Winche 1B **50** (5B **18**)
Newbury Cl. SO50: B'stke 3H **41**
New Farm Ind. Est.
SO24: New A 5D **14**
New Farm Rd. SO24: New A . . . 4D **14**
Newlands Cl. SO53: Cha F 6A **32**
New La. GU34: Holy 1H **47**
Newlyn Wlk. SO51: Rom 2G **29**
Newman La. GU34: Alt 4F **47**
Newman La. Ind. Est.
GU34: Alt 3F **47**
Newmarket Cl. SO50: Hor H . . . 6B **42**
New Odiham Rd.
GU34: Alt, Shal 1B **46**
New Paddock Cl.
GU34: Holy 1G **47**
Newport Cl. SO53: Cha F 1C **38**
New Rd. SO21: Col C 2F **35**
SO22: Lit 5F **9**
SO32: Bis W 3F **45**
SO50: B'stke 3H **41**
SO51: Rom 3G **29**
Newton La. SO51: Rom 4E **29**
Newton Rd. SO21: Twyf 2G **27**
NEWTOWN
GU34 . . . . 5C **46**
SO32 . . . . 5C **44**
Newtown Rd. SO50: E'leigh 1A **40**
Nichol Rd. SO53: Cha F 2F **33**
Nicholson Pl. SO24: New A 4D **14**
Nicholson Wlk. SO16: Rown . . . 6B **36**
Nickel Cl. SO23: Winche 5D **18**
Nickson Cl. SO53: Cha F 3D **32**
Nightingale Av.
SO50: E'leigh 4E **39**
Nightingale Cl.
SO22: Winche 1F **21**
SO51: Rom 4G **29**
Nightingale Ho. SO51: Rom . . . 3G **29**
Ninian Cl. SO50: Fair O 4A **42**
NOB'S CROOK 4G **35**
Nob's Crook SO21: Col C 3G **35**
NO MAN'S LAND 5H **19**
Nook, The SO50: E'leigh 6B **34**
Norbury Cl. SO53: Cha F 4D **32**
Norfolk Ct. SO53: Cha F 2E **39**
Norlands Dr. SO21: Ott 5C **26**
Normandy Cl. SO16: Rown 6C **36**
Normandy Ho. *SO51: Rom* *4G* ***29***
(off Chambers Av.)
Normandy St. GU34: Alt 4D **46**
Norman Rd. SO23: Winche 1B **22**
Normans Flats
SO23: Winche 1B **22**
Norris Cl. SO51: Rom 1A **30**
Norris Gdns. SO21: Sth W 5D **6**
Norsebury Ring 2H **5**
Northanger Cl. GU34: Alt 4C **46**
NORTH BADDESLEY 1F **37**
NORTHBROOK 5F **45**
Northbrook Av.
SO23: Winche 6D **18**
Northbrook Bower
SO32: Bis W 5F **45**
Northbrook Cl.
SO23: Winche 6E **19**
Northbrook Ct.
SO23: Winche 6E **19**
Northbrook Ho. SO32: Bis W . . . 5F **45**
North Cl. SO51: Rom 2A **30**
Northdene Rd. SO53: Cha F 6E **33**
North Dr. SO22: Lit 6F **9**
North End Cl. SO53: Cha F 1E **39**
Northerwood Cl.
SO52: N Bad 1D **36**
Northfield Cl. SO32: Bis W 4C **44**
Northfield La. GU34: Alt 2A **48**
Northfields SO21: Twyf 2G **27**
North Hill Cl. SO22: Winche . . . 3B **18**
North Hill Ct. SO22: Winche . . . 3B **18**
Northington Rd. SO21: Itc A . . . 3F **13**
Northlands Dr.
SO23: Winche 3C **18**
Northlands Rd.
SO50: E'leigh 2A **40**
SO51: Rom 5A **30**
Nth. Millers Dale
SO53: Cha F 2C **32**
North Rd. SO23: Kin W 2D **10**
NORTH STONEHAM 6F **39**
North Vw.
SO22: Winche 1A **50** (5A **18**)
North Walls
SO23: Winche 1D **50** (5C **18**)
Northwood Park 6C **8**
NORTON 1D **4**
Norton Welch Cl.
SO52: N Bad 1F **37**
Noyce Dr. SO50: Fair O 4B **42**
Nuns Rd. SO23: Winche 4C **18**
Nuns Wlk. SO23: Kin W 6E **11**
SO23: Winche 4C **18**
Nursery Gdns.
SO22: Winche 5H **17**
SO51: Rom 4G **29**
SO53: Cha F 2E **39**
Nursery Ho. SO53: Cha F 5E **33**
Nursery Rd. GU34: Alt 3E **47**
SO24: New A 4F **15**
Nurse's Path SO21: Twyf 3G **27**
Nutbeem Rd. SO50: E'leigh 3A **40**
NUTBURN 6F **31**
Nutburn Rd. SO52: N Bad 6F **31**
Nutfield Rd. SO16: Rown 6B **36**

O

Oakbank Rd. SO50: B'stke 1C **40**
Oak Coppice Cl.
SO50: B'stke 3G **41**
Oakdene GU34: Alt 3C **46**
Oakdene Ct. SO50: Fair O 3A **42**
Oak Dr. SO50: Fair O 3A **42**
Oakfields SO50: E'leigh 4A **34**
Oakgreen Pde.
GU34: Four M 3H **49**
Oakgrove Gdns.
SO50: B'stke 3E **41**
Oakgrove Rd. SO50: B'stke 3E **41**
Oak Hill SO24: New A 5F **15**
Oakhill Cl. SO53: Cha F 6G **33**
Oakhill Ct. SO53: Cha F 6G **33**
Oaklands SO21: Sth W 5D **6**
Oaklands, The SO53: Cha F . . . 2E **39**
Oaklands Cl. SO22: Winche 1F **21**
Oakleafe Pl. SO53: Cha F 5E **33**
Oakleigh Gdns. SO51: Rom 4G **29**
Oakmore Pk. SO50: Hor H 6B **42**
Oakmount Av. SO53: Cha F 1F **39**
Oakmount Rd. SO53: Cha F 4G **33**
Oak Rd. SO32: Bis W 5F **45**
Oak Tree Cl. SO21: Col C 3F **35**
Oak Tree Way SO50: E'leigh . . . 6A **34**
Oak Wlk. SO50: Fair O 3A **42**
Oakwood Av. SO21: Ott 6C **26**
Oakwood Cl. SO21: Ott 5C **26**
SO51: Rom 2H **29**
SO53: Cha F 2F **33**
Oakwood Ct. SO53: Cha F 2F **33**
Oakwood Dr. GU34: Alt 5B **46**
Oakwood Rd. SO53: Cha F 3F **33**
Oatlands SO51: Rom 3F **29**
O'Connell Rd. SO50: E'leigh . . . 3G **39**
Octavia Gdns. SO53: Cha F . . . 4H **33**
Octavia Hill SO22: Winche 1H **21**
Odiham Cl. SO53: Cha F 2D **38**
Oglander Rd. SO23: Winche . . . 3C **18**
Old Acre Rd. GU34: Alt 6C **46**
OLD ALRESFORD 1F **15**
Old Gardens SO22: Winche 3B **18**
Old Hillside Rd.
SO22: Winche 3G **17**
Old Kennels Cl. SO22: Oli B . . . 4E **21**
Old Kennels La. SO22: Oli B . . . 4E **21**
Old Odiham Rd. GU34: Alt 1C **46**
Old Parsonage Ct. SO21: Ott . . . 6C **26**
Old Rectory Gdns.
SO21: Abb W 5F **11**
Old Rectory La. SO21: Twyf . . . 2G **27**
Old Rd. SO51: Rom 2G **29**
Old Salisbury La.
SO51: Rom 1A **28**
(not continuous)
Old School, The
SO32: Bis W 6D **44**
Old Stable M. SO22: Lit 5E **9**
Old Station App.
SO23: Winche 3F **50** (6D **18**)
Old Station Rd. SO21: Itc A 5E **13**
Old Stoke Rd. SO21: Stoke C . . . 4G **7**
Oliver Ri. GU34: Alt 4D **46**
OLIVER'S BATTERY 3F **21**
Oliver's Battery Cres.
SO22: Oli B 3F **21**
Oliver's Battery Gdns.
SO22: Oli B 4F **21**
Oliver's Battery Rd. Nth.
SO22: Winche 2F **21**
Oliver's Battery Rd. Sth.
SO22: Oli B 4F **21**
Olympic Way SO50: Fair O 2G **41**
Omega Enterprise Pk.
SO53: Cha F 5E **33**
Omega Pk. GU34: Alt 5F **47**
Omni Bus. Cen. GU34: Alt 5F **47**
Orchard, The SO16: Chilw 4A **38**
SO32: Bis W 6F **45**
SO50: E'leigh 3A **40**
Orchard Av. SO50: B'stke 4F **41**
Orchard Cl. SO21: Col C 2F **35**
SO21: Sth W 5C **6**
SO24: New A 5F **15**
SO52: N Bad 6D **30**
Orchard Dean SO24: New A 3F **15**
Orchard Ho. *GU34: Alt* *5E* ***47***
(off Orchard La.)
Orchard La. GU34: Alt 4E **47**
SO51: Rom 4E **29**
Orchard Rd. SO21: Sth W 5C **6**
SO50: Fair O 3A **42**
Orchard Ter. *GU34: Alt* *4E* ***47***
(off Orchard La.)
Orchard Wlk. SO22: Winche . . . 3H **17**
SO23: Winche 1D **50**
Oriel Bus. Pk. GU34: Alt 4F **47**
Orient Dr. SO22: Winche 2G **17**
Ormesby Dr. SO53: Cha F 2D **32**
Ormond Cl. SO50: Fair O 2H **41**
Osborne Cl. GU34: Alt 5B **46**
Osborne Dr. SO53: Cha F 6G **33**
Osborne Gdns. SO50: Fair O . . . 3C **42**
Osborne M. SO50: E'leigh 4C **34**
OTTERBOURNE 1B **34**
Otterbourne Golf Course 4H **25**
Otterbourne Hill SO21: Ott 2A **34**
Otterbourne Ho. SO21: Ott 6B **26**
Otterbourne Ho. Gdns.
SO21: Ott 1B **34**
Otterbourne Park Wood &
Nature Reserve 2B **34**
Otterbourne Rd.
SO21: Comp, Ott, Shaw . . . 5C **26**
SO21: Comp, Winche 1D **26**
Otter Cl. SO50: B'stke 3G **41**
Ouse Cl. SO53: Cha F 3C **32**
Overbrook Way SO52: N Bad . . . 6C **30**
OVINGTON 5A **14**
Ovington Rd. SO50: E'leigh 4A **40**
Owen Rd. SO50: E'leigh 3H **39**
Owens Rd. SO22: Winche 4B **18**
Oxburgh Cl. SO50: E'leigh 6H **33**
Ox Drove SO21: Sth W 5F **7**
Oxford Rd. SO21: Sut S 4C **4**
Oxlease Cl. SO51: Rom 2G **29**

P

Packridge La. SO51: Toot 4C **36**
Paddock, The SO21: Itc A 5F **13**
SO23: Kin W 5E **11**
SO50: E'leigh 5B **34**
Paddock Cl. SO21: Sth W 5E **7**

Paddock Vw. SO22: Lit 6E **9**
Paddock Way SO24: New A 5E **15**
Paice La. GU34: Meds 2E **49**
Paimpol Pl. SO51: Rom 5E **29**
Painters Fld. SO23: Winche 3A **22**
Palace Cinema, The 4E **47**
Palace M. SO32: Bis W 6E **45**
Pallet Cl. SO21: Col C 3F **35**
Palmers Cl. SO50: Fair O 3B **42**
Palmerston Ct.
SO23: Winche 2B **22**
Palmerston Ho. *SO51: Rom 4G **29***
(off Fryers Cl.)
Palmerston St. SO51: Rom 4E **29**
Palm Hall Cl. SO23: Winche 6E **19**
Pantheon Rd. SO53: Cha F 4H **33**
Paper Mill La. GU34: Alt 4E **47**
Paradise La.
SO32: Bis W, Wal C 6H **45**
Parchment St.
SO23: Winche 3D **50** (6C **18**)
(not continuous)
Parham Dr. SO50: E'leigh 1H **39**
Park & Ride
East Winchester (Barfield)
1D 22
East Winchester (St Catherine's)
2D 22
South Winchester 6A 22
Park Av.
SO23: Winche 1E **50** (5C **18**)
Park Cl. SO23: Winche 3C **18**
Park Cl. Rd. GU34: Alt 3E **47**
Park Ct. SO23: Winche 3C **18**
SO51: Rom 6A **30**
Park Ho. SO23: Winche 1E **50**
Parklands Cl. SO53: Cha F 4E **33**
Park La. SO21: Abb W 5F **11**
SO21: Ott 2B **34**
SO21: Twyf 4G **27**
SO50: E'leigh 2B **34**
Park Mt. SO24: New A 3F **15**
Park Rd. SO22: Winche 3B **18**
SO23: Winche 3B **18**
SO32: Bis W 5C **44**
SO53: Cha F 3E **33**
Parkside Gdns.
SO22: Winche 3G **17**
Park Vw. SO21: Shaw 3E **27**
*SO50: E'leigh 2A **40***
(off Newtown Rd.)
Park Way SO50: Fair O 3C **42**
Parkway Ct. SO53: Cha F 4F **33**
Parkway Gdns. SO53: Cha F 4E **33**
Parliament Pl. SO22: Oli B 3G **21**
Parmiter Ho. SO23: Winche 2F **50**
Parnell Rd. SO50: E'leigh 3H **39**
Partridge Down SO22: Oli B 4F **21**
Partridge Grn. GU34: Alt 3D **46**
Partry Cl. SO53: Cha F 3C **32**
Passfield Av. SO50: E'leigh 4G **39**
Passfield Cl. SO50: E'leigh 3G **39**
Pastures, The SO23: Kin W 2D **10**
*SO50: E'leigh 3A **40***
(off Cranbury Rd.)
Paternoster Ho.
SO23: Winche 3E **50**
Paternoster Row
SO23: Winche 3E **50** (6C **18**)
Paulet Pl. SO22: Winche 2A **22**
Paulson Cl. SO53: Cha F 3E **33**
Pauncefoot Hill SO51: Rom 6C **28**
Pavilion Cl. SO50: Fair O 5A **42**
Pavilion on the Park 3F **39**
Paynes La. SO50: Fair O 2A **42**
Peacock Pl. SO23: Winche 5E **19**
Peacock Trad. Est.
SO50: E'leigh 1G **39**
Peak La. SO32: Bis W, Uph 1C **44**
Peel Cl. SO51: Rom 2A **30**
Pelican Ct. SO21: Hurs 2D **24**
Pembers Cl. SO50: Fair O 3B **42**
Pembroke Cl. SO50: E'leigh 6H **33**
SO51: Rom 4F **29**
Pemerton Rd.
SO22: Winche 2H **17**
Pendula Way SO50: B'stke 6E **35**
Penford Paddock
SO32: Bis W 6F **45**
Peninsula Rd.
SO22: Winche 4A **50** (6A **18**)
Peninsula Sq.
SO23: Winche 3B **50** (6B **18**)
Pennard Way SO53: Cha F 1C **38**
Pennine Way SO53: Cha F 1F **39**
Pennington Cl. SO21: Col C 3F **35**
Penrhyn Cl. SO50: E'leigh 6H **33**
Penrose Way GU34: Four M 4F **49**
Penshurst Way
SO50: E'leigh 5A **34**
Pentice, The SO23: Winche 3D **50**
Penton Pl. SO23: Winche 1D **22**
Penton Rd. SO21: Twyf 2G **27**
Pentons Cl. GU34: Holy 1H **47**
Percivale Rd. SO53: Cha F 1B **38**
Perins Cl. SO24: New A 5D **14**
Petersfield Rd.
SO21: Winche 6F **19**
SO23: Winche 6D **18**
Petty Cl. SO51: Rom 4G **29**
Petworth Gdns.
SO50: E'leigh 6A **34**
Peverells Rd. SO53: Cha F 4G **33**
Peverells Wood Av.
SO53: Cha F 4G **33**
Peverells Wood Cl.
SO53: Cha F 4H **33**
Pheasant Cl. GU34: Four M 5E **49**
Phi Ho. SO16: Chilw 4G **37**
Phoenix Ind. Pk.
SO50: E'leigh 3C **40**
Pigeonhouse Fld.
SO21: Sut S 3C **4**
Pigeonhouse Yd.
SO21: Sut S 3C **4**
Pilchards Av. SO50: Fair O 2H **41**
Pilgrims Cl. SO53: Cha F 6B **32**
Pilgrims Gate
SO22: Winche 1A **50** (4A **18**)
SO32: Bis W 5D **44**
Pilgrims Ho. SO22: Winche 4A **18**
Pine Cl. SO21: Sth W 5E **7**
SO22: Oli B 4F **21**
SO52: N Bad 6D **30**
Pine Ct. GU34: Four M 5G **49**
Pine Cres. SO53: Cha F 2E **33**
Pinehurst Rd. SO16: Bass 6B **38**
Pinelands Rd. SO16: Chilw 5B **38**
Pine Lea SO32: Bis W 4C **44**
Pine Rd. GU34: Four M 3H **49**
SO32: Bis W 5F **45**
SO51: Rom 5A **30**
SO53: Cha F 2D **32**
Pine Wlk. SO16: Chilw 6A **38**
Pine Way SO16: Bass 6B **38**
Pinewood Cl. SO51: Rom 2A **30**
Pinset Camp Site
SO22: Winche 5E **17**
Piping Cl. SO21: Col C 3F **35**
Piping Grn. SO21: Col C 3F **35**
Piping Rd. SO21: Col C 3F **35**
Pirelli Way SO50: E'leigh 3A **40**
Pitmore Cl. SO50: E'leigh 3B **34**
Pitmore Rd. SO50: E'leigh 3B **34**
PITT 2F **21**
Pitter Cl. SO22: Lit 6F **9**
Place La. SO21: Comp 1E **27**
Plaza Pde. SO51: Rom 4F **29**
Plaza Theatre, The 4F **29**
Plough Way SO22: Winche 3H **21**
Plovers Down SO22: Oli B 4F **21**
Plovers Way GU34: Alt 2E **47**
Plumpton Way GU34: Alt 6D **46**
Pluto Rd. SO50: E'leigh 2H **39**
Poets Way SO22: Winche 5H **17**
Point, The
Eastleigh 2A **40**
Polesden Cl. SO53: Cha F 3D **32**
Poles La. SO21: Hurs, Ott 3D **24**
Pondside La. SO32: Bis W 5D **44**
(not continuous)
Popes La. SO32: Lwr U 1G **43**
Poplar Way SO52: N Bad 6D **30**
Poppyfields SO53: Cha F 5C **32**
Portal Rd. SO23: Winche 1D **22**
SO50: B'stke 2D **40**
Portchester Ri.
SO50: E'leigh 4A **34**
Porteous Cres. SO53: Cha F 5H **33**
Portersbridge M.
SO51: Rom 4E **29**
Portersbridge St.
SO51: Rom 4E **29**
Port La. SO21: Hurs 2D **24**
Portsmouth Cl. GU34: Alt 1B **48**
Portsmouth Rd. SO50: Fis P 5H **35**
Potters Heron Cl.
SO51: Ampf 6A **24**
Potters Heron La.
SO51: Ampf 6A **24**
Pound Ga. GU34: Alt 3E **47**
Pound Hill SO24: New A 3E **15**
Pound La. SO51: Ampf 1F **31**
Pound Rd. SO23: Kin W 3E **11**
Premier Centre, The
SO51: Rom 5B **30**
Premier Way SO51: Rom 6B **30**
Priestlands SO51: Rom 3E **29**
Primrose Cl. SO53: Cha F 1B **38**
Primrose Way SO51: Rom 3A **30**
Prince Rd. SO16: Rown 6C **36**
Prince's Bldgs.
SO23: Winche 2E **50**
Princes Cl. SO32: Bis W 5D **44**
Prince's Pl. SO22: Winche 2A **22**
Prince's Rd. SO51: Rom 3E **29**
Princess Ct.
SO23: Winche 1D **50** (5C **18**)
Princess Dr. GU34: Alt 5B **46**
Princess Louise Sq.
GU34: Alt 1B **48**
Prince William Ct.
SO50: B'stke 3F **41**
Prinstead Cl. SO23: Winche 1D **22**
Printers Row SO23: Winche 2C **50**
Priors Barton SO23: Winche 2B **22**
Priors Dean Rd.
SO22: Winche 1H **17**
Priors Way SO22: Oli B 4F **21**
Priory, The SO32: Bis W 6D **44**
Priory Cl. SO32: Bis W 5D **44**
Priory Ct. SO32: Bis W 5D **44**
Priory Gdns. SO23: Winche 2D **50**
Priory Gate 4D **50**
Priory Rd. SO50: E'leigh 4H **39**
Proctor Dr. SO52: N Bad 2D **36**
Prospect Commercial Pk.
SO24: New A 5E **15**
Prospect Pl. SO53: Cha F 5E **33**
Prospect Rd. SO24: New A 5D **14**
Pudding La. SO23: Winche 6D **10**
Purkess Cl. SO53: Cha F 4F **33**
PYLEHILL 1A **42**

Q

Quadrangle, The
SO50: E'leigh 1A **40**
SO51: Rom 5B **30**
Quarry Rd. SO23: Winche 6D **18**
Queen's Cl. SO51: Rom 4G **29**
Queens Ct. SO23: Winche 2B **50**
Queens Gate SO22: Winche 4H **17**
Queens Lodge
*SO22: Winche 6G **17***
(off Highcroft Rd.)
Queens Mead SO22: Winche 1G **21**
Queens Ride SO52: N Bad 1C **36**
Queens Rd. GU34: Alt 5C **46**
SO22: Winche 6H **17**
SO53: Cha F 2F **33**
Queen St. SO21: Twyf 3F **27**

R

Rachel Cl. SO50: B'stke 3H **41**
Rack Cl. Rd. GU34: Alt 5C **46**
Raglan Cl. SO53: Cha F 1B **38**
Raglan Ct. SO50: E'leigh 5A **34**
Rakemakers GU34: Holy 1H **47**
Ralph La. SO51: Rom 2G **29**
RAMALLEY 3D **32**
Ramalley La. SO53: Cha F 3D **32**
Ramsay Rd. SO23: Kin W 4E **11**
Rances Way SO22: Winche 2A **22**
Randall Rd. SO53: Cha F 1F **33**
Ranelagh Rd. SO23: Winche 1B **22**
Rapide Cl. SO50: E'leigh 5A **40**
Rapids Swimming Pool, The
5F **29**
Rareridge La. SO32: Bis W 5F **45**
(not continuous)
RATLAKE 6B **24**
Ratlake La. SO21: Hurs 5B **24**
Raven Sq. GU34: Alt 2D **46**
(not continuous)
SO50: E'leigh 3F **39**
Read's Fld. GU34: Four M 4G **49**
Recess, The SO50: E'leigh 6B **34**
Rectory La. SO21: Itc A 3G **13**
Red Bushes Cl. GU34: Meds 1H **49**
Red Deer Ct.
SO22: Winche 1A **50** (5A **18**)
Red Hill GU34: Meds 2G **49**
Red House, The SO51: Rom 3F **29**
Red Lion St. *SO32: Bis W 6E **45***
(off Brook St.)
Red Lodge SO53: Cha F 2D **38**
Rees Rd. SO21: Wor D 1G **9**
Regal Wlk. SO50: E'leigh 2B **40**
Regent Cl. SO21: Ott 5C **26**
Regent Ct. *SO23: Winche 3C **18***
(off Northlands Dr.)
Regent Rd. SO53: Cha F 5F **33**
Reginald Mitchell Ct.
SO50: E'leigh 1H **39**
Reliant Cl. SO53: Cha F 6D **32**
Renown Cl. SO53: Cha F 6D **32**
Retreat, The SO50: E'leigh 1B **40**
Rewlands Dr. SO22: Winche 2G **17**
Rex Ind. Est. SO53: Cha F 6F **33**
Reynolds Ct. SO51: Rom 5G **29**
Reynolds Rd. SO50: Fair O 4B **42**
Rhinefield Cl. SO50: B'stke 3F **41**
Ribble Cl. SO53: Cha F 6F **33**
Richard Moss Ho.
SO23: Winche 1D **50**
Richmond Cl. SO53: Cha F 2E **33**
Richmond Ho.
SO22: Winche 1B **50** (5B **18**)
Richmond La. SO51: Rom 2G **29**
Richmond Pk. SO21: Ott 5D **26**
Ridgeway SO22: Winche 2G **21**
Ridgeway, The GU34: Alt 6D **46**
Ridgeway Cl. SO50: Fair O 2A **42**
SO53: Cha F 6G **33**
Ridgeway Wlk. SO53: Cha F 6G **33**
Ridings, The SO50: B'stke 3G **41**
Riley Rd. SO21: Wor D 1A **10**
Rimington Gdns.
SO51: Rom 1H **29**
Ring, The SO16: Chilw 6A **38**
Ringlet Way SO23: Winche 5E **19**
Ringwood Dr. SO52: N Bad 6C **30**
Ripon Ct. SO50: Hor H 6B **42**
River Cl. GU34: Four M 4G **49**
Rivermead Cl. SO51: Rom 4D **28**
Rivermead Ho. SO51: Rom 4D **28**
River M. SO50: B'stke 2D **40**
River Park Leisure Cen.
1E **50** (4C **18**)
Riverside GU34: Alt 5F **47**
SO50: B'stke 2D **40**
Riverside Gdns. SO51: Rom 5D **28**
Riverside Ho. SO23: Winche 2F **50**
Riverside Indoor Bowling Club
1E **50** (4C **18**)
River Vw. GU34: Alt 4E **47**
Riverwey Ind. Pk. GU34: Alt 4F **47**
Roberts Cl. SO23: Kin W 2D **10**
Robertson Cl. GU34: Alt 1B **48**
Robertson Rd. SO24: New A 5E **15**
Robert Whitworth Dr.
SO51: Rom 2F **29**
Robin Cl. GU34: Alt 2E **47**
Robins Ct. *SO24: New A 4F **15***
(off Station App.)
Robin Sq. SO50: E'leigh 3E **39**
Rockbourne Rd.
SO22: Winche 1H **17**
Rockford Ho. SO50: Fair O 5H **41**
Roe Downs Rd. GU34: Meds 1F **49**
Rogers Cl. SO50: B'stke 1E **41**
Rogers Ct. GU34: Alt 5D **46**
Rogers Rd. SO50: B'stke 1E **41**
Roke La. SO32: Bis W 3C **44**
Roker Way SO50: Fair O 4H **41**
Rolling Mill Mews
SO50: E'leigh 3H **39**
Roman Cl. SO53: Cha F 4G **33**
Roman Dr. SO16: Chilw 6A **38**
Roman Rd.
SO16: Bass, Chilw 5B **38**
SO21: Twyf 3G **27**
Roman Row SO32: Bis W 5F **45**
Roman's Rd. SO23: Winche 1B **22**
ROMSEY 4E **29**
Romsey By-Pass
SO51: Rom 5D **28**
Romsey Cl. SO50: E'leigh 2A **40**
Romsey Golf Course 6A **36**
ROMSEY HOSPITAL 3G **29**
Romsey Ind. Est.
SO51: Rom 3E **29**

Romsey Rd.
SO16: Nur, South 6A **36**
SO22: Pitt, Winche 3A **50** (3C **20**)
SO23: Winche 3A **50** (2F **21**)
SO50: E'leigh 2A **40**
Romsey Sports Cen. 5F **29**
Romsey Station (Rail) 3F **29**
Ronald Bowker Ct.
SO22: Winche 5A **18**
Rooks Down Rd.
SO22: Winche 2H **21**
Rookswood GU34: Alt 3D **46**
Rookwood Cl. SO50: E'leigh . . .5B **34**
Ropewalk Ho.
SO23: Winche 1D **50**
Rosebay Cl. SO50: Hor H 6A **42**
Rosebery Cres.
SO50: E'leigh 5B **34**
Rosebery Rd. SO24: New A 4E **15**
Rosedale Av. SO51: Rom 4G **29**
Rosehip Cl. SO50: Fair O 4G **41**
Roselands Cl. SO50: Fair O 2H **41**
Rosemary Cl.
SO23: Winche 2F **50** (5D **18**)
Rosemoor Gro. SO53: Cha F . . .2D **32**
Rosendale Rd. SO53: Cha F . . .1F **39**
Rosewarne Ct.
SO23: Winche 4C **18**
Rosslyn Cl. SO52: N Bad 1E **37**
Rothsbury Dr. SO53: Cha F 5D **32**
Rothville Pl. SO53: Cha F 1D **32**
Roundhuts Ri.
SO23: Winche 5E **19**
Routs Way SO16: Rown 6C **36**
Rowan Cl. SO21: Sth W 5E **7**
SO51: Rom 5A **30**
Rowan Ct. SO53: Cha F 5G **33**
Rowan Ind. Pk. GU34: Alt 4F **47**
Rowlands Cl. SO53: Cha F 1C **38**
Rowlings Rd. SO22: Winche . . .2H **17**
ROWNHAMS **6C 36**
Rownhams Ho. SO16: Rown . . .6C **36**
Rownhams La. SO16: Rown 4D **36**
SO52: N Bad 6D **30**
Rownhams Pk. SO16: Rown 5C **36**
Rownhams Rd. SO52: N Bad . . .2E **37**
ROWNHAMS SERVICE AREA **5D 36**
Rowse Cl. SO51: Rom 2F **29**
Royal Green Jackets Museum, The . . . .**2B 50 (5B 18)**
ROYAL HAMPSHIRE COUNTY HOSPITAL **6A 18**
Royal Hampshire Regiment Mus. . . . .**3C 50 (6B 18)**
Royal Oak Pas.
SO23: Winche 2D **50**
Royal Winchester Golf Course **6F 17**
Royal Winchester M.
SO22: Winche 5G **17**
Roydon Cl. SO22: Winche 2A **22**
Royston Av. SO50: E'leigh 6A **34**
Rozelle Cl. SO22: Lit 6E **9**
Ruffield Cl. SO22: Winche 3G **17**
Rufford Cl. SO50: E'leigh 5A **34**
Rufus Cl. SO53: Cha F 3G **33**
Ruskin Rd. SO50: E'leigh 1A **40**
Rusland Cl. SO53: Cha F 4D **32**
Russell Rd. SO23: Winche 3C **18**
Russet Cl. SO24: New A 5E **15**
Russett Rd. GU34: Alt 5E **47**
Rustan Cl. SO50: Fair O 3B **42**
Rutledge Dr. SO22: Lit 6F **9**
Rye Cl. SO53: Cha F 5B **32**
Ryedown La. SO51: E Wel 6A **28**

S

Saddlers Cl. SO21: Sut S 3C **4**
SO50: E'leigh 5A **34**
St Andrews Cl. SO52: N Bad . . .6C **30**
St Annes Cl. SO22: Winche 2G **21**
St Anne's Ho. *SO51: Rom 5E 29*
(off Banning St.)
St Aubins Cl. GU34: Four M . . .4G **49**
St Austell Cl. SO50: B'stke 2E **41**
St Barbe Cl. SO51: Rom 5G **29**
St Bede's Ct. SO23: Winche 4C **18**
St Blaize Rd. SO51: Rom 3H **29**
St Boniface Ct. SO52: N Bad . . .2E **37**
St Bonnet Dr. SO32: Bis W 5E **45**
St Catherine's Hill **3C 22**
St Catherine's Hill Nature Reserve **3C 22**
St Catherine's Rd.
SO23: Winche 1D **22**
SO50: E'leigh 6A **34**
St Catherine's Vw.
SO23: Winche 2D **22**
St Catherines Way
SO21: Winche 2E **23**
St Christophers Cl.
SO52: N Bad 1D **36**
St Clements Cl. SO51: Rom . . .3E **29**
St Clement St.
SO23: Winche 3C **50** (6B **18**)
St Clements Yd.
SO23: Winche 3D **50**
ST CROSS **2B 22**
St Cross Ct. SO23: Winche 2B **22**
St Cross Hospital
SO23: Winche 3B **22**
St Cross Mede
SO23: Winche 3A **22**
St Cross Rd.
SO23: Winche 4C **50** (4A **22**)
St David's Ct. SO52: N Bad 2E **37**
St Faith Cl. GU34: Four M 4F **49**
St Faith's Rd. SO23: Winche . . .2B **22**
St George's Ct. SO52: N Bad . . .2E **37**
St George's Sq.
SO32: Bis W 6E **45**
St George's St.
SO23: Winche 2D **50** (5C **18**)
(not continuous)
St Giles Cl.
SO23: Winche 4F **50** (6D **18**)
St Giles Hill
SO23: Winche 3F **50** (6D **18**)
ST GILES'S HILL **6E 19**
St Helens M. *SO50: Fair O 3B 42*
(off Stubbington Way)
St James' La.
SO22: Winche 3A **50** (6A **18**)
SO23: Winche 3A **50** (6A **18**)
St James Pk. SO52: N Bad 2C **32**
St James' Ter.
SO22: Winche 3B **50** (6B **18**)
St James' Vs.
SO23: Winche 4B **50** (6B **18**)
St John's Cen. SO52: N Bad . . .6E **31**
St Johns Cl. SO16: Rown 6C **36**
St John's Ct. SO52: N Bad 2F **37**
St Johns Gdns. SO51: Rom 3F **29**
St John's Glebe
SO16: Rown 6C **36**
St John's Nth.
SO23: Winche 3F **50** (6D **18**)
St John's Rd. SO23: Winche . . .5D **18**
SO50: E'leigh 1B **40**
St John's Sth.
SO23: Winche 3F **50** (6D **18**)
St John's St.
SO23: Winche 3F **50** (6D **18**)
St Lawrence Rd. GU34: Alt 4D **46**
SO50: E'leigh 1A **40**
St Leonards Cl. SO21: Sth W . . .5D **6**
St Leonard's Rd.
SO23: Winche 1E **23**
St Margaret's Rd.
SO50: B'stke 1C **40**
St Mark's Cl. SO53: Cha F 2H **33**
St Martin's Cl.
SO23: Winche 2F **50** (5D **18**)
SO50: B'stke 1D **40**
St Martin's Trade Pk.
SO23: Winche 1F **50** (4D **18**)
St Mary Magdalen Almshouses
SO23: Winche 4F **50** (6D **18**)
St Mary's *SO51: Rom 5E 29*
(off Banning St.)
St Marys Cl. GU34: Alt 6D **46**
SO23: Kin W 6E **11**
St Mary's Rd. SO50: B'stke 1D **40**
St Mary's Ter. SO21: Twyf 3G **27**
St Mary St. SO22: Winche 2H **21**
St Matthew's Rd.
SO22: Winche 3H **17**
St Michael's Gdns.
SO23: Winche 4C **50** (6B **18**)
St Michael's Pas.
SO23: Winche 1C **22**
St Michael's Rd.
SO23: Winche 1B **22**
St Nicholas Ri. SO23: Kin W . . .5D **10**
St Patrick's Ct. SO52: N Bad . . .2E **37**
St Paul's Ct. SO23: Winche 2C **50**
St Paul's Hill
SO22: Winche 1B **50** (5B **18**)
St Paul's Pl. SO23: Winche 2C **50**
St Peter's St. SO32: Bis W 5E **45**
St Peter St.
SO23: Winche 2D **50** (5C **18**)
(not continuous)
St Stephen's Rd.
SO22: Winche 3H **17**
St Swithun Cl. SO32: Bis W . . .5D **44**
St Swithun's Cl. SO51: Cram . . .2B **30**
St Swithuns Ter.
SO23: Winche 4C **50** (6B **18**)
St Swithun St.
SO23: Winche 4C **50** (6B **18**)
St Swithuns Vs.
SO23: Winche 4D **50** (6C **18**)
St Thomas Ct. SO50: Fair O 3B **42**
St Thomas M.
SO23: Winche 3C **50**
St Thomas' Pas.
SO23: Winche 3C **50** (6B **18**)
St Thomas St.
SO23: Winche 4C **50** (6B **18**)
St Vigor Way SO21: Col C 2F **35**
ST WALERIC **3C 18**
Salcombe Cl. SO53: Cha F 1D **38**
Salcot Rd. SO23: Winche 3C **18**
Salerno Ho. *SO51: Rom 4H 29*
(off Chambers Av.)
Salisbury Cl. GU34: Alt 6E **47**
SO50: E'leigh 1B **40**
Salisbury Ct. SO50: E'leigh 1B **40**
Salisbury Rd. SO24: New A 4E **15**
SO51: Rom 4A **28**
Salmon Dr. SO50: B'stke 3F **41**
Salona Cl. SO53: Cha F 4H **33**
Salters Acres SO22: Winche . . .2G **17**
Salters La. SO22: Winche 3F **17**
Sam Ford Pl. SO50: E'leigh 3A **40**
Sand Martin Cl.
SO50: E'leigh 4F **39**
Sandown Cl. GU34: Alt 6E **47**
Sandringham Cl. GU34: Alt 5B **46**
SO53: Cha F 1B **38**
Sandy La. SO50: Fair O 3H **41**
SO52: N Bad 6F **31**
(not continuous)
Saracens Rd. SO53: Cha F 4H **33**
Sarum Cl. SO22: Winche 6G **17**
Sarum Ct. SO22: Winche 6H **17**
Sarum Rd. SO22: Winche 6B **16**
SO53: Cha F 5G **33**
SARUM ROAD BMI HOSPITAL **6G 17**
Sarum Vw. SO22: Winche 6F **17**
Savernake Cl. SO51: Rom 2H **29**
Saville Cl. SO50: B'stke 6D **34**
Sawyers Cl. SO22: Winche 4F **17**
Saxon Ct. SO50: Hor H 6A **42**
Saxon Rd. SO23: Winche 4C **18**
Saxon Wlk. SO53: Cha F 6G **33**
Saxon Way SO51: Rom 4H **29**
Sayers Rd. SO50: B'stke 3D **40**
Scantabout Av. SO53: Cha F . . .4G **33**
School Cl. SO53: Cha F 6D **32**
School La. SO21: Itc A 4F **13**
SO23: Winche 6C **10**
SO53: Cha F 1C **38**
School Rd. SO21: Twyf 3F **27**
SO51: Rom 2A **30**
Scivier's La.
SO32: Durl, Lwr U 2G **43**
Scotland Cl. SO50: Fair O 3C **42**
Scotter Rd. SO50: B'stke 2D **40**
Scotter Sq. SO50: B'stke 2D **40**
Scott Rd. SO50: E'leigh 3H **39**
Scotts Cl. SO21: Col C 3G **35**
SCRAG HILL **5D 30**
Searles Cl. SO24: New A 4F **15**
Sedgewick Ct. SO50: B'stke . . .2D **40**
Sedgwick Rd. SO50: B'stke 2D **40**
Segars La. SO21: Twyf 4F **27**
Selborne Ct. SO51: Rom 2A **30**
Selborne Pl. SO22: Winche 2H **21**
Selborne Rd. GU34: Alt 1C **48**
Selbourne Dr. SO50: E'leigh . . .1A **40**
Seldon Cl. SO22: Oli B 3F **21**
Selhurst Way SO50: Fair O 4A **42**
Selsdon Av. SO51: Rom 3H **29**
Selwyn Gdns. SO50: E'leigh . . .6A **34**
Senlac Rd. SO51: Rom 4H **29**
Serendipity Sam's Play & Party Cen. **2E 29**
Sermon Rd. SO22: Winche 4F **17**
Setters Cl. SO21: Col C 3F **35**
Seward Ri. SO51: Rom 3A **30**
Seymour Cl. SO53: Cha F 6G **33**
Seymour La. SO52: N Bad 1D **36**
Shaftesbury Av. SO53: Cha F . . .1E **39**
Shakespeare Bus. Cen.
SO50: E'leigh 1B **40**
Shakespeare Rd.
SO50: E'leigh 6H **33**
Shannon Way SO53: Cha F 5C **32**
SHAWFORD **3E 27**
Shawford Down Nature Reserve **2D 26**
Shawford Rd.
SO21: Shaw, Twyf 3E **27**
Shawford Station (Rail) **3E 27**
Shears Rd. SO50: B'stke 2E **41**
Sheddon Pl. SO21: Spar 3B **16**
Sheffield Cl. SO50: B'stke 6D **34**
Shelley Cl. SO21: Itc A 5E **13**
SO22: Winche 5H **17**
Shelley Rd. SO50: E'leigh 4H **39**
Shepherds Cl. SO22: Oli B 3F **21**
Shepherds Down
SO24: New A 5E **15**
Shepherds Fld.
SO21: Mar W 4B **12**
Shepherds La.
SO21: Comp, Hurs 3H **25**
Shepherds Rd.
SO23: Winche 5E **19**
Sherborne Ct. SO50: E'leigh . . .5H **33**
Sherbrooke Cl. SO23: Kin W . . .3E **11**
Sheridan Cl. SO22: Winche 2G **21**
Sherwood Rd. SO53: Cha F 2G **33**
Sherwood Ter. *GU34: Alt 5E 47*
(off Kingsmead)
Shipcote La. SO32: Bis W 3E **45**
Shipley Cl. GU34: Alt 3E **47**
Shipley Rd. SO21: Twyf 2G **27**
Shore Cres. SO32: Bis W 6F **45**
Shore La. SO32: Bis W 6F **45**
Short Hill SO51: Rom 1A **30**
Short's Rd. SO50: Fair O 3H **41**
Shrave, The GU34: Four M 2H **49**
Shroner Vw. SO23: Kin W 1D **10**
Silchester Pl.
SO23: Winche 1D **50** (4C **18**)
SILKSTEAD **3H 25**
Silkstead La. SO21: Hurs 4G **25**
Silver Hill
SO23: Winche 3E **50** (6C **18**)
Silver Hill Sq.
SO23: Winche 3E **50**
Silverlake Stadium **6G 39**
Silverweed Cl. SO53: Cha F . . .4B **32**
Silverwood Cl.
SO22: Winche 2H **21**
Silwood Cl. SO22: Winche 4H **17**
Simonds Ct. SO23: Winche 3C **18**
Sir Galahad Rd.
SO53: Cha F 5B **32**
Sir Lancelot Cl. SO53: Cha F . . .5B **32**
Siskin Cl. SO32: Bis W 5C **44**
Six Oaks Rd. SO52: N Bad 1E **37**
Skintle Grn. SO21: Col C 3F **35**
Skipton Rd. SO53: Cha F 1F **39**
Skylark Cl. GU34: Alt 3D **46**
Skys Wood Rd. SO53: Cha F . . .5B **32**
Sleepers Delle Gdns.
SO22: Winche 1A **22**
SLEEPER'S HILL **6H 17**
Sleeper's Hill SO22: Winche . . .1G **21**
Sleeper's Hill Gdns.
SO22: Winche 1H **21**
Sleeper's Hill Ho.
SO22: Winche 1H **21**
Smiths Fld. SO51: Rom 2G **29**
Smithy Cl. GU34: Holy 1H **47**
SOKE, THE
SO23 . . . .**4F 50 (6D 18)**
SO24 . . . .**3F 15**
Soke, The SO24: New A 3F **15**
Soke Hill GU34: Four M 5E **49**
Soldridge Rd. GU34: Meds 2E **49**
Solent Cl. SO53: Cha F 5G **33**
Somers Cl. SO22: Winche 2H **21**
Somerset Cres. SO53: Cha F . . .2F **39**
Somers Way SO50: E'leigh 5H **39**
Somerville Rd. SO23: Kin W . . .2E **11**
Sopwith Rd. SO50: E'leigh 2H **39**

Sorrel Cl. SO51: Rom 2A **30**
Southampton Airport Parkway Station (Rail) 6H **39**
SOUTHAMPTON INTERNATIONAL AIRPORT 6A **40**
Southampton Rd.
SO50: E'leigh 5A **40**
SO51: Rom 4F **29**
Southbrook M. SO32: Bis W . . .5E **45**
South Cl. SO24: New A 4D **14**
SO51: Rom 2A **30**
Southdale Ct. SO53: Cha F 5E **33**
Southdene Rd. SO53: Cha F . . .6E **33**
SOUTH DOWN 4D **26**
Southdown Pl. SO21: Comp . . .3C **26**
Southdown Rd. SO21: Shaw . . .3D **26**
South Dr. SO22: Lit 1E **17**
SO51: Rom 1B **28**
South End Cl. SO21: Hurs 3D **24**
Southfields Cl. SO32: Bis W . . .5E **45**
South Front SO51: Rom 4F **29**
Southgate M.
SO23: Winche 4C **50** (6B **18**)
Southgate St.
SO23: Winche 3C **50** (6B **18**)
Southgate Vs.
SO23: Winche 4C **50**
SOUTH HILL 1G **39**
Sth. Millers Dale
SO53: Cha F 4D **32**
South Rd. SO24: New A 4D **14**
South St. SO50: E'leigh 5A **40**
SOUTH TOWN 1E **49**
Sth. Town Rd. GU34: Meds 1E **49**
South Vw.
SO22: Winche 2A **50** (5A **18**)
South Vw. Cl. SO21: Sut S 4D **4**
Southview Pk. Homes
SO22: Oli B 4G **21**
Southview Ri. GU34: Alt 3C **46**
South Vw. Rd. SO22: Oli B 4F **21**
Southwick Cl. SO22: Winche . . .1H **17**
South Winchester (Park & Ride) 6A **22**
South Winchester Golf Course 3E **21**
Southwinds SO21: Stoke C 4H **5**
SOUTH WONSTON 5D **6**
Southwood Rd. GU34: Shal 1A **46**
Sovereign Ct. SO50: E'leigh . . .3A **40**
Sovereign Way
SO50: E'leigh 5H **33**
Sparkford Cl.
SO22: Winche 4A **50** (1A **22**)
Sparkford Rd. SO22: Winche . . .1A **22**
Sparrowgrove SO21: Ott 5C **26**
Sparrow Sq. SO50: E'leigh 3F **39**
SPARSHOLT 2B **16**
Sparsholt La. SO21: Hurs 5A **20**
SO21: Spar 1A **20**
SO22: Winche 1A **20**
Speedwell Cl. SO53: Cha F 6D **32**
Spencer Cl. GU34: Four M 3G **49**
Spencer Gdns. SO52: N Bad . . .6E **31**
Spencer Rd. SO50: E'leigh 3G **39**
Spenser Cl. GU34: Alt 3E **47**
Spicers GU34: Alt 5E **47**
Spicers Ct.
SO22: Winche 1B **50** (5B **18**)
Spinney, The SO16: Bass 6B **38**
SO21: Comp 2C **26**
SO50: B'stke 3G **41**
*SO50: E'leigh 3A **40***
(off Desborough Rd.)
Spinney Caravan Park, The
SO24: New A 3E **15**
Spirit Health Club Eastleigh 2G **39**
Spitalfields Rd. GU34: Alt 4D **46**
SPITALHATCH 4F **47**
Spital Hatch GU34: Alt 4F **47**
Spitfire End SO23: Winche 5F **19**
Spitfire Link SO21: Winche 6F **19**
Spitfire Loop SO18: S'ton A . . .6H **39**
Spring Cl. SO50: Fair O 3A **42**
Springfields Cl. SO21: Col C . . .2F **35**
Spring Gdns. SO24: New A 5E **15**
SO52: N Bad 6D **30**
Springhill Rd. SO53: Cha F 5E **33**
Spring Ho. Cl. SO21: Col C 2G **35**
Spring La. SO21: Col C 2F **35**
SO50: B'stke 1D **40**
Spring Pl. SO51: Rom 4E **29**
SPRINGVALE 3E **11**
Springvale Av. SO23: Kin W . . .4D **10**
Springvale Rd.
SO23: Kin W, Winche 6D **10**
Spring Way SO24: New A 5E **15**
Spruce Cl. SO21: Sth W 4E **7**
Square, The
SO23: Winche 3D **50** (6C **18**)
SO50: Fair O 3A **42**
Squirrel Cl. SO50: B'stke 3F **41**
Stag Cl. SO50: B'stke 3F **41**
Stainers La. SO21: Sth W 5C **6**
Stakes La.
SO32: Bis W, Durl, Uph . . .3A **44**
Stamford Way SO50: Fair O 4A **42**
STANDON 5A **20**
Stanham Cl. SO21: Wor D 1H **9**
STANMORE 2H **21**
Stanmore La. SO22: Winche . . .1G **21**
Stanstead Rd. SO50: E'leigh . . .1H **39**
Stapleford Cl. SO51: Rom 2H **29**
Staple Gdns.
SO23: Winche 2C **50** (5B **18**)
Starling Sq. SO50: E'leigh 3F **39**
Station App.
GU34: Four M, Meds 3F **49**
(not continuous)
SO21: Itc A 4E **13**
SO24: New A 4F **15**
SO51: Rom 3F **29**
Station Cl. SO21: Itc A 4E **13**
Station Hill SO21: Itc A 5E **13**
SO23: Winche 1C **50** (5B **18**)
Station La. SO53: Cha F 5E **33**
Station M. SO51: Rom 3F **29**
Station Rd. GU34: Alt 4E **47**
SO23: Winche 1B **50** (5B **18**)
SO24: New A 3F **15**
SO32: Bis W 6E **45**
SO51: Rom 4E **29**
Station Ter. SO21: Shaw 3E **27**
Stavedown Rd. SO21: Sth W 5C **6**
Steele Cl. SO53: Cha F 1F **39**
Steeple Dr. GU34: Alt 4D **46**
Stephens Ct. SO51: Rom 5E **29**
Step Ter.
SO22: Winche 2A **50** (5A **18**)
Stewart Ho. SO53: Cha F 2E **33**
Stillions Cl. GU34: Alt 5E **47**
Stinchar Dr. SO53: Cha F 6C **32**
Stirling Wlk. SO51: Rom 4E **29**
Stockbridge Rd.
SO21: Craw, Spar 4A **8**
SO21: Sut S 3B **4**
SO22: Lit, Winche 1A **50** (4A **8**)
SO23: Winche 1C **50** (4A **8**)
Stockers Av. SO22: Winche 3H **17**
Stockwell Pl. SO21: Spar 2B **16**
STOKE CHARITY 4H **5**
Stoke Charity Rd.
SO21: Kin W 4G **7**
SO23: Kin W 4G **7**
STOKE COMMON 6E **35**
Stoke Comn. Rd.
SO50: B'stke 6E **35**
Stoke Hgts. SO50: Fair O 2H **41**
STOKE PARK 3F **41**
Stoke Pk. Dr. SO50: B'stke 1D **40**
Stoke Pk. Rd. SO50: B'stke 1D **40**
Stoke Rd. SO23: Winche 2C **18**
Stoke Wood Cl.
SO50: Fair O 3H **41**
Stoneham Golf Course 6D **38**
Stoneham La. SO16: S'ing 6G **39**
SO50: E'leigh 4G **39**
Stonemasons Ct.
SO23: Winche 2D **50**
Stone Ter. SO21: Ott 2A **34**
Stoney Ct. SO22: Winche 3A **18**
Stoney Croft Rise
SO53: Cha F 3E **39**
Stoney La. GU34: Meds 2G **49**
SO22: Winche 3H **17**
Stoney M. SO22: Winche 3A **18**
Stourvale Gdns.
SO53: Cha F 6F **33**
Stragwyne Cl. SO52: N Bad . . .6D **30**
Straight Mile SO51: Ampf 2B **30**
Stranding St. SO50: E'leigh 2H **39**
Stratfield Dr. SO53: Cha F 2D **32**
Stratford Ct. *SO23: Winche 3C **18***
(off Northlands Dr.)
Stratford Pl. SO50: E'leigh 1B **40**
Stratton Rd. SO23: Winche 6D **18**
Strawberry Mead
SO50: Fair O 4G **41**
STREET END 1F **45**
Street End SO52: N Bad 6F **31**
Strongs Cl. SO51: Rom 3H **29**
Stroudwood Rd.
SO32: Lwr U 2E **43**
Stuart Cres. SO22: Winche 1A **22**
Stuart Ho. *SO22: Winche 6G **17***
(off Highcroft Rd.)
Stubbington Way
SO50: Fair O 3B **42**
Suetts La. SO32: Bis W 6H **45**
Suffolk Cl. SO53: Cha F 3E **39**
Suffolk Dr. SO53: Cha F 2E **39**
Suffolk Grn. SO53: Cha F 3E **39**
Summerlands Rd.
SO50: Fair O 3A **42**
Sun Hill Cres. SO24: New A . . .5F **15**
Sun La. SO24: New A 5F **15**
Sunningdale Cl.
SO50: B'stke 3F **41**
Sunningdale Mobile Home Pk.
SO21: Col C 2F **35**
Sunnydown Rd. SO22: Oli B . . .4E **21**
Sun Valley Ind. Pk.
SO23: Winche 4E **19**
Surbiton Rd. SO50: E'leigh 6B **34**
Surrey Ct. SO53: Cha F 2F **39**
Surrey Rd. SO53: Cha F 2E **39**
Sussex Rd. SO53: Cha F 2F **39**
Sussex St.
SO23: Winche 2C **50** (5B **18**)
Sutherland Cl. SO51: Rom 2H **29**
Sutherlands Ct. SO53: Cha F . . .5E **33**
Sutherlands Way
SO53: Cha F 4D **32**
Sutton Gdns.
SO23: Winche 2D **50** (5C **18**)
Sutton Manor M. SO21: Sut S . . .3C **4**
Sutton Pk. Rd. SO21: Sut S 3C **4**
SUTTON SCOTNEY 3C **4**
SUTTON SCOTNEY SERVICE AREA 2B **4**
Swale Dr. SO53: Cha F 4C **32**
Swallow Cl. GU34: Alt 2E **47**
Swallow Sq. SO50: E'leigh 3F **39**
Swan Centre, The
SO50: E'leigh 3B **40**
Swan La.
SO23: Winche 1C **50** (5B **18**)
Swanley Cl. SO50: E'leigh 6A **34**
Swanmore Cl.
SO22: Winche 2G **17**
Swanmore Rd.
SO32: Bis W, Swanm 6H **45**
Swanton Gdns. SO53: Cha F . . .4D **32**
Swift Cl. SO22: Winche 2H **21**
SO50: E'leigh 3F **39**
Sycamore Av. SO53: Cha F 2E **33**
Sycamore Cl. SO51: Rom 5A **30**
SO52: N Bad 6D **30**
Sycamore Dr. SO23: Kin W 3D **10**
Sycamore Pk. GU34: Alt 4F **47**
Sycamore Rd. SO32: Bis W 6G **45**
Sydmanton Rd. SO51: Rom 5G **29**
Sydney Rd. SO50: B'stke 1D **40**
Sylvan Dr. SO52: N Bad 1D **36**
Symes Rd. SO51: Rom 4H **29**
Symonds Cl. SO53: Cha F 1F **39**
Symonds St.
SO23: Winche 4D **50** (6C **18**)

T

Tadburn Cl. SO51: Rom 4G **29**
SO53: Cha F 6F **33**
Tadburn Grn. SO51: Rom 5E **29**
Tadburn Meadows Local Nature Reserve . . .3H **29**
Tadburn Rd. SO51: Rom 4G **29**
Tadfield Cres. SO51: Rom 4G **29**
Tadfield Rd. SO51: Rom 4G **29**
Tangier La. SO32: Bis W 6B **44**
Tangmere Ri. SO53: Cha F 1F **39**
Tanhouse La. GU34: Alt 5D **46**
Tanners Rd. SO52: N Bad 2E **37**
Tanner St.
SO23: Winche 3E **50** (6C **18**)
Tansy Mdw. SO53: Cha F 1B **38**
Tanyards, The SO53: Cha F 2D **32**
Taplings Cl. SO22: Winche 2H **17**
Taplings Rd. SO22: Winche 2H **17**
Tavistock Cl. SO51: Rom 2H **29**
Tavy Cl. SO53: Cha F 5D **32**
Taw Dr. SO53: Cha F 4D **32**
Tawny Gro. GU34: Four M 4F **49**
Taylors Cnr. SO23: Winche 6D **10**
Team-Sport Indoor Karting Eastleigh 2B **40**
Tees Cl. SO53: Cha F 4C **32**
Tees Farm Rd. SO21: Col C 3F **35**
Tees Grn. SO21: Col C 3F **35**
Teg Down Meads
SO22: Winche 4F **17**
Telegraph La. GU34: Four M . . .3H **49**
Templars Mede SO53: Cha F . . .2D **38**
Templars Way SO53: Cha F 1B **38**
Templecombe Rd.
SO50: B'stke 4F **41**
Temple Dr.
SO21: Avin, Winche 6E **13**
Tenby Dr. SO53: Cha F 1C **38**
Tench Way SO51: Rom 3F **29**
Tennyson Cl. SO32: Bis W 5G **45**
Tennyson Rd. SO50: E'leigh . . .4H **39**
Terrace, The GU34: Alt 2B **48**
SO21: E'ton 6A **12**
Terriote Cl. SO53: Cha F 4E **33**
Test Mill SO51: Rom 3D **28**
Test Valley Bus. Pk.
SO52: N Bad 6E **31**
Teviot Rd. SO53: Cha F 6C **32**
Texas Dr. SO22: Oli B 5F **21**
Thacking Grn. SO21: Col C 3F **35**
The . . . .
Names prefixed with 'The' for example 'The Abbey' are indexed under the main name such as 'Abbey, The'
Theatre Royal Winchester 1C **50** (5B **18**)
Thetford Gdns. SO53: Cha F . . .3C **32**
Thicket, The SO51: Rom 5A **30**
Thirlmere SO50: E'leigh 3H **39**
Thirlstane Firs SO53: Cha F . . .1D **38**
Thistledown Cl.
SO22: Winche 3G **17**
Thistle Rd. SO53: Cha F 6B **32**
Thomas Rd. SO52: N Bad 1E **37**
Thornbury Hgts.
SO53: Cha F 2H **33**
Thornbury Wood
SO53: Cha F 2H **33**
Thorn Cl. GU34: Four M 3H **49**
SO50: E'leigh 6A **34**
Thorn Ct. GU34: Four M 4G **49**
Thorn Cres. GU34: Four M 4G **49**
Thorn Dr. GU34: Four M 4G **49**
Thorn La. GU34: Four M 4G **49**
Thornton Cl. SO24: New A 4E **15**
Thornton End GU34: Holy 2G **47**
Thornybush Gdns.
GU34: Meds 2H **49**
Thorold Rd. SO53: Cha F 2G **33**
Thorpe Gdns. GU34: Alt 4B **46**
Thurmond Cres.
SO22: Winche 1G **21**
Thurmond Rd.
SO22: Winche 1G **21**
Thurston Cl. SO53: Cha F 4F **33**
Tichborne Down
SO24: New A 5E **15**
Tichborne Rd. SO50: E'leigh . . .5H **39**
Tilden Rd. SO21: Comp 4D **26**
Tilney Cl. GU34: Alt 4C **46**
Timbercroft Cl.
GU34: Four M 5F **49**
Tinker All. SO18: S'ton A 6A **40**
Tiptree Cl. SO50: E'leigh 6A **34**
Tithe Mead SO51: Rom 2F **29**
Tithewood Cl. SO53: Cha F 1D **32**
Tivoli Cl. SO53: Cha F 4H **33**
Tolefrey Gdns. SO53: Cha F 5B **32**
Tollgate SO53: Cha F 3E **39**
Tomkyns Cl. SO53: Cha F 5B **32**
Tommy Grn. Wlk.
SO50: E'leigh 2H **39**
TOOTHILL 4C **36**
Toothill Rd. SO51: Toot 4A **36**
Torch Cl. SO50: B'stke 3H **41**
Tornay Gro. SO52: N Bad 1D **36**
Torre Cl. SO50: E'leigh 5A **34**
Torwood Gdns. SO50: B'stke . . .3F **41**
Totnes Cl. SO50: E'leigh 6H **33**
Tottehale Cl. SO52: N Bad 2D **36**

Tourist Info. Cen.
Romsey 4E 29
Winchester 3E 50 (6C 18)
Tovey Pl. SO23: Kin W 4E **11**
Tower Arts Cen. 1F 21
Tower Ct.
SO23: Winche 1C **50** (5B **18**)
Tower La. SO50: E'leigh 3C **40**
Tower Lane Ind. Est.
SO50: E'leigh 4C **40**
Tower Rd.
SO23: Winche 1C **50** (5B **18**)
Tower St. GU34: Alt 6C **46**
SO23: Winche 2C **50** (5B **18**)
Toynbee Cl. SO50: E'leigh 2A **40**
Toynbee Rd. SO50: E'leigh 2A **40**
Trafalgar Cl. SO53: Cha F 6D **32**
Trafalgar St.
SO23: Winche 3C **50** (6B **18**)
Trafford Rd. SO50: Fair O 4H **41**
Traveller's End
SO22: Winche 4H **17**
Treasury Ct. SO23: Winche 2C **50**
Treble Cl. SO22: Oli B 3F **21**
Treloyhan Cl. SO53: Cha F 1F **39**
Trevose Cl. SO53: Cha F 1F **39**
Trevose Cres. SO53: Cha F 6F **33**
Trinity Ct. SO21: Col C 3H **35**
SO53: Cha F 5F **33**
Trinity Gdns.
SO23: Winche 2E **50** (5C **18**)
Tristram Cl. SO53: Cha F 1B **38**
Triton Centre, The
SO51: Rom 6B **30**
Trowbridge Ct.
SO23: Winche 2D **50**
Truncheaunts La.
GU34: E Wor 6F **47**
Truro Ri. SO50: B'stke 2E **41**
Trussell Cl. SO22: Winche 2H **17**
Trussell Cres.
SO22: Winche 2H **17**
Tudor Way SO23: Kin W 3D **10**
Turk St. GU34: Alt 5D **46**
(not continuous)
Turnpike Down
SO23: Winche 5E **19**
Tuscan Wlk. SO53: Cha F 5G **33**
Tutland Rd. SO52: N Bad 1D **36**
Tweed Cl. SO53: Cha F 4C **32**
Twiss Sq. SO23: Winche 2C **18**
TWYFORD 3G 27
Twyford Ct. SO23: Winche 3C **18**
Twyford Rd. SO50: E'leigh 5B **34**
Twyford Waterworks 3H 27
Tyleshades, The SO51: Rom ...5G **29**
Tyne Cl. SO53: Cha F 6C **32**
Tyrrel Rd. SO53: Cha F 4E **33**

U

Ullswater SO50: E'leigh 4A **40**
Ullswater Gro. SO24: New A ...5F **15**
Underwood Rd.
SO50: B'stke 1D **40**
Union St.
SO23: Winche 2F **50** (5D **18**)
Unity Ct. SO50: E'leigh 3B **40**
University of Southampton
Sports Ground 6H 39
Winchester School of Art
.............1E 50 (5D 18)
University of Winchester
King Alfred Campus
.............4A 50 (6A 18)
West Downs Campus 5H 17
University Parkway
SO16: Chilw 4G **37**
Upham St.
SO32: Lwr U, Uph 1G **43**
Uphill Rd. SO22: Lit 6F **9**
Uplands La. GU34: Four M 5F **49**
Uplands Rd. SO22: Winche 2A **18**
Up. Anstey La. GU34: Alt 1D **46**
Up. Barn Copse
SO50: Fair O 2H **41**
Up. Brook St.
SO23: Winche 3D **50** (6C **18**)
(not continuous)
Up. Crescent Rd.
SO52: N Bad 6D **30**
UPPER FARRINGDON 6C 48
Up. Grove Rd. GU34: Alt 6D **46**
Up. High St.
SO23: Winche 1B **50** (5B **18**)
Upper Mkt. St.
SO50: E'leigh 2B **40**
Up. Mead Cl. SO50: Fair O 3B **42**
Up. Moors Rd. SO50: B'dge 3F **35**
Up. Neatham Mill La.
GU34: Holy 2G **47**
Up. Toothill Rd. SO16: Rown ...4C **36**
UPTON 6A 36
Upton Cres. SO16: Nur 6B **36**
Upton Grey Cl.
SO22: Winche 2H **17**
Upton La. SO16: Nur 6A **36**

V

Valdean Home Pk.
SO24: New A 3F **15**
Valerian Cl. SO50: Hor H 6A **42**
Vale Rd. SO23: Winche 1E **23**
Vale Way SO23: Kin W 2D **10**
Valley, The SO22: Winche 1G **21**
Valley Cl. SO21: Col C 3F **35**
Valley Court, The
SO22: Winche 1H **21**
Valley Rd. SO22: Lit 6F **9**
SO53: Cha F 4E **33**
Vanburgh Way SO53: Cha F ...2D **32**
Vaughans GU34: Alt 5E **47**
Vear's La. SO21: Col C 3G **35**
Vectis Cl. GU34: Four M 4F **49**
Velmore Rd. SO53: Cha F 1D **38**
Venture Rd. SO16: Chilw 4H **37**
Vernham Rd. SO22: Winche ...3H **17**
Vernon Cl. SO32: Bis W 3F **45**
Vernon Hill SO32: Bis W 3E **45**
Verona Rd. SO53: Cha F 4G **33**
Vespasian Way SO53: Cha F ...5G **33**
Vesta Way SO53: Cha F 4G **33**
Vian Pl. SO23: Kin W 3E **11**
Vicarage Farm Bus. Pk.
SO50: Fair O 6H **35**
Vicarage Hill GU34: Alt 5D **46**
Vicarage Rd. GU34: Alt 6C **46**
Victena Rd. SO50: Fair O 3A **42**
Victoria Bldgs. SO32: Bis W ...5D **44**
Victoria Ct. SO32: Durl 6G **43**
Victoria Gate
SO23: Winche 1C **50** (4B **18**)
Victoria Ho. SO23: Winche 1C **50**
Victoria Pl. *SO51: Rom 4E 29*
(off Love La.)
Victoria Rd. GU34: Alt 4D **46**
SO23: Winche 1C **50** (4B **18**)
SO32: Bis W 5D **44**
SO50: E'leigh 6B **34**
Victoria Rd. E. GU34: Alt 4E **47**
Victory Cl. SO53: Cha F 6D **32**
Victory Way SO16: Rown 6C **36**
Vikings, The SO51: Rom 4A **30**
Villeneuve St. SO50: E'leigh ...2G **39**
Villiers Ct. SO23: Winche 3C **50**
Vindomis Cl. GU34: Holy 1H **47**
Vine Gdns. SO32: Bis W 5D **44**
Vineyards, The SO52: N Bad ...1E **37**
Viney Av. SO51: Rom 3H **29**
Violet Cl. SO53: Cha F 5C **32**
Viscount Gdns.
SO50: E'leigh 5H **39**
Vue Cinema
Eastleigh 3B 40
Vyne Cl. GU34: Alt 4D **46**

W

Wagtail Cl. SO50: E'leigh 3F **39**
Wakeford Ct. SO51: Rom 4F **29**
Wales St.
SO23: Winche 2F **50** (5D **18**)
Walk, The
SO22: Winche 2B **50** (5B **18**)
Walkers Cl. SO50: Fair O 3B **42**
Wallington Dr. SO53: Cha F 3D **32**
Walmer Cl. SO50: E'leigh 4A **34**
Walnut Cl. GU34: Alt 3D **46**
SO53: Cha F 1E **33**
Walnut Gro. SO22: Winche 4H **17**
Walnut Tree Cl. SO21: Sth W ...5D **6**
Walpole Rd. SO22: Winche 2G **21**
Walton Pl. SO22: Winche 2H **21**
Wansbeck Cl. SO53: Cha F 6D **32**
Warblington Cl.
SO53: Cha F 2C **38**
Wardle Rd. SO50: Highb 4D **34**
Warner Ct. *SO23: Winche 3C 18*
(off Northlands Dr.)
Warren Av. SO53: Cha F 6G **33**
Warren Cl. SO53: Cha F 6G **33**
Warren Gdns. SO51: Rom 2H **29**
Warren Rd. SO23: Winche 5E **19**
Warrior Cl. SO53: Cha F 1D **38**
Warrior Pk. Ind. Est.
SO53: Cha F 1D **38**
Warwick Cl. SO23: Winche 3B **18**
SO53: Cha F 1C **38**
Warwick Ct. *SO23: Winche 3C 18*
(off Northlands Dr.)
Waterbrook Est. GU34: Alt 4G **47**
Waterbrook Rd. GU34: Alt 4F **47**
Water Cl.
SO23: Winche 4E **50** (6C **18**)
Watercress Ct. *GU34: Alt 4E 47*
(off Dickers La.)
Watercress Line (Mid-Hants Railway)
Alresford Station 4F 15
Medstead and
Four Marks Station 3G 49
Watercress Mdw.
SO24: New A 5D **14**
Watercress Way
GU34: Meds 2H **49**
Waterhouse Cl.
SO21: Twyf 2G **27**
Water La. GU34: Alt, E Wor 6F **47**
SO21: Abb W 6F **11**
SO23: Winche 3F **50** (6D **18**)
SO24: Itc S 4A **14**
Waterside Ct. GU34: Alt 4E **47**
Waterside Rd. SO51: Rom 2G **29**
Watersmeet SO23: Winche 4F **50**
Waterworks Rd. SO21: Ott 5C **26**
Watley La. SO21: Spar 2B **16**
SO21: Twyf 3H **27**
Wavell Way SO22: Winche 2G **21**
Waverley Cl. SO51: Rom 2H **29**
Waverley Dr. SO21: Sth W 5E **7**
Wayneflete Pl.
SO22: Winche 1G **21**
Waynflete Cl. SO32: Bis W 5E **45**
Weardale Rd. SO53: Cha F 1F **39**
Weavers Pl. SO53: Cha F 2D **32**
Weavills Rd. SO50: B'stke 3G **41**
Webster Rd. SO22: Winche 4F **17**
Wedmore Cl. SO22: Oli B 4E **21**
WEEKE 3H 17
Weeke Mnr. Cl.
SO22: Winche 3H **17**
Weeks Ct. *SO32: Bis W 6F 45*
(off Shore La.)
Weirs, The SO23: Winche 4F **50**
Wellbrooke Gdns.
SO53: Cha F 4D **32**
Welles Rd. SO53: Cha F 5F **33**
Wellhouse La. SO22: Winche ...6H **9**
SO23: Winche 6H **9**
Wellowbrook Cl.
SO53: Cha F 5C **32**
Wells Pl. SO50: E'leigh 3A **40**
Wells Rd. SO50: E'leigh 3B **40**
Welshers La. SO21: Comp 1C **26**
Wembley Way SO50: Fair O ...4A **42**
Wentworth Gdns. GU34: Alt ...4C **46**
Wentworth Grange
SO22: Winche 1A **22**
Wesley Ho.
SO23: Winche 2D **50** (5C **18**)
Wesley Rd. SO23: Kin W 4E **11**
Wesseden Bus. Cen.
SO24: New A 5E **15**
Wessex Bus. Pk.
SO21: Col C 3G **35**
Wessex Dr. SO22: Winche 3A **18**
Wessex Gdns. SO51: Rom 4H **29**
WESSEX NUFFIELD
HEALTH HOSPITAL 2A 34
Wessex Pk. SO21: Sut S 2C **4**
Wessex Way SO21: Col C 3G **35**
Westbroke Gdns.
SO51: Rom 2F **29**
Westbrooke Rd. GU34: Alt 5C **46**
Westbrook Wlk. *GU34: Alt.....5D 46*
(off High St.)
West Downs Student Village
SO22: Winche 5H **17**
West Dr. SO50: B'stke 1D **40**
West End Cl.
SO22: Winche 2A **50** (5A **18**)
West End Ter.
SO22: Winche 2A **50** (5A **18**)
Westering SO51: Rom 2A **30**
Western Rd.
SO22: Winche 1A **50** (5A **18**)
SO53: Cha F 2G **33**
Westfield Cl. SO50: Hor H 6B **42**
Westfield Cres. SO53: Cha F ...1E **39**
West Fld. Rd. SO23: Kin W 2E **11**
Westfield Rd. SO22: Lit 6F **9**
SO53: Cha F 2E **39**
Westgate Mus. 2C 50
West Hayes SO22: Winche 6H **17**
WEST HILL 3A 50 (6A 18)
West Hill Dr. SO22: Winche ...5A **18**
West Hill Pk. SO22: Winche ...5H **17**
West Hill Rd. Nth.
SO21: Sth W 4E **7**
West Hill Rd. Sth.
SO21: Sth W 5E **7**
W. Hoe La. SO32: Bis W 5H **45**
W. Horton Cl. SO50: B'stke 3F **41**
W. Horton La. SO50: B'stke 4F **41**
West La. SO52: N Bad 6C **30**
WESTLEY 1A 16
Westley Cl. SO22: Winche 4H **17**
Westley La. SO21: Spar 1A **16**
Westman Rd. SO22: Winche ...3H **17**
Westminster Ga.
SO22: Winche 2F **21**
Westmorland Way
SO53: Cha F 5G **33**
Weston Rd. SO50: E'leigh 2A **40**
West St. SO24: New A 3F **15**
Westview Rd. SO22: Spar 3E **17**
Westwood Gdns.
SO53: Cha F 3G **33**
Weyside Pk. GU34: Alt 3F **47**
Whalesmead Cl.
SO50: B'stke 4F **41**
Whalesmead Rd.
SO50: B'stke 3F **41**
WHARF HILL 1C 22
Wharf Hill SO23: Winche 1D **22**
Wharf Mill *SO23: Winche 1D 22*
(off Wharf Hill)
Wheat Cl. SO53: Cha F 5B **32**
Wheatland Cl.
SO22: Winche 2H **21**
Wheelers Yd. SO21: Sut S 3C **4**
Wheelhouse Pk. Caravan Pk.
SO52: N Bad 2C **32**
Whitebeam Cl. SO21: Col C ...3G **35**
Whitebeam Way
SO52: N Bad 6E **31**
Whitedown GU34: Alt 6C **46**
Whitedown La. GU34: Alt 6B **46**
White Hart Rd. SO50: Fair O ...4A **42**
Whitehill La.
SO24: Bis S, New A 5G **15**
White La. SO21: Twyf 1G **27**
WHITENAP 5A 30
Whitenap Cl. SO51: Rom 5H **29**
Whitenap La. SO51: Rom 5H **29**
White Rd. SO50: B'stke 1D **40**
Whiteshute La.
SO22: Winche 4H **21**
SO23: Winche 2A **22**
White Swan Ct. SO21: Sut S 3C **4**
White Tree Cl. SO50: Fair O ...5B **42**
Whyteways SO50: E'leigh 1A **40**
Wickham Cl. GU34: Alt 6B **46**
Wicklow Dr. SO53: Cha F 6C **32**
Wide La. SO50: E'leigh 6H **39**
Wide Lane Sports Complex ...6H 39
Widgeons GU34: Alt 3D **46**
Wilberforce Cl.
SO22: Winche 1G **21**
Wilcon Ct. SO50: Hor H 6B **42**
Wild Arum Way SO53: Cha F ...6B **32**
Wild Cherry Way
SO53: Cha F 5C **32**
Will Hall Cl. GU34: Alt 6B **46**
Will Hall Farm GU34: Alt 5B **46**
William Panter Ct.
SO50: E'leigh 3A **40**
William Way GU34: Alt 3E **47**
Willis Av. SO52: N Bad 1F **37**
Willis La. GU34: Four M 6H **49**
Willis Waye SO23: Kin W 5D **10**
Willoughby Cl. GU34: Alt 4C **46**
Willow Ct. GU34: Alt 5C **46**

Willow Gdns. SO52: N Bad 6D **30**
Willow Grn. SO21: Col C 3G **35**
Willow Gro. SO50: Fair O 3B **42**
Willow Rd. SO32: Bis W 6G **45**
Willows, The SO53: Cha F 2E **39**
Wills Way SO51: Rom 5G **29**
Wilmer Rd. SO50: E'leigh 3A **40**
Wilmot Cl. SO50: B'stke 6E **35**
WILSOM **5F 47**
Wilsom Cl. GU34: Alt 5E **47**
Wilsom Rd. GU34: Alt 5F **47**
Wiltshire Rd. SO53: Cha F 2F **39**
Wincanton Cl. GU34: Alt 6E **47**
WINCHESTER . . . .**2B 50 (5B 18)**
Winchester By-Pass
SO21: Kin W, Wor D 6B **6**
SO22: Kin W, Winche 1F **9**
SO23: Winche 2E **19**
Winchester Cathedral
. . . .**3D 50 (6C 18)**
Winchester Cathedral
Triforium Gallery
. . . .**4E 50 (6C 18)**
Winchester Cathedral Vis. Cen.
. . . .**3D 50 (6C 18)**
Winchester Cl. SO51: Rom 2H **29**
Winchester Discovery Cen.
. . . .**1D 50 (5C 18)**
Winchester Gallery . . .**1E 50 (5D 18)**
Winchester Great Hall
. . . .**3C 50 (6B 18)**
Winchester Hill SO21: Sut S 4C **4**
SO51: Rom 4G **29**
Winchester M.
GU34: Four M 3H **49**
Winchester Rd. GU34: Alt 3B **48**
(not continuous)
GU34: Four M 5E **49**
SO16: Chilw 5C **38**
SO21: Comp 1D **26**
SO24: New A 4C **14**
SO32: Bis W, Wal C 6F **45**
SO32: Lwr U 1F **43**
SO50: Fair O 5H **35**
SO51: Cram, Rom 2A **30**
SO51: Rom 4F **29**
SO53: Cha F 5E **33**
Winchester Sports Stadium . . .**1E 23**
Winchester Station (Rail)
. . . .**1B 50 (5B 18)**
Winchester Trade Pk.
SO23: Winche 4E **19**
Windermere Gdns.
SO24: New A 5F **15**
Windfield Dr. SO51: Rom 3H **29**
Windmill Ct. GU34: Alt 6D **46**
Windmill Flds.
GU34: Four M 3G **49**
Windmill Hill GU34: Alt 5E **47**
Windmill La. GU34: Alt 6F **47**
Windmills, The GU34: Alt 5D **46**
Windsor Cl. GU34: Alt 5B **46**
Windsor Ct. SO50: B'stke 1D **40**
Windsor Gate SO50: E'leigh . . .5A **34**
Windsor Ho. SO23: Winche 2F **50**
Windsor Pk. GU34: Alt 6D **46**
Windsor Pl. SO21: Col C 2F **35**
Windsor Rd. GU34: Meds 2G **49**
SO24: New A 5E **15**
Winifred Cl. SO50: Fair O 2A **42**
WINNALL **4E 19**
Winnall Cl. SO23: Winche 4E **19**
Winnall Mnr. Rd.
SO23: Winche 5E **19**
Winnall Moors Nature Reserve
. . . .**1F 50 (5D 18)**
Winnall Trad. Est.
SO23: Winche 4E **19**
Winnall Valley Rd.
SO23: Winche 5E **19**
Winsford Av. SO50: B'stke 4G **41**
Winsford Cl. SO50: B'stke 4G **41**
Winsford Gdns.
SO50: B'stke 4G **41**
Winslade Rd. SO22: Winche . . .1G **17**
Winston Cl. SO50: E'leigh 1A **40**
Winstone Cres. SO52: N Bad . . .2E **37**
Winston Ri. GU34: Four M 3F **49**
Winstreet Cl. GU34: Alt 1B **48**
Winterbourne Rd.
SO51: Rom 2H **29**
WINTERSHILL **4B 44**
Winters Hill SO32: Durl 5H **43**
Winters Pl. SO50: E'leigh 3B **34**
Winton Cl. SO22: Winche 3B **18**
Winton Ct. SO22: Winche 3B **18**
Winton Mews SO22: Winche . . .3B **18**
Wisteria M. *GU34: Holy 1H* ***47***
(off London Rd.)
Witham Cl. SO53: Cha F 5C **32**
Withy Cl. SO51: Rom 3F **29**
Witton Hill SO24: New A 5E **15**
Witt Rd. SO50: Fair O 3A **42**
Woburn Cl. SO50: E'leigh 5A **34**
Wolfe Cl. SO22: Winche 2G **21**
Wolf's La. GU34: Alt 2C **48**
Wolvesey Castle . . . . .**4E 50 (6C 18)**
Wolvesey Palace . . . . .**4E 50 (6C 18)**
Wolvesey Pl. SO53: Cha F 1C **38**
Wolvesey Ter.
SO23: Winche 1D **22**
WONSTON **3E 5**
Wonston Cl. SO21: Sut S 4D **4**
Wonston La. SO21: Wons 2C **6**
Wonston Rd. SO21: Sut S 4C **4**
Wood End Way SO53: Cha F . . .5C **32**
Wooderson Cl.
SO50: Fair O 2H **41**
Woodfield Dr. SO22: Winche . . .1F **21**
Woodgreen Rd.
SO22: Winche 1H **17**
Woodland, The SO53: Cha F . . .2C **32**
Woodland Drove
SO21: Col C 6G **27**
WOODLANDS **4D 14**
Woodlands, The
SO23: Kin W 5E **11**
Woodlands Cl. SO53: Cha F 1F **33**
Woodlands Ct. GU34: Alt 6B **46**
SO23: Winche 4C **18**
Woodlands Gdns.
SO51: Rom 2H **29**
Woodlands Way
SO52: N Bad 1D **36**
Woodlea Cl. SO22: Winche 3A **18**
Woodlea Pk. GU34: Meds 3G **49**
Woodlea Way SO51: Ampf 1B **32**
WOODLEY **1A 30**
Woodley Cl. SO51: Rom 1A **30**
Woodley Cl. Flats
SO51: Rom 1A **30**
Woodley Grange
SO51: Rom 2A **30**
Woodley La. SO51: Rom 3G **29**
Woodley Way SO51: Rom 1A **30**
Woodman Cl. SO21: Spar 3B **16**
Woodman La. SO21: Spar 2B **16**
Woodpeckers SO23: Winche . . .3C **18**
Woodpeckers Dr.
SO22: Winche 3G **17**
Woodpecker Way
SO50: E'leigh 3F **39**
Woodside SO16: Chilw 3A **38**
Woodside Av. SO50: E'leigh . . .2G **39**
Woodside Cres.
SO16: Chilw 3A **38**
Woodside La.
GU34: Lwr Farr 6A **48**
Woodside Rd. SO50: E'leigh . . .1G **39**
SO52: N Bad 1D **36**
Woodstock Ct.
SO22: Winche 2A **18**
Woolford Cl. SO22: Winche . . .1G **21**
Woolverton SO22: Winche 4H **17**
Wooteys Way GU34: Alt 3D **46**
Wordsworth Cl.
SO22: Winche 5H **17**
SO32: Bis W 5G **45**
Worldham Golf Course **6G 47**
WORTHY DOWN **1G 9**
Worthy La.
SO23: Winche 1C **50** (4B **18**)
Worthy Rd. SO23: Winche 4C **18**
Wren Cl. GU34: Alt 3E **47**
SO22: Winche 2H **21**
Wren Rd. SO50: E'leigh 4G **39**
Wrights Cl. SO21: Sth W 5D **6**
Wrights Way SO21: Sth W 5D **6**
Wychwood Gro.
SO53: Cha F 3G **33**
Wychwood Pl.
SO22: Winche 3B **18**
Wyeth Ho. SO23: Winche 1D **50**
Wykeham Ind. Estate, The
SO23: Winche 3E **19**
(not continuous)
Wykeham Pl. SO22: Winche . . .2H **21**
Wyke Mark SO22: Winche 3G **17**
Wynyards Gap SO52: N Bad . . .1D **36**
Wyre Cl. SO53: Cha F 5D **32**
Wyvern Cl. SO53: Cha F 5F **33**
Wyvern Leisure Cen. **4A 42**

Y

Yarnhams Cl.
GU34: Four M 4G **49**
Yellowhammers GU34: Alt 2D **46**
Yewberry Way SO53: Cha F 5A **32**
YEW HILL **5E 21**
Yew Tree Cl. SO50: Fair O 2A **42**
Yonge Cl. SO50: E'leigh 2B **40**
York Cl. SO50: Hor H 6B **42**
SO53: Cha F 1B **38**
York M. GU34: Alt 4E **47**
York Rd. SO50: E'leigh 5A **40**
Youngs Rd. GU34: Alt 4D **46**

The representation on the maps of a road, track or footpath is no evidence of the existence of a right of way.

SAFETY CAMERA INFORMATION

PocketGPSWorld.com's CamerAlert is a self-contained speed and red light camera warning system for SatNavs and Android or Apple iOS smartphones/tablets. Visit www.cameralert.co.uk to download.

Safety camera locations are publicised by the Safer Roads Partnership which operates them in order to encourage drivers to comply with speed limits at these sites. It is the driver's absolute responsibility to be aware of and to adhere to speed limits at all times.

By showing this safety camera information it is the intention of Geographers' A-Z Map Company Ltd., to encourage safe driving and greater awareness of speed limits and vehicle speed. Data accurate at time of printing.